NRA
AN AMERICAN LEGEND

Painting courtesy Army Art Collection/Robert Bruce Military Photos

NRA

AN AMERICAN LEGEND

JEFFREY L. RODENGEN

Edited by Melody Maysonet
Design and layout by Sandy Cruz

Write Stuff Enterprises, Inc.
1001 South Andrews Avenue
Second Floor
Fort Lauderdale, FL 33316
1-800-900-Book (1-800-900-2665)
(954) 462-6657
www.writestuffbooks.com

Publisher's Cataloging in Publication

Rodengen, Jeffrey L.
    NRA: An American Legend/ Jeffrey L.
Rodengen. — 1st ed.
    p. cm.
    Includes index.
    LCCN 00131246
    ISBN 0-945903-81-2

    1. National Rifle Association of America —
History. I. Title.

GV1163.N25R63 2002   799.3'1'06073
                          QBI02-200556

Library of Congress
Catalog Card Number 00131246

ISBN 0-945903-81-2

Completely produced in the
United States of America
10 9 8 7 6 5 4 3 2 1

Also by Jeffrey L. Rodengen

The Legend of Chris-Craft

*IRON FIST: The Lives
of Carl Kiekhaefer*

*Evinrude-Johnson and
The Legend of OMC*

*Serving the Silent Service:
The Legend of Electric Boat*

*The Legend of
Dr Pepper/Seven-Up*

The Legend of Honeywell

The Legend of Briggs & Stratton

The Legend of Ingersoll-Rand

*The Legend of Stanley:
150 Years of The Stanley Works*

The MicroAge Way

The Legend of Halliburton

*The Legend of
York International*

*The Legend of
Nucor Corporation*

*The Legend of Goodyear:
The First 100 Years*

The Legend of AMP

The Legend of Cessna

The Legend of VF Corporation

The Spirit of AMD

The Legend of Rowan

*New Horizons:
The Story of Ashland Inc.*

*The History of
American Standard*

The Legend of Mercury Marine

The Legend of Federal-Mogul

*Against the Odds:
Inter-Tel—The First 30 Years*

The Legend of Pfizer

*State of the Heart:
The Practical Guide to
Your Heart and Heart Surgery*
with Larry W. Stephenson, M.D.

*The Legend of
Worthington Industries*

*The Legend of
Trinity Industries, Inc.*

The Legend of IBP, Inc.

*The Legend of
Cornelius Vanderbilt Whitney*

The Legend of Amdahl

The Legend of Litton Industries

The Legend of Gulfstream

The Legend of Bertram
with David A. Patten

*The Legend of
Ritchie Bros. Auctioneers*

The Legend of ALLTEL
with David A. Patten

*The Yes, you can of
Invacare Corporation*
with Anthony L. Wall

*The Ship in the Balloon:
The Story of Boston Scientific
and the Development of
Less-Invasive Medicine*

*The Legend of
Day & Zimmermann*

The Legend of Noble Drilling

*50 Years of Innovation:
Kulicke & Soffa*

*Biomet—From Warsaw
to the World*
with Richard F. Hubbard

*The Heritage and Values
of RPM, Inc.*

TABLE OF CONTENTS

FOREWORD

by

Tom Clancy

AMERICANS AND THEIR GUNS

You know, it's pretty easy—if you can read.

The people who decided in 1776 that they wanted no further part of being subjects of the British Crown were not all lawyers, reporters, or professional politicians. They were something new in the world, and they called themselves Americans. Their professional backgrounds? Ben Franklin was a writer, printer, and inventor. John Hancock was a smuggler who made a good living avoiding British taxes. Thomas Jefferson was a planter, a member of the aristocracy, and, to his personal shame, a slave owner. John Adams was an attorney who even defended the British soldiers accused of killing his fellow citizens in the Boston massacre, and from that case comes a memorable line: "Facts are stubborn things." They are indeed, and they are the first things some people try to discard in an argument.

Their collective heritage was that of England—America remains the spiritual and intellectual child of Britain, from which we get our legal code and sense of fair play. But the England of the 18th century was a place ruled by an aristocracy. Someone whose great to-the-nth grandfather swung a sword in the right way at the right time and place, and was seen to do so by the king of the moment, and as a result ended up with a peerage—an earl, say—and from that came the hereditary right to tell people what to do. Those peasants or maybe a few tradesmen who lived on his land had to call him m'lord, and take his orders in a social contract that had lasted a millennium or more.

But with the discovery of America, things changed. Those tired of bending down in the presence of those who thought themselves their betters risked their lives to take a trip in small wooden ships across what could be a violent and dangerous ocean to a new land. The new land was a place where the land had as yet no titles, and so a man without a peerage was able there to own his own land, on which he could raise crops to sell and rear children to either inherit what was his or strike out on their own to pursue their own dreams. Most farmed, but some followed other lines of work, and in the climate of opportunity that was as boundless as the land itself, they thrived according to their abilities and their effort, which was all they'd ever asked for.

Living on the frontier of civilization, most of them owned arms. They used those to hunt for meat—which was plentiful, and not the property of the local earl, as things are reckoned in Europe—and for personal protection in the uncertainty that came along with new opportunities. You see, on the European continent, the aristocracy preferred that the serfs did not have arms. They might use them to kill an earl's deer when their children were hungry—or, worse, use them to seek political freedom when the nobility got a little too oppressive to bear. They couldn't have that. Were they not those anointed by God to rule the peasants?

And so, over time, the brave and the bright came west to start what became a thriving new country that remained the property of someone else, someone they'd never chosen as they'd chosen their own destinies. And unlike their second-class ancestors to the east, they also had the ability to enforce their desires and their needs with arms.

Then in 1776, these new Americans decided collectively that they could look after their own affairs, thank you. They would be happier, they thought, ruling themselves than with having someone 3,000 miles away try to do it by remote control. In this they were thinking in full accord with the Enlightenment, during which the idea of human freedom and self-determination started to flower. The difference was that in America the soil was a lot less rocky.

The American Revolution was more complex than that, and it is not correct to think that it began and ended with our own desires. But it is similarly true to remember that American ideas drove the event, even if we needed help from the King of France to see things through. And along the way, the British army learned that Americans armed with firearms were a lot more dangerous than the rabble they expected their opponents to be. At least one British regiment, the Royal Green Jackets, has that name to this date because their former red tunics invited too many casualties, and many were British officers who learned too late that a rifle was much less random a tool on the battlefield than the Brown Bess of the British infantryman. The use of precision firepower on the battlefield remains an American invention. And the rifles made mainly for Pennsylvania hunters are as much a part of our history as the document drafted by Jefferson and signed by the Founding Fathers in Philadelphia on a hot summer day.

And in due course, America became free. Our land became something entirely new in the world. We became a country whose first citizen, having won the war, gave the army back to the people's congress and rode back home to Mount Vernon to raise his crops instead of doing what a European would have probably chosen—replaced George III with himself as George I. The rights of the people are our country's only foundation. George Washington fought for those, not for himself.

It's never been easy. How easily we've forgotten the political and philosophical battles which defined our first 20 years as a nation. The Founding Fathers—Founding Brothers is a more recent term worth remembering—were split on the issue of just how much the common folk could be trusted to manage any affairs, but in this what prevailed were the views of that most enlightened of aristocrats, Thomas Jefferson. Flawed as he was, he knew that the average man or woman had the common sense to make good decisions, or to learn from the bad ones and move on.

But by the War of 1812, America had sufficient confidence to declare war on Britain, again, for the mother country's disrespect. That was a political move of more courage than intelligence, and when Britain invaded us again, we had not the power at first to do much more than sting our adversary. The British army burned Washington, but then when it re-embarked and came to Baltimore, their ground-force commander was shot and killed by an ordinary citizen using his personal hunting rifle. That broke up the land attack, effectively ending the Battle of Baltimore, and let London know that this war was not worth the trouble—other American seamen were savaging Britain's maritime trade as free-agent privateers, and that, really, is what turned the trick. In the final major combat action—actually taking place after the treaty of Ghent—the British regiments that had come to ravage New Orleans were savaged by American citizens using their personally owned Pennsylvania/Kentucky rifles from behind cotton bales. England learned a valuable lesson. America was better to have as a friend than as an enemy, and so it has remained ever since.

Along the way a diminutive giant named James Madison drafted a federal Constitution to replace the failed Articles of Confederation. That document was—and largely remains—unique in the human experience. The United States Constitution spends virtually all of its time telling the government what it may not do rather than letting the citizens know what they are allowed to do.

But even that wasn't quite right. Thomas Jefferson, by this time America's Minister to France, read the draft over and wrote frantically back to James Madison to let him know what he'd left out—and those things Thomas Jefferson thought were important. Madison agreed, and so did the several states, almost instantly adopting the first 10 amendments, collectively known as the Bill of Rights. Just a reminder, really, to let the government know a few more things that it was not allowed to do, lest it become another tyranny such as the revolution had been fought over. Freedom of speech, freedom of religion, and freedom of the press were taken care of by Amendment #1. You couldn't be free if a casual remark about the current idiot in the White House might land you in jail. The most fundamental of all human freedoms is how one chooses to see his God. And a free press is always an important check on those who think that being elected to office is the same thing as being anointed by God's own hand.

But what was the next amendment?

"A well regulated Militia, being necessary to the security of a free State, the right of the people to keep and bear Arms, shall not be infringed."

And from that comes a lot of modern controversy.

There are those who say that the existence of the National Guard invalidates the meaning of Amendment #2. Well, there are people who like to twist words.

But first, back up a little. Nowhere does the Constitution talk about the need of setting up a professional army. Why not? Aren't armies useful tools for international affairs? The Constitution talks about building a navy, doesn't it? Yes, it does, but look back a little further at American history. To the Founding Fathers, a professional army was a tool of tyranny. Quite a few of them had dodged musket balls fired by professional soldiers—English and German—and the idea of an American professional army beholden only to the President (the Constitution makes him Commander in Chief, which means that he answers to no one at all) was not terribly appealing. A professional navy, another useful tool, couldn't threaten people on land very much. But an army could walk right through your front door. So, no, the modern National Guard—whose uniform fatigues say "U.S. Army" on them—probably wasn't quite what Madison and his friends had in mind.

The next thing to remember, "Militia" back then had a meaning to the drafters rather different from what we recognize today. Back then the militia was —us. The militia was your average citizens standing together with their firearms to defend their country from all enemies, foreign and domestic. Such bodies elected their own leaders, and while they might be subject to guidance from their Governor, they remained free citizens defending their country.

And finally, the Second Amendment does not say: because the militia is so useful, the central government graciously grants the peasantry (us) the right to own firearms for so long a time as it serves the government's purpose.

The Constitution, remember, tells the government what it may not do. So, the preexisting right of the people to keep and bear arms (we are not peasants under the rule of the nearest earl) shall not be infringed. That right predates the Constitution, the Second Amendment recognizes. That's an entirely sensible reading of the document, because the right to bear arms was freely undertaken by Americans even before the Revolution.

Now, people can dispute that—in recent memory, the meaning of the word "is" was publicly nitpicked—but while the Constitution is a legal document, one need not be a lawyer to know how to read. The drafters all spoke English, after all.

The right to keep arms of any reasonable type for the purpose of hunting, personal enjoyment, or self-defense is manifestly a right recognized by the Founding Fathers. Otherwise, why does #2 precede eight other restrictions of government power in the Bill of Rights? Somebody—somebody important to the history of our nation—thought it to be important.

But there are those who oppose this right. Well, there were those who opposed the rights of people with different skin color—in fact the right to bear arms was one that some so-called Americans didn't want freed slaves to have. We couldn't have them thinking they were citizens, after all. They might want political rights next!

But we've grown out of that sort of thing, haven't we?

No, I think the ones who dislike the idea of firearms in civilian hands are those who, unlike Thomas Jefferson, do not think the average citizen can be trusted. And in our country they are as entitled to their opinions as anyone else, but we need to remind them that distrust of the individual was the very reason why people left the repression of Europe to start a new nation, conceived in liberty. Distrust of the individual citizen is something of the distant past, a thing of aristocracies and self-awarded superiority over the lesser folk, the right to tell the serfs what to do and how to live.

America has prospered by the reverse of that. In ratifying the rights given to us at birth by a loving God, America was the first to sanctify the sovereignty of the individual man or woman over his or her own life, the right to live that life in any way that does not infringe upon the rights of others, to establish a political and economic system which rewards people for doing well.

And part of that was a Constitution, ordained and established by the people, whose purpose it is to protect us from the government, not to protect the aristocracy from us.

© 2002 TOM CLANCY

ACKNOWLEDGMENTS

DRAWING UPON NUMEROUS RESOURCES, especially the 1967 history, *Americans and Their Guns*, by James B. Trefethen and James E. Serven, a great number of people assisted in the research, preparation, and publication of *NRA: An American Legend*.

Special thanks are due to NRA Secretary Edward Land Jr., who got the project off the ground and provided valuable oversight, and Mark Ness, Operations Research Analyst, who provided extensive coordination and support. John Grubar, NRA Archivist and retired Director of Competitions, helped locate many archival photographs. This book would not have been possible without the immense knowledge and talents of many NRA staff members including: John R. Robbins, Communications Manager of the Community Service Programs Division; Mark Keefe IV, Editor of *American Rifleman*, and Talmadge G. Rutledge, Chief Photographer, NRA Publications.

Much of the initial research was conducted by Jim Casada, outdoor writer, whose immeasurable skills went a long way toward making the book a success.

Thanks are also extended to staff members of Write Stuff Enterprises: Richard F. Hubbard, Co-executive Author and David Patten, former Co-executive Author; Melody Maysonet, Senior Editor; Mary Aaron, Transcriptionist; Erica Orloff, Indexer; Sandy Cruz, Senior Art Director; Bruce Borich, Production Manager; Marianne Roberts, Vice President of Administration; Linda Edell, Executive Assistant to the Author; Lars Jessen, Director of Marketing; Joel Colby, Sales and Promotion Manager; Sherrie Hasso, Bookkeeper; Rory Schmer, Distribution Supervisor; and Jennifer Walter, Administrative Assistant.

In July 1872, Creed's Farm on Long Island was deeded to the National Rifle Association for $26,250. Renamed Creedmoor, NRA's first range hosted its inaugural match on June 21, 1873.

1871: The National Rifle Association is formed by a group of New York National Guardsmen who are concerned about marksmanship training and national defense.

1874: NRA sponsors an American rifle team in the country's first-ever international match. Shooting becomes an immensely popular spectator sport as English-speaking people around the world follow the match.

1880: Believing there will be no more wars in his lifetime, the Governor of New York slashes state funding in the National Guard, at the same time cutting deeply into NRA's shooting program.

1872: NRA acquires Creedmoor, the organization's first shooting range.

1876: The Palma Trophy is introduced in NRA's Centennial Match as a symbol of excellent marksmanship.

PART ONE

EARLY FOUNDATION AND DEVELOPMENT

WHAT STARTED AS A TINY ORGANI-
zation representing mainly the state
of New York had, by the early 1900s,
evolved into a truly national Association. NRA's
program during its youthful years centered
mainly on improving marksmanship among
the military. Rifle tournaments at ranges in
Creedmoor, Sea Girt, and Camp Perry captured
the country's spirit of nationalism and resulted
in key improvements in rifles and target scoring. NRA also set standards for military rifle
training and even inspired the federal government to form its own segment within the War
Department to focus on promoting rifle practice among soldiers as well as civilians.

1903: The War Department creates
a National Board for the Promotion
of Rifle Practice to promote
military and civilian
marksmanship. The
NBPRP's objectives
are a major boon
to NRA's program.

1907: NRA and the NBPRP begin holding
their Annual Matches at Camp Perry in Ohio,
a location that will
endure well into
the next century.

CAMP PERRY, 1910.

1892: Lacking support from New
York, NRA transfers its Annual
Matches to
Sea Girt in
New Jersey.

1903: In what would become a long-term
agenda for NRA, the organization begins
working with America's youth.

The
National Rifle Association.

President: William C. Church.
Vice President: Alexander Shaler.
Secretary: Geo. W. Wingate.
Corresponding Secretary: Fred. M. Peck.
Treasurer: John Powell Jr.

New York, 1st October 1873

Dear Sir:

The Officers and Directors of The National Rifle Association would be pleased to have you honor them with your presence at their First Annual Prize Meeting at Creedmoor, L.I., on Wednesday, October 8th; the first day of the meeting which concluded October 11th.

The boat leaves James Slip at Nine Thirty a.m., and the foot of Thirty Fourth St. East River, at Nine forty-five a.m., to connect with the Ten o'clock train from Hunters Point, L.I.

Very Respectfully Yours

Wm. C. Church President N.R.A.

General Stryker
& Staff
Trenton
N.J.

Colonel William C. Church, one of the founders of NRA and later its President, wrote personal letters of invitation for NRA's "First Annual Prize Meeting" at Creedmoor, which began on October 8, 1873.

CHAPTER ONE

BIRTH OF NRA

1870–1873

. . . [T]he general ignorance concerning marksmanship which I found among our soldiers during the Civil War appalled me, and I hoped that I might better the situation. I believed that if I could help to dispel the prevalent ignorance about rifle shooting I might bring our American Rifleman nearer in actuality to his legendary stature.

—General George W. Wingate, circa 1901

NOT OFTEN WILL WORDS PUBLISHED in a newspaper actually change the course of history, but that is exactly what happened in 1870 and 1871, when William C. Church, Editor of the *Army and Navy Journal*, published a series of editorials about the need for better rifle marksmanship to support national defense. Those editorials and the subsequent *Manual for Rifle Practice* written by George W. Wingate inspired a group of National Guard officers to realize the dire need for Americans to improve their marksmanship. In November 1871, these men created history with the formation of one of America's finest, most productive, and most necessary organizations—the National Rifle Association.

The Instigators

The group of National Guard officers who formed NRA had firsthand knowledge of how far American marksmanship had declined during the Civil War, but it was Lieutenant Colonel William Conant Church and Captain George Wood Wingate who were most responsible for bringing that knowledge to the public. Church and Wingate, in fact, shouldered most of the organizational groundwork for the National Rifle Association.

Church was born in Boston in 1836 of a generally literary family and gravitated naturally to a career in journalism. In 1860, he became acting publisher of the *New York Sun*, then the largest daily newspaper in the United States.

During the Civil War, Church was a freelance war correspondent covering activities of the Army of the Potomac. No rear-echelon reporter, he was wounded at Fair Oaks while gathering material on the Peninsula Campaign. In 1862, he accepted a commission as Captain of Volunteers on the staff of General Silas Casey.

During the early years of the war, prominent citizens of the North were alarmed over what they considered a disloyal and subversive press. They determined to sponsor a newspaper for servicemen "to diffuse knowledge and stimulate a broad national patriotism." To guide this enterprise, launched on June 18, 1863, they selected young Captain William Church, who resigned his commission to accept the assignment. The first edition of the *United States Army and Navy*

Church's editorials concerning the need for better marksmanship were published in the *Army and Navy Journal*. Later, after Church cofounded NRA, the publication donated on his behalf the Regimental Trophy, awarded to "the regiment making the best shooting of any in the United States at the range of the National Rifle Association."

It was during the Civil War that William Church (left) and George Wingate, among others, began to see the lack of rifle marksmanship. There were some notable exceptions to poor federal marksmanship, including Berdan's sharpshooters as pictured above in Dale Gallon's "Breechloaders and Greencoats." Armed principally with Model 1859 Sharps breechloaders (top), each "sharpshooter" was expected to be able to hit a 5" target 10 times at 200 yards.

Journal and Gazette of the Regular and Volunteer Services appeared on August 29, 1863. Under Church's guidance, the paper prospered and soon became a running encyclopedia of contemporary military affairs. By the end of the war, Church was known by name or personally to practically every officer and enlisted man in the Union Army and Navy.

In nearly every issue of his newspaper up to 1871, Church published articles on rifles and editorials decrying the lack of marksmanship training in America's volunteer militia units. After watching a parade of the New York National Guard, he commented on the precision with which the troops ran through their manual of arms. They were far better than the British volunteers, he said, who had impressed him as sloppy marchers. Then he observed that every member of the British volunteers was expected to be able to place bullets on a

six-foot target at 1,000 yards, and he questioned how many of the well-drilled New Yorkers could do the same. This, and a running barrage of similar editorials, helped point out the need for organizing a National Rifle Association.

George Wingate was born in New York City on July 1, 1840, and received his education in the city's public schools. After graduation, he worked his way into a supervisory position in the building of Brooklyn's elevated railway. Soon after the war began, he enlisted in New York's Twenty-second Regiment and saw action in the campaigns in Pennsylvania and northern Virginia. Later he became the regimental historian. At the end of the war, with the rank of Captain, Wingate retained his affiliation with the Twenty-second and studied law. He was admitted to the bar in New York state shortly before the National Rifle Association was founded.

FROM THE OLD WORLD TO THE NEW

TWENTY-YEAR-OLD JOHN ALDEN, SEEK-ing freedom in a new world, brought his wheellock carbine to Plymouth Colony on the *Mayflower* in 1620. Like most of the able-bodied men in the new colony, Alden was a member of Captain Miles Standish's Militia unit and carried his own musket to the regular drills.

The manifest of the *Mayflower* and Alden's will both show that he owned a number of firearms. One, a wheellock of Italian origin, was found during a restoration of Alden's home in Duxbury, Massachusetts, in 1924. It is a short, smoothbore carbine and of a finely made Italian wheellock design. The few markings on the gun have not yet yielded further clues as to its origins. According to the few written records available for this gun, it is thought to have been restocked with American walnut at some point in the New England area.

It was not uncommon for early settlers to keep their potential enemies at arms length while remaining cordial to them to their faces. It was not uncommon for firearms to be hidden amongst the wall boards and in closets to hide them from view but where they were handy in case of a raid by Indians or other hostiles. The Aldens were particularly blessed with the fact that their home was one of very few to survive nearly 350 years without being ravaged by fire. It was in the Aldens' second home (the one built in Duxbury in 1653), where the now famous wheellock was discovered.

Records kept by the Pilgrim Society indicate that the Alden home was occupied by members of the Alden family from 1653 through 1896—a remarkable feat in and of itself. Additional records also indicate the transfer of numerous firearms in the wills of John Alden and his subsequent heirs.

The Alden wheellock can be found in a special exhibition in the NRA's National Firearms Museum. It symbolizes the transition from the firearms of old Europe to the new freedoms and heritages that were found in the New World. *(Rifle courtesy National Firearms Museum)*

Wingate was deeply impressed by Church's editorials. Since boyhood, Wingate had taken a keen interest in shooting, both as a hunter and as a target shooter, and he had been appalled by the poor marksmanship of the average American soldier that he had seen in battle. As a conscientious officer, he felt that his duties included preparing his unit for possible combat rather than merely making an impression on the parade ground. But when he began to search for published material that might help teach his men to shoot, he discovered that neither the War Department nor any other logical sources could provide anything of value.

Lieutenant Colonel Church was one of the men Wingate contacted. Church suggested that Wingate prepare a manual on target practice for publication by the *Army and Navy Journal.* The result was Wingate's *Manual for Rifle Practice,* which appeared serially in six installments in the *Journal* in late 1870 and early 1871 and in expanded booklet form in 1872; it was the first full treatise on rifle practice published in the United States.

The Founding Members

Many other American Army and militia officers recognized the need for improving the marksmanship of their men, and Wingate's *Manual for Rifle Practice* helped fill that need. Church's running barrage of editorials pricked the conscience of many officers, and Wingate's manual received immediate acceptance and its author national recognition as the leading authority on military marksmanship.

Capitalizing on the interest in rifle practice that his editorials and the publication of Wingate's manual had stimulated, Church, on August 12, 1871, wrote in the *Army and Navy Journal:*

> *An association should be organized in this city to promote and encourage rifle shooting on a scientific basis. . . . It only requires hearty cooperation and an actual start to make the organization successful. . . .*

On August 19, 1871, one week after the release of his editorial, Lieutenant Colonel Church invited

General George Wingate, who cofounded NRA and later served as its President, became the leading authority on military marksmanship after writing his *Manual for Rifle Practice,* first published in 1870. By 1879, it was in its sixth printing and remained the United States' only official handbook on individual and team shooting.

all officers of the New York National Guard who were interested in forming an association to improve marksmanship of state troops to meet informally at his office at 192 Broadway, on the first Monday in September. Including Church, 15 men, almost all of them officers of the First and Second divisions of the New York National Guard, crowded into the editorial office of the *Army and Navy Journal.*

Colonel Frederick E. Mason of the Thirteenth Infantry was elected Chairman of a 10-man

Committee on Organization whose members included Major General John B. Woodward; Brigadier Generals Augustus Funk and Thomas S. Dakin; Colonels Church, Harry Rockafellar, and Henry G. Shaw; Major George Moore Smith; Captains Bird W. Spencer and George Wingate; and Adjutant William J. Harding.

The men also discussed the need to establish a rifle range, which would be essential to the proposed organization. Several of those present had visited ranges in Canada and Great Britain or had studied the British National Rifle Association and were well informed on suitable ranges, targets, and rifles. These men were organized under Colonel Church as a committee to draw up rules for the proposed range and to obtain any further information on target shooting that they could find.

On September 12, 1871, the Committee on Organization met again in the offices of the *Army and Navy Journal.* The entire meeting was devoted to the reading, section by section, by Church of the tentative constitution and bylaws. These documents, with a few verbal amendments, were adopted by the full committee. The original bylaws specified a 15-member Board of Directors. Annual dues were two dollars with an admission fee of three dollars for each new member. A special rate was given to military units who joined *en masse.* Range rules were established, including a rule that "No betting shall be allowed on the grounds of the Association."

The committee drew up a certificate of incorporation as required by the state of New York. On November 17, 1871, the certificate was approved and the charter issued for the fledgling National Rifle Association "to promote rifle practice, and for this purpose to provide a suitable range or ranges in the vicinity of New York, and a suitable place for the meetings of the association in the city itself, and to promote the introduction of a system of aiming drill and target firing among the National Guard of New York and the militia of other states."

General Ambrose Burnside, who gained fame as a great leader during the Civil War, served as NRA's first President from 1871 to 1872. The prestige of his name lent credence to NRA's mission.

The First President

Even before NRA's incorporation was approved, the Committee on Organization invited Major General Ambrose Everett Burnside to serve as the first President of the National Rifle Association. Burnside, who then lived in New York City, was a logical choice, as many members of NRA had served under him during the recent war, and Church knew him well.

Burnside had emerged from the war as a national hero. While modern historians are inclined to remember only his two major defeats, his contemporaries knew the big, handsome Hoosier with the distinctive whiskers (from which the term "sideburn" originated) as a gallant and brave soldier and as a modest, forthright, and impeccably honest man.

Burnside became President of the Association on November 24, 1871. On the same day, Colonel Church was elected Vice President; Captain Wingate Secretary; Frederick M. Peck Corresponding Secretary; and Major General John Woodward, Commanding General of the Second Division, New York National Guard, was elected Treasurer.

Burnside served just long enough to see the new organization smoothly launched. At the spe-

BURNSIDE AND HIS CARBINE

IN ADDITION TO BEING NRA'S FIRST PRESident, Ambrose E. Burnside was the inventor of a .54 caliber, breechloading percussion carbine made first by the Bristol Firearms Company and later by the Burnside Rifle Company in Providence, Rhode Island.

More than 50,000 Burnside carbines of various models were accepted for service with Union troops during the Civil War, and they featured a breechblock that swings down with the under lever to allow access to the block's chamber for loading.

cial meeting called on July 22, 1872, the Board of Directors elected Church to fill the vacated office, and Major General Alexander Shaler became Vice President.

NRA's First Range

NRA's leaders knew that the future of the Association hinged largely on finding a rifle range where members could practice marksmanship. At that time, however, NRA's total monetary assets comprised only $485, mostly in pledges for Life Memberships made by the first members themselves. Such funds were inadequate to buy the needed land, so the men decided to seek public funds.

On February 7, 1872, the Board of Directors drafted a bill that proposed state assistance without endangering the private nonpolitical status of the Association. The state was asked to appropriate $25,000 for the purchase of land on the condition that NRA would raise $5,000 and assume its ownership, development, maintenance, and management. The state also was obligated to contribute prizes to stimulate competition among the members of the National Guard.

Church immediately publicized the bill in the pages of his *Journal* and encouraged his military friends and acquaintances to write letters of support. The bill passed the lower house by an overwhelming 84–19 vote, and just before adjournment, with the help of Senator James O'Brien, the bill was squeezed through the State Senate.

The NRA Range Committee's search for affordable land that would be suitable for a rifle range was not easy, but at last Colonel Church found what NRA had been looking for. The President of the Central and North Side Railroad of Long Island, a man named Hermann C. Poppenhusen, had acquired a 70-acre farm that adjoined the right of way of a railroad line that was being built the length of Long Island. Poppenhusen was willing to sell the land known as Creed's Farm at low cost to any group that might stimulate travel into that part of the island. His price was $375 an acre, where neighboring landowners were asking at least $500. In late July, Creed's Farm was deeded to the National Rifle Association for the price of $26,250.

The name Creed's Farm didn't last long, thanks to Colonel Henry Shaw, one of the members of the Range Committee. Shaw was also a member of the Board of Directors, Editor of the *New York Sun,* and a much-traveled man with a gift for words. Stepping from the special railroad train that Poppenhusen had put at the committee's disposal, Shaw surveyed the brushy fields with the morning mists sifting across them. "Just like the moors of southern England," he observed. "Perhaps we should call it Creed's Moor, rather than the Creed Farm." And so Creedmoor, one of the most famous names in

The first formal matches at Creedmoor were widely anticipated, as evidenced by this artist's rendering of enthusiastic spectators who would gather at the Long Island range to witness NRA's hosting of the historical shooting events.

shooting history, became the official name of the range before the first spade of earth had been moved to develop it.

As soon as construction on the range began, NRA ordered 50 targets, with necessary accessories, from England, for no American manufacturer then produced such equipment. It also ordered marking equipment like that developed at England's Wimbledon range. When NRA adopted targets and scoring procedures already in use by the National Rifle Association of Great Britain and its subsidiaries throughout the British Empire, target shooting throughout the English-speaking world became a standardized sport.

NRA grew quickly during its first months. In January 1872, it had fewer than 100 members and little more than $1,000 in assets. By the end of the year, a number of military companies and nearly all of the officers of the local National Guard divisions had become members.

Creedmoor Marks Improvement

The inaugural Creedmoor match on June 21, 1873, in addition to providing scores against which future improvement could be measured, was a perfect proving ground for Colonel Church and George Wingate's theories about marksmanship training. The teams finished almost in the exact order of the time they had spent in aiming drill. Shooters of the Twenty-second Regiment, which had practiced most religiously, made almost a clean sweep of the match. In addition to the team prize of $50, its members walked away with seven of the individual prizes offered, including a gold-mounted Model 1866 Winchester rifle valued at $100.

After that, the men began to practice. During August and September, the range was filled with tents and wagons of encamped military units, all preparing for NRA's first full-scale Annual Matches on October 8, 1873.

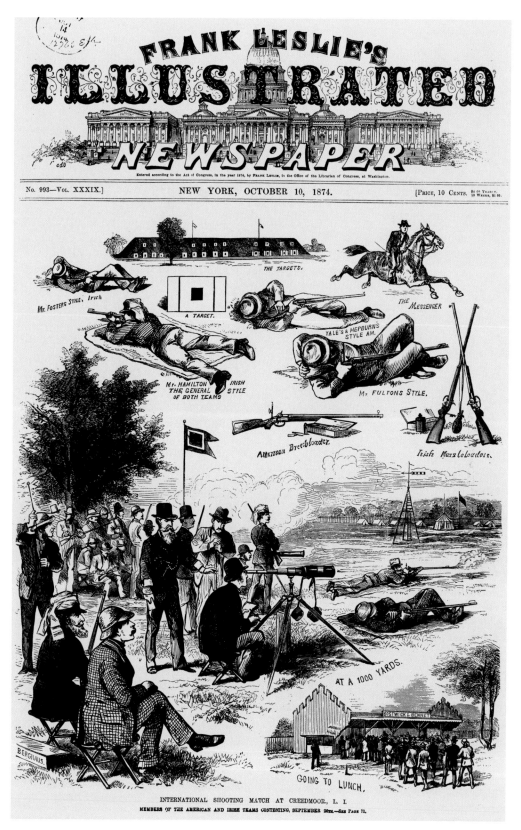

Much like modern-day sporting events, the first shooting matches at Creedmoor drew spectators in droves and were widely covered in the media. This newspaper captures the excitement of the 1874 match against the Irish, depicting everything from shooting positions of various team members to the layout of Creedmoor.

CHAPTER TWO

INTERNATIONAL FAME

1874–1876

We have not only successfully inaugurated rifle practice in this coun-
try, but . . . we have established for the National Rifle Association a
record so brilliant that the name of Creedmoor has become a synonym
the world over . . . for the highest skill in marksmanship yet attained.

—Colonel William C. Church, January 1875

THE EVENTS AT CREEDMOOR were so popular that by the end of 1873, Wingate's office was being bombarded with letters from other states asking how they might join NRA's shooting program. Similarly, the military, the Army in particular, began looking more critically at its rifle training methods. But it was the international competition for the Elcho Shield that truly inspired Americans to show their enthusiasm and support for shooting competition.

The Irish Challenge

The Elcho Shield had originated in 1862 when Lord Elcho, the tenth Earl of Wemyss, commissioned silversmiths in England to produce a massive silver shield to be awarded each year to the winner of a rifle match between Scotland and England. Ireland had not been included because at the time it was considered in a state of rebellion against the crown.

By 1865, however, the Irish, largely through the efforts of Major Arthur Blennerhasset Leech, had been permitted to enter the Elcho Shield Match. For eight successive years they had placed second to the English, but in 1873 the Irish team of eight produced the highest score ever made in the match—1,195—which topped the English by 20 points and beat the Scots by a resounding 67. That

night the coveted trophy was paraded through the streets of Dublin on a gun carriage, and the victory celebration spread all over Ireland.

The Irish began looking for new marksmen to conquer, and in November 1873 a letter signed by Major Leech on behalf of the Irish Rifle Association appeared in New York's *Herald.* It was an open challenge for any team of Americans to meet the Irish team, on American soil, in 1874. The match would be conducted under the general rules of the Elcho Shield Match, with the Americans using American-made rifles.

Because the letter had not been sent directly to the Association, NRA chose to dismiss the invitation. The Amateur Rifle Club, the first rifle club to be affiliated with NRA, was less constrained, and it wrote to Major Leech accepting his challenge. Organized in October 1872 by George Wingate, who became its first President, and Judge Henry A. Gildersleeve, who was its first Vice President, the Amateur Rifle Club was made up entirely of NRA members. With the honor of the nation at

The Elcho Shield was symbolic of the rifle championship of the British Isles. When the Irish won the trophy in 1873, they sought to test their skill against an American rifle team, thus initiating America's first international rifle match.

stake, NRA threw its full support behind the club and placed Creedmoor at its disposal. The international match was to be held there on September 26, 1874, four days before the Annual Matches of the National Rifle Association.

Although both the Irish and the Americans were then unaware of the fact, the Amateur Rifle Club's acceptance in the fall of 1873 was akin to a small-town sandlot baseball club picking up a challenge from the World Series champions. The Irish Rifle Association had several thousand members, most of whom had been practicing for years

Harper's Weekly devoted several pages to the 1874 international match against the Irish, including this drawing of the Irish team members. From left: Dr. J. B. Hamilton, Major Arthur B. Leech, Captain Philip Walker, J. K. Millner, John Rigby, Edmund Johnson, and James Wilson.

and many of whom had engaged in international competition. By contrast, the Amateur Rifle Club boasted a total membership of 67, only a few of whom had competed in formal matches at distances beyond 500 yards and at least half of whom had not attained proficiency at that range. In the first annual competition of the National Rifle Association on October 8, only one match had approximated the long-range conditions of the Elcho Shield Match, and this had been won by a Canadian.

Priming Up

To select the best shooters, the Amateur Rifle Club initiated a series of matches beginning in May 1874, and the six men who made the highest scores were selected to form the American team with Colonel Wingate as Captain. (The Captains of the respective teams

THE "CREEDMOOR" RIFLES

Above: The Grade C Remington No. 1 Long-Range Military Creedmoor Target rifle (circa 1875) has a military ladder sight on the barrel, a long-range vernier rear tang sight, and a front target sight. *(Rifle courtesy National Firearms Museum)*

Below: The Grade A Remington No. 1 Long-Range Creedmoor Target Rifle featured a long-range vernier rear sight and an adjustable front sight. *(Rifle courtesy National Firearms Museum)*

WHEN IT WAS AGREED THAT AMERIcan marksmen of the Amateur Rifle Club—with the backing of the fledgling NRA—would face the world-champion Irish team at Creedmoor on September 26, 1874, one of the stipulations was that the Americans would use rifles of American manufacture. The problem was no suitable rifles existed. E. Remington & Sons of Ilion, New York, and the Sharps Rifle Manufacturing Company of Hartford, Connecticut, agreed to provide target rifles suitably accurate for 1,000-yard competition. Louis L. Hepburn of Remington and G. W. Yale of Sharps headed up their companies' respective efforts to adapt their existing designs for Creedmoor. The rifles would be .44-77 center-fire, single-shot breechloaders and had to meet the international restrictions set down by the Elcho Shield rules. The rifles were not to exceed 10 pounds in weight and were to have trigger pulls of three pounds. No set or hair-triggers were allowed; no artificial rests were allowed; and only iron sights were permitted. Thus developed a new class of American rifles dubbed "Creedmoors." With their Remington and Sharps rifles, the Americans would establish themselves as the preeminent marksmen in later decades of the 19th century.

The Remingtons were made in several different grades, and a host of features could be custom ordered. The rifles generally featured 34" half-round-half-octagon barrels and vernier rear sights. Some were fitted with vernier sights on the comb of the buttstock. It is estimated that fewer than 500 Remington Creedmoors were made. The Sharps rifles were based on the firm's Model 1874. Again, there were a host of custom features that could be ordered, but they generally had 32" octagonal barrels and vernier tang sights. Other calibers, including .40-90 and .44-105 were made by both makers.

Above: Captain Henry Fulton, Secretary of NRA, participated in the first international match for the Leech Cup. His unorthodox shooting position (shown on page 22) drew attention at the match, as did his style of loading his breechloader through the muzzle.

Right: Even with a badly cut hand, Colonel John Bodine managed to finish the 1874 Leech Cup Match with a bullseye at the 1,000-yard target, bringing victory to the American team with a score of 934 to Ireland's 931. NRA's goal to improve marksmanship was truly becoming a reality.

functioned as managers and coaches and did not themselves participate in the shooting.) The team was made up of Lieutenant Henry Fulton, G. W. Yale, Colonel John Bodine, Lieutenant Colonel Gildersleeve, L. L. Hepburn, and General Thomas S. Dakin.

The Irish team, consisting of John Rigby, James Wilson, Dr. J. B. Hamilton, J. K. Millner, Edmund Johnson, and Captain Philip Walker, with Major Leech as Captain, arrived in New York in time to size up the American competition and came away not overly impressed.

The Leech Cup

The big day finally arrived, and on that hot, dry morning, the trains of the Central Railroad were filled to capacity with the cream of New York society mingling with denim-clad Irish laborers who had come to watch the lads from the Old Country clobber the Yankees. Clouds of dust hung over the unpaved roads leading to Creedmoor as streams of cyclists and horse-drawn vehicles converged. By 11 A.M. the crowd had swelled to nearly 8,000.

As the match progressed, tension mounted, not only on the range but in New York, London, and Dublin. The *Herald* and other newspapers telegraphed shot-by-shot scores to New York City, where they were posted on public bulletin boards and relayed to Great Britain by cable.

At the end of the 800-yard stage, the Americans were in the lead with a score of 326 to 317. It was noon by the time the first stage of the match ended, and the two teams and dignitaries from both countries adjourned to a large tent to dine. During lunch Major Leech toasted the Americans and

Above: The Arthur B. Leech Cup was donated on behalf of the Irish team by Major Leech on the day of the big 1874 international match. It would become the trophy of many other rifle matches.

Right: The media also covered the return Leech Cup Match, which took place at Ireland's Dollymount range in 1875. Portrayed here is the American team at practice.

presented them with a handsome silver tankard. This token of international friendship became known as the Leech Cup, one of the oldest and most coveted of shooting trophies.

Won by a Long Shot

The match resumed after lunch, with young Millner opening for the Irish at the 900-yard line. He lay on his back, took careful aim, and fired. Seconds later, the sharp "ping" of a solid hit drifted back to the spectators. He had made a perfect bullseye—but on the adjacent target, a solid miss.

To even matters, Thomas Dakin's fourth shot, following a clean bullseye, hit the dirt halfway to the target. The teams at this point were so close that either shot could have been decisive. At the end of the 900-yard round, the score was 636 to 629, with the Americans clinging to a slim lead.

Midway through the final, 1,000-yard phase, the crowd began to pay special attention to 28-year-old Henry Fulton, the youngest man on the American team, whose unorthodox shooting position had already attracted their notice. Now, with almost monotonous regularity, the white disc rose over the distant bullseye every time he pulled the trigger.

The match came down to the final shot, and it was up to John Bodine to win or lose for the American team. A friend handed him a bottle of soda to wash the dust from his mouth, but when he tugged at the cork the crowd heard a report like a pistol shot, followed by a tinkle of glass. The sun-heated beverage had exploded. Broken glass

had sliced deeply into the tall Colonel's right
hand, and he stood in momentary shock watching the blood drip from his fingers. Doctor
Hamilton of the Irish team rushed over to exam-
ine the wound and recommended that it be given
prompt medical attention. Major Leech generously offered to postpone the final shot of the match
until Bodine had recovered.

Wrapping a handkerchief around his hand,
Bodine waved back his well-wishers and assumed
his shooting position. He waited until the wind
and light were exactly right. Then, with blood drip-
ping from the white handkerchief, he squeezed off
the shot. The crowd held its collective breath. There
was a long pause, and then the sharp, unmistak-

able sound of a hit drifted back to the crowd, and
the white marker went up over the bullseye. Bodine
had made a perfect shot, and America won the
match 934 to 931.

The American victory set off a wave of excitement that began in the front ranks of the spectators and spread by telegraph over much of the
world. Bodine, bloody but beaming like a school-
boy, was carried on the shoulders of his cheer-
ing audience.

Small wonder that Colonel Church, the retiring President of the National Rifle Association, was
still in an exultant mood when he addressed the
annual meeting on January 12, 1875:

Above right: In 1876, the National Rifle Association amended
its charter to add the words "of America" to its name. This
remains its official logo.

Below: A few days after the Americans won the return rifle
match at Dollymount, *Harper's Weekly* published this cartoon
with the caption, "Uncle Sam beats all."

> *We have not only successfully inaugurated
> rifle practice in this country, but in connection
> with one of our subsidiary organizations, the
> Amateur Rifle Club, we have established for
> the National Rifle Association a record so brilliant
> that the name of Creedmoor has become a syn-
> onym the world over . . . for the highest skill in
> marksmanship yet attained.*

Famous Trophies

After winning a return match the following
year at Ireland's Dollymount range, the American
team, captained by NRA Secretary Gildersleeve,
asked the National Rifle Association of Great
Britain for permission to compete in the Elcho
Shield Match. But the original terms under which
the Elcho Shield had been donated restricted the
competition to teams representing Scotland and

England; Ireland had been admitted only under a special dispensation from the donor.

The National Rifle Association of Great Britain stuck rigidly to those terms but presented NRA with a fine silver tankard trophy to be awarded each year to the champion long-distance rifleman of the United States. This was the famous Wimbledon Cup, which has remained a coveted award in American rifle competition. Henry Fulton, who scored 133 out of a possible 150, was the Wimbledon Cup's first winner.

In 1876, the centennial of American independence, NRA amended its charter to add the words "of America" to its name, making the official name of the organization the "National Rifle Association of America." It also invited all nations "having rifle associations or clubs" to a match that would determine the long-range shooting championship of the world in a competition that would become known as the Centennial Match. Though the National Rifle Association of Great Britain declined the invitation due to trouble with the Irish and Scots, teams from Scotland, Ireland, Canada, and Australia journeyed to New York, where NRA unveiled the magnificent Grand Centennial Trophy. The trophy was a full-sized replica of an ancient Roman legionary standard executed in silver, gold, and bronze. On its silver banner were engraved the words, "In the name of the United States of America to the Riflemen of the World." Below the beautifully sculptured crowning eagle, which clutched in its claws a wreath of palm leaves, was a plaque bearing the single word, PALMA, the Latin word for palm tree, which was used by Romans to signify victory or the ultimate in excellence. Although the trophy was known initially as the Grand Centennial Trophy, it became known in 1878 as the Palma Trophy.

As with previous matches at Creedmoor, the 1876 Centennial Match stirred intense excite-

The Palma Trophy, originally called the Grand Centennial Trophy, was won first by the United States in 1876, the year marking America's centennial. Over the years, the Palma Match became one of the most exciting international contests.

ment. The Americans won the match with a score of 3,126 to Ireland's second-place score of 3,104. For the record, the Irish still swore by their Rigby rifles, and the Scots, Canadians, and Australians stood by their Metfords, but nearly every member of each of the foreign teams placed an order for a Remington or Sharps Creedmoor match rifle before leaving for home.

The 1891 matches signaled an end to Creedmoor's prominence in the American shooting scene.

CHAPTER THREE

TUMULTUOUS TIMES

1877–1892

It should not be forgotten that to the National Rifle Association belongs the credit for elevating the use of the rifle to the dignity of the present service; of directing popular attention to its importance as part of the national military training; of stimulating American patriotism through the international matches; and finally causing a revolution in army target-practice.

—The *New York Graphic,* 1891

THOUGH AMERICANS HAD proven themselves as champion shooters of the world, largely through the efforts of the National Rifle Association, an editorial appeared in October 1877 in the *Army and Navy Journal* that criticized the current NRA program. The editorial was unsigned, but it could have come from only one pen, that of Colonel William Church.

Church felt that the existing NRA represented only the state of New York, although its officers and directors had striven, with some success, to encompass all formal rifle shooting in America. He also thought NRA was overemphasizing long-range shooting at the expense of practical military exercise.

While some of these arguments held validity, critics of match shooting overlooked the value that the long-range matches already had brought to military training. Not only had the match rifle inspired a search for more accurate military firearms, but the international matches had given more impetus to military training in marksmanship. Creedmoor rules had become standards for marksmanship training throughout America, and ranges patterned after Creedmoor were being built all over the country.

Church's criticism helped NRA realize that its management and membership were weighted in favor of New Yorkers and that Creedmoor shooters represented most of the international team. To remedy this, in January 1878 the Board of Directors passed a resolution: The General commanding the Army, the Commanders of the various Army departments, the Superintendent of West Point, the Chief of Ordnance of the United States, the Adjutants General of the several states and territories, and the Presidents of all affiliated state rifle associations would become honorary directors *ex officio* of NRA. These individuals were "allowed a voice in all matters relating to the association, but will only be entitled to vote upon general rules of the association in relation to rifle practice, and all rules governing international and interstate rifle matches."

The Hilton Trophy, presented to NRA by the Honorable Henry Hilton of New York, was awarded to a winning international military rifle team in what became known as the Hilton Trophy Match. Creedmoor-trained shooters of the New York National Guard won the first Hilton Match in 1878.

THE 1875 OFFICER'S MODEL "TRAPDOOR"

Rifle courtesy National Firearms Museum

THE U.S. SPRINGFIELD ARMORY MADE a special version of the Trapdoor with a 26" barrel. This was for private purchase by Army officers for their hunting, target shooting, or personal sporting use. The rifles featured folding tang sights, single-set triggers, and oil-fin-ished and checkered walnut stocks with a half-pistol grip stock. Based on the U.S. Model 1873, these exquisite rifles had factory-engraved scroll-work on the hammer, receiver, breechblock, and other metal components. This particular rifle, chambered in .45-80, was once owned by NRA cofounder and later NRA President General George Wingate. From 1875 through 1885, less than 500 Officer's Model Trapdoors were made.

Church was also displeased with NRA's refusal to offer the Palma Trophy for an international rifle match with standard infantry firearms. While adamant about keeping the existing rules for the Palma Match, NRA voted to hold a separate international military match during its fall meetings with a special trophy to be offered to the winner. The first such match was held on September 17, 1878, with a massive silver shield called the Hilton Trophy as the prize.

No More Wars

Unfortunately, by this time, interest in international match shooting had languished, partially because American teams had been so thoroughly dominant in the competition. But a more serious threat to NRA's mission to improve marksmanship came after Alonzo B. Cornell was elected Governor of New York in 1880.

Wingate learned through Frederick Townsend, Cornell's newly appointed Adjutant General, that the Governor held little regard for the National Guard and was already sharpening his knife to cut into its funding. Wingate tried to persuade the Governor to change his mind, but Cornell would hear none of his arguments, telling Wingate, "There will be no war in my time or in the time of my children. The only need for a National Guard is to show itself in parades and ceremonies. I see no reason for them to learn how to shoot if their only function will be to march a little through the streets. Rifle practice for these men is a waste of money, and I shall not countenance in my presence anything as foolish as a discussion of the rifle shooting at Creedmoor."

Military training in New York was to revert to its spit-and-polish status before the days of NRA, when marksmanship was considered secondary to fancy close-order drill. The sudden shift of state support along with the abrupt withdrawal

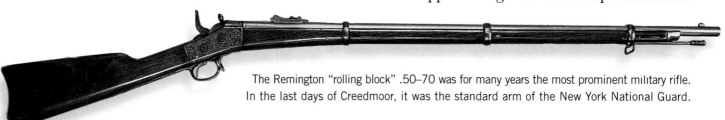

The Remington "rolling block" .50–70 was for many years the most prominent military rifle. In the last days of Creedmoor, it was the standard arm of the New York National Guard.

of the Army teams in NRA matches nearly destroyed NRA's existing program, but the organization was a long way from giving up.

A Need for Improvement

NRA's first move was to seek a nationally known figure, who, like General Burnside had, would provide firm support and emblematic leadership to guide the Association toward renewed national prestige. In January 1881, the Executive Committee chose General Winfield Scott Hancock, who had become a national hero during the Civil War and was one of the most prominent men in American public life, to serve as the new NRA President.

To help renew enthusiasm for shooting and the importance of military marksmanship, NRA agreed to a British-American military rifle competition using standard military rifles to be held at Creedmoor in September 1882. To help finance

the match, NRA sought contributions from the National Guard and the public.

As it turned out, the international match of 1882 was a resounding disappointment to all of America but especially to NRA, for the British won the match by a crushing 170 points. The defeat dramatized the relatively poor quality of available American military rifles as well as the need for marksmanship training at longer distances, and NRA was determined to remedy both of these problems at a return match in Wimbledon.

E. Remington & Sons rose to the occasion and assigned its best craftsmen to design a new rifle model based on the time-tested Hepburn patent. The new Remington Long-Range Military Rifle was of .44 caliber but chambered to accept a .45 caliber cartridge case for greater powder capacity behind the 550-grain bullet. The barrel was improved by deepening the grooves and narrowing the lands. John Bodine and Thomas J. Dolan of the 1882 team spent several weeks at the Remington factory experimenting to determine the most reliable load.

At the same time, J. H. Brown, a member of NRA's Board of Directors, had developed another rifle with a falling block action and a half-concealed hammer. The Brown Standard Rifle was of .45 caliber with an eight-groove bore, chambered for a Winchester case using a 550-grain bullet. In his test, Brown shot one group of 10 shots from the back position at 200 yards that he could cover with his watch.

When the subcommittee to select the rifle couldn't decide between the Brown and the Remington, the individual team members were permitted to choose between the two rifles. These team members were more representative of the entire United States than previous teams had been. National Guard organizations across America had been selecting contenders for the team, and only five members of the 1882 team won places in 1883.

The second British-American military match was held over two days in July 1883, and though

After Governor Cornell cut funding for the New York National Guard, General George Wingate wrote this letter to a member of Congress, asking for support of an appropriations bill that would set aside funds to send state teams to NRA's Annual Matches.

PRESIDENTIAL COLT 1883 SIDE-BY-SIDE

Rifle courtesy National Firearms Museum

GROVER CLEVELAND HOLDS THE DIS-tinction of being the only U.S. President to serve two nonconsecutive terms as the President of the United States. Elected first in 1884, he was defeated by Benjamin Harrison in 1888 and in turn defeated Harrison in 1892. Cleveland was born in Caldwell, New Jersey, on March 18, 1837, and enjoyed waterfowling.

This Colt Hammerless 1883 side-by-side shotgun, serial number 7624, is the only known 8 gauge made by Colt and bears the name "GROVER CLEVELAND" inlaid in gold on the bottom of the trigger guard. The Model 1883, one of the finest American shotguns ever produced, was manufactured from 1883 until 1895. Less than 8,000 1883s were manufactured, and the vast majority were 10 or 12 gauges.

the Americans were leading on the first day, they lost the match by 45 points with a score of 1,906. Still, the Americans' skill had improved drastically from the previous year, and the public's interest in international matches had been somewhat revived.

As a result, the 1884 showing at Creedmoor was one of the strongest in years. To further bolster the organization, a committee headed by Wingate urged General Ulysses S. Grant to accept the presidency of NRA. Inaugurated in April 1883, the war hero and former President of the United States maintained a close interest in the affairs of NRA, but poor health prevented his active partic-ipation. He was succeeded the following year by

General Philip H. Sheridan, the Commander-in-Chief of the Army.

Throughout the administrations of Hancock, Grant, and Sheridan, the actual direction of the National Rifle Association fell on the shoulders of George Wingate. In January 1886, Wingate, his once long beard now close-cropped and iron gray, became the 10th President of NRA.

Goodbye to Creedmoor

This was a period of severe economic crisis for the nation as well as for NRA. The economy of the United States was still reeling under the

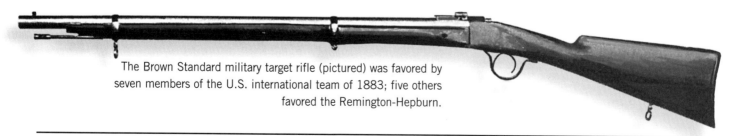

The Brown Standard military target rifle (pictured) was favored by seven members of the U.S. international team of 1883; five others favored the Remington-Hepburn.

General Winfield Scott Hancock (left), who had become a national hero in the Civil War, served as NRA President from 1881 to 1883. He was succeeded by General Ulysses S. Grant (below), also a Civil War hero and former President of the United States. General Philip H. Sheridan (right), Commander-in-Chief of the U.S. Army, followed Grant's two-year term, serving as NRA President from 1885 to 1886.

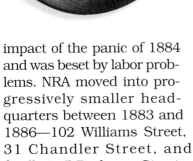

impact of the panic of 1884 and was beset by labor problems. NRA moved into progressively smaller headquarters between 1883 and 1886—102 Williams Street, 31 Chandler Street, and finally to 5 Beekman Street.

Disgusted with the lack of appreciation for what had been accomplished for the benefit of the National Guard, and to eliminate the financial burdens, NRA finally voted in January 1890 to deed Creedmoor to the state of New York with the understanding that the Association would be permitted to hold its customary matches on the range and to issue its marksmanship qualification medals to members of the National Guard.

A crowning blow came in January 1892, when Captain B. M. Whitlock was appointed Inspector General of Rifle Practice with the rank of Brigadier General by New York's Governor Roswell Flower. Whitlock's first official act was to withdraw the state's recognition of the marksmanship badges issued by NRA. He also adopted a new policy of free use of Creedmoor by state troops, which eliminated the entrance fees that NRA had charged to help finance the Creedmoor program. Deliberately or unintentionally he also ordered various units of the state National Guard to practice on the range at times customarily occupied by NRA matches.

On June 16, 1892, NRA's Board of Directors met to discuss the very serious problems the Association faced. The board voted to place NRA's records in storage and to enter into negotiations with the New Jersey State Rifle Association to see if the Annual Matches could be transferred from Creedmoor to the new Sea Girt range of that state organization. Though the turn of the century was still eight years away, this was the last formal meeting of the Board of Directors during the 19th century.

In 1903, the year the National Board for the Promotion of Rifle Practice was created, Americans brought the prestigious Palma Trophy back to American soil. Sergeant J. H. Keough (pictured) was given special media coverage for making the top score.

CHAPTER FOUR

NATIONAL SCOPE AND FEDERAL RECOGNITION

1892–1905

[A] soldier who cannot shoot is a soldier who counts for very little in battle, and all credit is due to those who keep up the standard of marksmanship.

—President Theodore Roosevelt, 1904

GEORGE WINGATE MUST have felt the loss of Creedmoor as a crushing defeat. The organization that he had helped to create seemed to be fighting a losing battle, a victim of economic depression, political apathy, and changing times. But Creedmoor and NRA had succeeded far beyond his realization.

For starters, the National Rifle Association had altered basic military attitudes toward the rifle. Before 1871, infantry tactics were based largely on the concentration of fire, aimed or unaimed, by massed troops against a general target. Individual skill in shooting, although considered a useful attribute in a recruit, was rarely thought of as a skill that could be taught or improved. After its early drubbings at the hands of Creedmoor-trained citizen-soldiers, the Army abruptly awakened and initiated training in marksmanship for combat troops. By 1890, it was holding regular rifle matches at all levels of command and had elevated skill in rifle shooting to an important requirement of the foot soldier. The militia organizations of the various states had started comparable training programs.

NRA was largely responsible for initiating these reforms. As late as 1890, the basic Army and Navy training manuals on marksmanship were only modifications of Wingate's *Manual for Rifle Practice.* Until 1885, the Army used targets identical to those that were standardized under rules laid down by NRA. The Army also had appointed inspectors of rifle practice through all levels of command.

Matches at Sea Girt

Although its program continued, the National Rifle Association as an organization became relatively dormant for eight years after 1892. Its strength was dispersed among many small but enthusiastic groups of riflemen organized in local clubs and state associations throughout the nation. By the time NRA deeded Creedmoor to New York, nearly every state in the union had a state rifle association that had been organized under rules established by NRA.

The one with the closest ties to NRA was the New Jersey State Rifle Association, which had been founded on March 11, 1878, by a group of Creedmoor-trained marksmen from the New Jersey National Guard. Its shooting range near Sea Girt was readily accessible by rail from Trenton and the northern cities and was less than 60 miles from New York City.

In 1901, NRA placed the Members Trophy into competition and awarded a miniature of the silver pitcher to each winner.

NRA transferred its Annual Matches to Sea Girt in 1892. As a result, the New Jersey State Rifle Association, for all practical purposes, assumed the functions of NRA. Such historic events as the Wimbledon Cup, Hilton Match, and interstate military team matches received a major boost, and at each annual meeting the New Jersey organization presented a well-balanced medley of long-range, short-range, and skirmishers' events. These Annual Matches attracted relatively modest crowds and only a few teams, but they spread the reputation of Sea Girt and the New Jersey State Rifle Association throughout the shooting world.

Limited Reach

In 1893, the *New York Sun* published an editorial applauding the continuation of the NRA Matches under sponsorship of the New Jersey Association and calling for more representation in the Matches by the states and federal services.

More editorials came from Arthur Corbin Gould, publisher of *Shooting and Fishing,* a sportsman's journal that was originally published as the *Rifle* in 1885 and was a predecessor of NRA's *American*

Rifleman. Gould was a Bostonian and a long-standing member of the Massachusetts Rifle Association. A student of ballistics and an authority on military marksmanship, he had written two books on rifles and was widely respected as a spokesman for shooting interests. In 1886, he campaigned through the *Rifle* for a standard target and published ballots for shooters and rifle clubs to vote for their favorite. The result was adoption of the Standard American Target.

After moving his offices to New York City in 1894, Gould attended all of the Matches at Sea Girt and took a close personal interest in the New Jersey State Rifle Association. Although he applauded the success of the Sea Girt matches and was impressed with their management, he was disturbed, as were others, by the lack of direction and coordination at the national level. Early in 1899, Gould ran a series of articles and editorials calling public attention to this deficiency.

Inspired by Gould's editorials, Lieutenant Albert S. Jones of the New Jersey National Guard and also the Secretary of the New Jersey State Rifle Association began corresponding with the officers of other state and local shooting organizations in the United States, asking their views on supporting a national society that would represent all of the nation's riflemen. The response was almost universally favorable. Among those who endorsed Jones's proposal was Theodore Roosevelt, then Governor of New York.

With this support, Jones, in July 1900, mailed a letter to the officers of every shooting association and National Guard organization in the nation. The letter urged each to be present or to send representatives to a convention of riflemen at Sea Girt on the following September 5 to discuss the formation of a "League of American Riflemen."

Above: When NRA transferred its Annual Matches to Sea Girt, the New Jersey State Rifle Association, in effect, assumed NRA's role of promoting shooting competition and marksmanship.

Left: In his sportsman's journal *Shooting and Fishing*, Arthur Corbin Gould inspired NRA's leaders to elevate the Association to a national level. *Shooting and Fishing* was originally published as the *Rifle* and evolved into NRA's *American Rifleman.*

At the convention, Jones had scarcely finished stating the purpose of the meeting before George Wingate rose and asked to be heard. The need for an active organization, as proposed by Mr. Gould and Lieutenant Jones, he said, was more than apparent. But the organization that these gentlemen proposed already existed. It had been established nearly 30 years before. Its Matches had been held almost continuously since that time and were internationally known and recognized. Its constitution and bylaws were already written, and it had traditions that no new organization could hope to acquire. Should the delegates not first try to breathe new life back into the old organization?

Wingate's proposal was accepted, and he returned to New York City to begin the task of reviving the dormant NRA.

THE KRAG

Rifle courtesy Robert Daly

FIRST ADOPTED IN 1892, THE U.S. Krag-Jorgensen rifle was the first smallbore breechloading magazine rifle adopted for use by the U.S. military. Chambered in the smokeless .30 Government (.30-40 Krag), it was fed by a five-round, side-loading magazine. The cartridges had to be loaded individually, and the design proved inferior during the Spanish-American War when compared to the clip-fed bolt-action Mauser rifles employed by the Spanish. The Krag was the last U.S. military arm that had separate rifles for the infantry (with 30" barrels) and carbines for the cavalry (with 22" barrels).

This is the Model 1899 Carbine, the last American military carbine to be issued. Many models of Krags were later disposed of through the Director of Civilian Marksmanship and made available to NRA members. Well into the 1920s and 1930s, Krags could be found on the firing lines of NRA matches all across the country.

New Life for NRA

On December 20, 1900, the first meeting of the Board of Directors of the National Rifle Association since 1892 was held in New York City. At this meeting the board elected Major General Wesley Merritt of the U.S. Army as honorary President and Brigadier General Bird Spencer, former President of the New Jersey State Rifle Association, as President. Albert Jones became Secretary. Wingate, although accepting an appointment to the Board of Directors, declined office, feeling that the new officers were quite capable. The number of vice presidents was increased to three, and the *ex officio* board membership was expanded to include the Secretary of War and all general officers of the U.S. Army, including the Chief of Ordnance and the Adjutant General of the United States.

Once established, the new officers began an immediate membership drive and organized a superb summer shooting program in August 1901.

A National Board

NRA received another welcome boost when, in 1902, Congressman Frank Mondell of Wyoming sponsored a bill that would create a "National Board for the Promotion of Rifle Practice" (NBPRP) in the War Department.

The bill incorporated several suggestions from General Bird Spencer: that the federal government sell surplus government arms to militia organizations of the various states, that it authorize annual appropriations for transporting qualified teams from the state and federal forces to an annual national rifle and pistol competition, and that it establish machinery under which such National Matches might be held.

Though the Mondell Bill had the active support of President Roosevelt and Secretary of War Elihu Root, it failed to pass. Early in 1903, however, Spencer outlined the proposal to his friend, Senator John Dryden of New Jersey. Dryden immediately enlisted the support of Senator Redfield Proctor of Ohio, who reintroduced most of the wording of the old Mondell Bill as an amendment to the War Department Appropriations Bill. It became law in February 1903 and authorized the establishment of the National Board for the Promotion of Rifle Practice, the National Matches, and appropriations to transport teams of marksmen to the National Matches from the various branches of the armed services and the National Guard organization of the states.

Elihu Root appointed the first members of the newly born NBPRP on March 31, 1903. At its first meeting on April 21, 1903, the NBPRP recommended "that every facility should be offered citizens outside of the Army, Navy, Marine Corps, and organized militia to become proficient in rifle shooting, and that this purpose can best be accomplished by means of rifle clubs. The board therefore respectfully recommends the encouragement by the War Department of the organization of rifle clubs composed of those who would be eligible for service in time of war, but without special obligation for war service on account of such membership, under such regulations as may be prescribed by the Secretary of War."

Above right: Secretary of War Elihu Root was dedicated to marksmanship training and strongly supported the legislation that created the National Board for the Promotion of Rifle Practice, which went a long way toward bringing NRA's scope to a national level.

Opposite: General Bird Spencer, one of NRA's founders, was elected President of NRA in 1902. He was involved in the creation of the National Board for the Promotion of Rifle Practice, and throughout his six-year tenure as President he helped keep NRA alive during some of its leanest years.

Formation of the NBPRP had two lasting effects on NRA. First, the federal government had approved and lent its support to the principles and program of the National Rifle Association of America. And whereas NRA's main goal since 1871 had been to promote marksmanship training among military types, the NBPRP and its accompanying National Matches triggered NRA to begin offering shooting programs for nonmilitary Americans as well.

The first National Matches authorized by an act of Congress were held at Sea Girt on September 8 and 9, 1903. Fifteen teams, including those from the Navy, Marine Corps, Infantry, and Cavalry entered the event, which was won by the New York National Guard with a score of 2,988.

The National Matches were sponsored by the National Board for the Promotion of Rifle Practice, and NRA still held its own Annual Matches. It was customary, however, that these matches be held jointly, a practice recognized by provisions of the National Defense Act.

The 1903 NRA Annual Matches, which immediately followed the NBPRP's National Matches, were the largest yet held and introduced the Dryden Match, sponsored by Senator Dryden. It was won by an Infantry team, whose members included Lieutenant Townsend Whelen, who was destined to take a place among the all-time greats of the shooting sports.

More Federal Support

Rifle practice, meantime, gained even more credence when President Theodore Roosevelt began a tradition that made a letter from the President of the United States the first prize in the President's Match. In a letter dated September 25, 1904, the winner of the 1904 President's Match at Sea Girt,

Competitors test their rifles on bench-rest blocks at Sea Girt, where NRA began holding its Annual Matches in 1892. At that time, Sea Girt was one of the most modern and best equipped ranges in the world.

Private Howard Gensch of the First Regiment of New Jersey's National Guard, received the President's personal congratulations:

I have just been informed that you have won the President's Match for the military championship of the United States of America. I wish to congratulate you in person, and through you not only the First Regiment of the National Guard of New Jersey, but the entire National Guard of New Jersey. As a nation we must depend upon our volunteer soldiers in time of trial; and, therefore, the members of the National Guard fill a high function of usefulness. Of course, a soldier who cannot shoot is a soldier who counts for very little in battle, and all credit is due to those who keep up the standard of marksmanship. I congratulate you, both on your skill and upon your possession of the qualities of perseverance and determination in long practice by which alone this skill could have been brought to its high point of development.

Then in 1905, Congress passed Public Law 149, which authorized the sale at cost of surplus military rifles, ammunition, and other military equipment to rifle clubs that met specifications laid down by the National Board for the Promotion of Rifle Practice and approved by the Secretary of War. NRA had only to make some minor word changes to its bylaws that would permit NRA-affiliated clubs to purchase government equipment.

Additionally, the NBPRP adopted a resolution in 1904 that

entitled members of all NRA-affiliated clubs to compete for a National Marksmen's Reserve qualification. Those making a total of 50 points in five shots each at the 200-, 300-, and 500-yard ranges were awarded a lapel button from the National Rifle Association and were recorded by the War Department as members of the nation's "second line of defense." In the event of a national emergency, members of the Marksmen's Reserve were promised "first consideration" by the War Department after volunteering for active duty.

Since 1871, NRA had functioned primarily as a national organization to promote marksmanship training in the militia and reserves of the states. But it had operated under severe difficulties until the federal government lent its support and launched an expanded, attractive program for all American shooters. The new laws permitted the National Rifle Association to greatly broaden its services and were an important milestone in the proud role it was destined to play.

The New Jersey State Rifle Association's first venture into civilian shooting was in 1895 with the *schuetzen* match, a stylized form of shooting with customized small-caliber rifles. Introduced in the mid-1800s by Swiss and German immigrants, the *schuetzen* match was one of the oldest forms of organized shooting and remained popular for many years. Cans of Du Pont *schuetzen* smokeless powder featured a figure copied from an old Swiss drinking cup.

CAMP PERRY, 1910.

In a show of sportsmanship, the U.S. Cavalry team of 1910 forfeited $150 in prize money to reinstate the Marine team to second place. (The Marines had committed a minor infraction of the rules.) The Marines were so appreciative that the team donated its $350 prize money toward a Cavalryman Cup to be awarded to the high-scoring cavalryman in the President's Match.

CHAPTER FIVE

NEW HORIZONS:
FROM SOLDIERS TO CIVILIANS

1906–1910

It seemed to just naturally be right at the right place.

—Ammon Critchfield, future NRA President,
on discovering Camp Perry

BY 1906, MOST OF NRA'S ORIGINAL objectives had been achieved. Each member of the armed forces was required to shoot his firearm on the range at least once a year, and nearly every military post and camp had some form of rifle range based on the standards developed by NRA.

Similar progress had been made in the advancement of military firearms, developments that were quickened by the Matches at Creedmoor and Sea Girt.

Training the Country's Youth

Although it had no inclination to reduce its interest in military marksmanship or to relinquish sponsorship of military matches, the National Rifle Association in 1906 had traveled about as far as it could along the military route. Already, it had begun to affiliate more closely with civilian marksmen and had even adopted a code of rifle instruction in 1903 to help qualify citizens in the War Department's National Marksmen's Reserve.

NRA adopted another resolution in 1903, saying it would work more closely with schools to encourage rifle practice in America's youth. Secretary Albert Jones sent letters to the presidents of all the major colleges and universities and the superintendents of the United States military and naval academies asking their cooperation in establishing rifle clubs.

Around the same time, George Wingate had become military instructor in the public schools of New York City, where he founded the Public School Athletic League to stimulate interscholastic competition in sports. In 1905, Wingate started a rifle shooting program in the public schools, and by early 1906 he had organized teams that were competing intramurally in 10 of the city's high schools. At Wingate's suggestion, the *Brooklyn Daily Eagle* sponsored an interscholastic marksmanship match in 1906, open to students of New York high schools. President Theodore Roosevelt wrote Wingate a letter to commend him.

The success of the Eagle Interscholastic Rifle Match inspired the National Rifle Association to add a comparable event to its annual shooting program. The opening match at Sea Girt in August 1906 was conducted under adult supervision and found more than 200 teenage boys encamped at Sea Girt all anxiously awaiting their turn on the firing line.

By 1911, NRA had 14 major trophies in competition, including the Enlisted Men's Trophy, which was presented to NRA in 1910.

James Drain and *Arms and the Man*

Although NRA made great progress under General Bird Spencer's administration, conditions in America were changing, and the time was ripe for a fresh outlook. That's when James A. Drain and Ammon B. Critchfield arrived on the scene. Although in personality and appearance they were near opposites, the two men shared boundless energy, a love of shooting, and a capacity for hard work. Each also had a wealth of political, social, and business experience and a host of powerful friends.

Brigadier General James Drain was a youthful, bustling, handsome man who at age 34 had been appointed Adjutant General of the state of Washington, the youngest man in history to attain that post. Drain was largely responsible for the legislation that gave NRA its official recognition as the mouthpiece for America's marksmen. In 1903, when this crucial legislation was pending in Congress, Drain contacted at his own expense most of the adjutants general of the other states, asking their support. He went to Washington to speak on behalf of the bill with congressmen and military leaders. He obtained enthusiastic support of the bill from Elihu Root, William Howard Taft, and other prominent people.

Although the New York City–based *Shooting and Fishing* magazine had no direct connection with NRA, it had long been the Association's unofficial organ, reporting all of its matches and meetings in detail. But since the death of its founder, Arthur Corbin Gould, the magazine had been languishing. In 1906, Drain purchased the periodical, renamed it *Arms and the Man,* and became Editor and Publisher so that he could continue Gould's work. Drain was elected a Vice President of NRA that same year.

The Father of Camp Perry

Ammon Critchfield of Ohio became a Vice President of NRA at the same time as Drain, and like Drain he was one of the youngest state adjutants

As NRA President from 1907 to 1910, General James A. Drain promoted civilian, youth, and international programs. His personal touch brought in many new members and affiliated clubs.

general in history. He had also built an outstanding shooting program in the Ohio National Guard.

Largely through General Critchfield's effort, the Ohio State Legislature in 1905 appropriated $25,000 toward the purchase and development of a state National Guard rifle range and camp. Critchfield found a level plain a mile long and a half mile deep along the southwestern shore of Lake Erie. It had ready access from rail lines and was less than 45 miles east of Toledo and just south of Put-in-Bay, the site of Commodore Perry's great triumph over the British in the War of 1812. As level as a tabletop, the land was only lightly wooded; it

would require almost no clearing and a minimum of grading. The Governor of Ohio had scarcely signed the appropriation bill before the Ohio State Rifle Association and the Ohio National Guard Association agreed to join in purchasing 30 additional acres as the site of a clubhouse.

Dissatisfaction with Sea Girt was growing both within NRA and within the War Department. The 1906 program was a great success in terms of interest, but the facilities were swamped. With so many teams on the field for the National Matches, the Annual Matches of NRA were delayed and disrupted. The camping facilities, once the most modern of any military installation in the United States, had become dated and dangerously overcrowded. Either a new site had to be found for future Matches, or the NBPRP's National Matches had to be divorced from those of NRA.

There seemed to be two alternatives to separating the Matches. One was to transfer them to the Army's range being built at Fort Riley, Kansas. The War Department, including a strong element in the National Board for the Promotion of Rifle Practice, favored transfer to Kansas because the range was near the geographic center of the nation and would be most accessible from all points in the country. But to the still eastern-oriented NRA, this suggestion was not acceptable. The range experts within NRA examined the range plans and branded them a monstrosity, poorly planned and badly executed. The second alternative was to transfer both Matches to the new installation that Critchfield was building on the shores of Lake Erie. Critchfield's plan called for the most modern facilities in running water, sewage, and electric lights. Its spacious campgrounds, easy access from all eastern and midwestern cities, and the quality of range plans were major points in its favor. Critchfield promised to have 150 targets for known-distance shooting at 200, 600, and 800 yards, four revolver ranges, and 50 skirmish targets installed by the summer of 1907.

NRA's Executive Committee, led by Critchfield and Drain, voted to transfer to Ohio. Spencer subsequently resigned as President of the National Rifle Association, and Drain was elected to succeed him. With the installation at Fort Riley still languishing, the NBPRP had little choice but to transfer the National Matches to Ohio. Just before the 1907 Matches began that August, the new installation was dedicated as Camp Perry, in honor of Commodore Perry, the hero of Lake Erie.

Ohio Adjutant General Ammon B. Critchfield (right) built the range at Camp Perry, Ohio, after personally walking the shores of Lake Erie to find an appropriate site. NRA and the National Board for the Promotion of Rifle Practice held their Annual Matches at Camp Perry in 1907 (below). Years later, Critchfield served as NRA President from 1936 to 1937.

"I HEARTILY ENDORSE THE GOALS AND PROGRAMS…"

WHEN IT CAME TO GUN KNOWLEDGE or shooting skill, no Chief Executive, now or ever, was the equal of Theodore Roosevelt, the 26th and youngest President of the United States. He was an avid hunter, a Nobel Prize winner, a wildlife conservationist, a war hero, and a Life Member of the National Rifle Association.

In 1902, a small wooden box arrived at 1600 Pennsylvania Avenue, Washington, D.C. It was addressed "Theodore Roosevelt, The Executive Mansion." Inside was perhaps the finest Browning Model 1900 pistol ever produced (right). The pistol was to be kept by the President next to his bed for personal protection in his new home, which he dubbed "The White House." The Belgian-made, Fabrique Nationale pistol was chambered in .32 ACP and featured tight banknote engraving and gold-ribbon inlay. The stocks were pearl, and it came in a fitted colt-covered and velvet-lined case.

Possibly one of the finest and most historic gifts given by Roosevelt was a Winchester Model 1895, serial number 23576 (below). This rifle was embellished with a gold plate and inscribed "To Leonard Wood, Governor of Cuba, 12-29-99

Firearms courtesy National Firearms Museum

from TR." At the time of the rifle's presentation, Roosevelt was Governor of New York and General Wood was Governor of Cuba. Wood had been Roosevelt's commanding officer during the Spanish-American War.

Another Roosevelt gun of note is a Rudolph Kornbrath engraved side-by-side double rifle imported by Frederick Adolph. Above each chamber are U.S. presidential seals. The exquisite rifle is chambered in .450-500 and was made for Roosevelt in 1910.

Drain's Campaign

When James Drain became President of the National Rifle Association on January 9, 1907, he declared in his inaugural speech to the Board of Directors that he wanted "to accomplish everything possible toward making the Association one of genuinely national scope and to increase its usefulness to the country as an agency for the promotion of rifle practice."

He began by moving NRA's headquarters to Washington, D.C., where it could be closer to the federal government. Then he started a campaign to sign as many prominent citizens as possible as Life Members, and he began at the top with President Theodore Roosevelt. A letter to Drain from President Roosevelt in February 1907 underscored Roosevelt's enthusiasm: "I am so heartily interested in the success of the National Rifle Association of America and its work done in cooperation with the National Board for the Promotion of Rifle Practice that I take pleasure in sending you herewith my check for $25 for life membership therein."

Drain also approached most of the members of the President's cabinet. Secretary of War William Howard Taft became a Life Member, as did Secretary of State Elihu Root, who sent his check along with a message to Drain saying that young men knowing "how to shoot straight is one of the fundamental requirements of our scheme of national defense." In addition, Drain toured all of the states of the West and Southwest, where NRA had the weakest representation, urging states that were already participating in NRA programs to increase their activities and encouraging those that had no state rifle association affiliated with NRA to create one.

The results of this personal approach were highly successful. Between 1900 and January 1907, NRA had received only 72 new Life Memberships. In 1907 alone Drain had added 87. In January 1907, the organization had 20 affiliated state organizations; one year later the total stood at 29. The number of affiliated regimental clubs increased from 57 to 79, affiliated civilian rifle clubs from 63 to 72, college rifle clubs from 5 to 15, and school clubs from 11 to 29.

TRIUMPH AT THE OLYMPIC GAMES

SHOOTING HAD BECOME A PART OF the Olympic Games in Athens in May 1906, but neither Great Britain nor the United States had sent teams. The next Olympic Games were held in London in 1908, and the British Olympic Association invited the United States to compete in a series of international rifle and pistol matches.

Using star-gauged Model 1903 rifles and 180-grain bullets, the American team outshot rival teams from the United Kingdom, Canada, France, Sweden, Norway, Greece, and Denmark at every distance except 600 yards, where they trailed the British by a single point. That year, the United States won its first gold medal in an Olympic shooting match, with a final score of 2,531 to 2,497 for the second-place British. Canada won the bronze medal. The Americans also swept the Olympic pistol matches.

A New Class of Marksmen

General Drain also gave George Wingate and Ammon Critchfield the task of expanding NRA's school shooting program. Drain appointed a committee to draw up qualifications for both indoor and outdoor rifle matches, and NRA appropriated funds for suitable badges to be awarded to qualifying youngsters. The school program, thanks to a built-in base of 6,000 young marksmen trained under General Wingate's Public School Athletic League, was an immediate success.

In addition, NRA had been trying to increase emphasis on individual marksmanship at the United States Military Academy. Through *Arms*

BREAKING THE GENDER BARRIER

NRA's 1906 ANNUAL MATCHES, WHICH introduced a youth competition and NRA-sponsored pistol matches, laid the groundwork for some of NRA's future programs. But another, unexpected occurrence was to crack the barrier for a program that was still years in the future—a program for female enthusiasts.

As part of its plan to associate more closely with civilians, NRA scheduled a qualification event in 1906 that was open to anyone who wished to compete for a place in the National Marksmen's Reserve. Each competitor was required to shoot the standard-issue Krag rifle at 200, 300, and 500 yards, five shots at each distance. A minimum of 50 points out of a possible 75 was required for qualification, and many of those who had lined up so confidently failed to make the grade.

Then, within the preeminently masculine environment of Sea Girt, a figure appeared in line who caused numerous eyebrows to raise, for this hopeful competitor was a woman. Officials drew together in heated consultation, but try as they might, they could find nothing in the rules barring female shooters. For the first time in history, a woman was about to compete in an NRA match.

Under the existing bylaws, it would have been highly improbable for a woman to join NRA. But nothing in the rules barred women from entering any all-comers' match open to civilians. A scattering of women had been at all of the larger matches, and some had ventured a trial shot or two with revolvers and light rifles. But no woman had ever competed shoulder to shoulder with male shooters on the firing line of a military rifle match.

Elizabeth Servaty Topperwein may have lacked the fame of Little Annie Oakley, but "Plinky" Topperwein was an amazing sharpshooter. She could handle rifle, shotgun, or pistol with equal authority. Two months before arriving at Sea Girt, she had broken 485 out of 500 clay pigeons, shooting in gusty wind at the trap range of the Texas Gun Club in San Antonio. She had shattered nearly all the records made by Annie Oakley both with the shotgun and with the rifle at thrown targets. She could clip tossed coins consistently with the pistol, using either hand. She and her husband, Adolph, were exhibition shooters of the Winchester Repeating Arms Company and formed the most spectacular husband-and-wife shooting team in history.

Shooting rapidly because of her training in exhibition work, Topperwein ran up 61 points to receive her medal—to the cheers of the admiring men.

and the Man, Drain circulated a report to the academy in which General Bird Spencer detailed the conditions at West Point, decrying the lack of shooting facilities and the shortsightedness of the faculty in failing to train future Army officers in this basic military skill. Unfortunately, the Commandant of cadets stood firmly on his decision that the cadets could not spare time from formal studies to engage in anything but rudimentary rifle practice and no time at all for interscholastic competition. "Expert shooting," he insisted, "is postgraduate work."

The future admirals at Annapolis, however, were shooting regularly on a first-class range, competing with teams from Maryland and the District of Columbia National Guard and building one of the strongest rifle teams in the armed services of the United States.

Smallbore Gets Bigger

Aside from its involvement in school competitions, the National Rifle Association had shown little interest in .22 rifles. That changed in January 1909, when NRA accepted a challenge from the Miniature Rifle Association of Great Britain to engage in a championship smallbore rifle match to be known as the Dewar Match, named after the silver Dewar Cup that was given as a trophy to the winning team. Though Great Britain was victorious that year, the Americans won the Dewar Cup in 1910 by a margin of 100 points.

The popularity of the Dewar Match spurred NRA to establish a national smallbore rifle league in which competing teams could shoot on home ranges and exchange the results by cable. This removed transportation problems faced by civilian marksmen who wanted to compete nationally. It

The Dewar Cup was presented to the Miniature Rifle Association of Great Britain in 1909 by Sir Thomas Dewar for the first international Dewar Match. The American Dewar Cup entered competition in 1930.

also limited the competition to indoor shooting, where the variables of wind, weather, and lighting would not influence the comparative scores. NRA supplied and scored marked targets, and a local NRA member supervised the shooting of each team.

Around the same time as the smallbore rifle leagues were formed, NRA initiated a league of college rifle clubs and expanded the public schools program. This in turn led to the formation of another 73 NRA-affiliated school rifle clubs in 1910, most of which would have been unable to compete in NRA matches through any other medium than the postal tournament.

A Lasting Legacy

As the organization moved increasingly toward civilian interests, in 1909 NRA offered an annual membership class, open to any civilian or soldier, which entitled them to all reports, publications, and privileges except a vote in the elections of the organization. (NRA had experimented briefly with annual memberships 10 years earlier but had dropped the class because of lack of public interest.)

Before he stepped down as President in January 1910, Drain spearheaded an amendment to NRA's bylaws that required 36 members of the Board of Directors to be elected from Life Members, members of any affiliated organization, and honorary directors. In addition, each year the Secretary of War would appoint three directors, one of whom was to be a member of the general staff, one representing the Infantry, and another the Cavalry. Two more were to be appointed by the Secretary of the Navy— one from the Navy and one from the Marine Corps. The adjutants general of all states were also added to the board.

Despite this military slant among NRA's leaders, James Drain would be known as the President who succeeded in extending NRA's support for marksmanship and competition beyond the military realm into the wide dominion of civilian interests.

ARMS AND  THE MAN

FORMERLY
SHOOTING AND FISHING.

WASHINGTON, D. C., SEPTEMBER 17, 1914.

$3 a year.   10 cents a copy.

VOLUME LVI. No. 25.

Shooting Stars.

Mr. John W. Hessian.

MR. HESSIAN is so well known to the world of shots that he needs no introduction.

Answering our sixteen interrogations he says:

1. Clinton, Ontario, Canada, Sept. 8, 1877. Travelling representative, Remington Arms-Union Metallic Cartridge Co.

2. The fact that when I first tried to shoot I could not hit anything, and a consequent desire to overcome this lack of ability on my part.

3. Twenty-four.

4. My first rifle was a Stevens Ideal, Model 44, .22 L. R. Cal., that I bought in 1901 from a Mr. Charles Schraum, of Greenville, Pa. In 1905 I sold this gun. Later on I realized what a desirable relic it would be in after years, and after an interesting hunt, I located it in 1911, and it is now in my possession.

5. The first regular match in which I competed was the 100-shot Championship match of the .22 Caliber Indoor League, of the United States, at the Iroquois Rifle Club range at Pittsburg, Pa., 1904. In this match, I made 2,411 points out of 2,500.

6. The trials held at Winthrop, Md., in 1912, to select the members of United States team in the Pan-American matches at Buenos Aires, Argentina. Killed a crow with a revolver at about 150 yards, from a bogie near Mars, Pa. (A luck shot, of course.)

7. Matches won (list attached herewith) gives matches won up to end of 1912-1913.—Marine Corps Match (Con.) Camp Perry, Ohio. New York State, R. A. Championship, Sea Girt, N. J., 1913.

Member of:

U. S. Olympic Rifle Team	1908
U. S. Argentina Rifle Team	1912
U. S. Palma Rifle Team	1912
U. S. Pan-American Team	1913
U. S. Individual Representative International Matches	1913
U. S. North America Rifle Team	1913
U. S. International Small Bore Rifle Team, 1910, 1912	1913

and of numerous other teams of less importance.

8. Long range shooting with the military rifle. Cannot answer all paragraphs of this question.

9. I have always considered Dr. W. G. Hudson the greatest shot that I have ever met or that ever lived. Given anything like the same amount of practice that the other stars usually receive, he would be a hard proposition to beat at any part of the game, while at the offhand position with any kind of a rifle, he is in a class by himself.

10. Yes; very. Have never hunted big game, so cannot say.

11. Yes. Remington Pump gun at the traps, and the Remington Autoloading at game.

12. Two weeks of quail shooting in Virginia over good dogs, with three good friends, viz.: John and Owen Fisher and "Nimrod" Watson, of Lynchburg, Va., in the fall of 1909.

13. I do not believe that there can be a great improvement made in the firearms of the present day. I do think, however, that we may expect a considerable improvement in high-power ammunition.

14. I think that the desire will always be for higher velocity and to obtain this, it will be necessary to secure a powder that, while increasing the velocity, will not increase the breech pressure beyond reasonable limits. It may be that a bullet of different shape and construction will be found that will aid materially in securing this increased velocity.

Mr. John W. Hessian.

15. Yes, decidedly. They allow the concentration of the shooter's mind upon one thing, viz.: pulling the trigger when the aim is correct, at the same time, giving more time in which to secure that aim.

16. By getting more influential people interested in rifle shooting. By making it more spectacular by providing matches that the spectator can watch and follow intelligently, such as Evans skirmish match; and by getting the newspapers to give it more publicity than it now receives.

I believe firmly in the European system of 300-metre ranges built right in the city, easy of access, with free rifles and ammunition at the range for the use of those entitled to shoot there, the place always open (Sundays included), and in charge of a competent corps of instructors. These ranges are so constructed as to be absolutely safe and the Argentine Team gave ample proof of the fact that men who have been taught to shoot well on the short ranges can, with coaching, give a good account of themselves at the long ranges.

At all events, it is so much better to shoot a great deal at 300 metres than once a year at long ranges, as many of the members of our National Guard do now, and I fear that some not even that often. I believe the government should annually give matches for civilian riflemen, and the National Guard only, with very large money prizes at the different divisional matches, of say, not less than $5,000.00 for first place, and other substantial prizes for the first 100 men. There would then be some incentive for the young men to put in their spare time shooting instead of playing baseball, although when one considers the salaries paid to ball players, present conditions are not to be wondered at.

Those of us who saw the beautiful prizes put up by the Argentinos for competition at Buenos Aires, could not help but compare them to those of our own country, and ours suffered by the comparison. These remarks will probably reap criticism, for I know that much has been said against the giving of large money prizes, principally by people who, themselves, know nothing about rifle shooting, and who were drawing lucrative salaries from the government or state for duties much less arduous than shooting a rifle in the blazing hot sun for glory.

These same commentators are loud in proclaiming that large money prizes would tend to lower the standing of rifle shooting as a sport. Anyone at all familiar with military rifle shooting in this country, knows that the prime reason for holding these matches is not for sport but to promote and spread the knowledge of how to shoot our military arm among the men who will be called upon to defend the flag in time of war.

War can hardly be classed as a sport, and it is useless for some citizens to try to induce other citizens to prepare themselves for it at their own expense, with glory alone, and that of doubtful quantity and value as the sole prize.

The return to this country of the 1912 Pan-American team, so ably captained by General Gaither, is till fresh in my mind. This team, after winning first prize in the team match and some one of its members first in every open event at Buenos Aires, after an absence of two months and a half, arrived at New York, and save for the immediate relatives of some of the team members, not a soul there to meet them.

That is a sample of the glory that falls to the rifleman who succeeds. What to those who try and fail? What encouragement is

After purchasing *Shooting and Fishing,* James Drain renamed the publication *Arms and the Man.* (It later evolved into *American Rifleman.*) Though it had been eight years since the name change, the masthead of this 1914 issue reminds readers that it was formerly *Shooting and Fishing.*

CHAPTER SIX

BIGGER AND BETTER

1910 – 1915

Never mind whether they know anything about drill. It doesn't matter whether they know their right foot from their left. Teach them how to shoot and do it quickly.

—Lord Kitchener, Commander of the British armed forces,
September 2, 1914

JAMES DRAIN WAS SUCCEEDED in the presidency by Lieutenant General John Coalter Bates of St. Louis, Missouri. Few men knew better the value of well-aimed rifle fire in battle than Bates. He began a long and distinguished military career as a First Lieutenant in the Eleventh Infantry of the U.S. Army in 1861 and ended it in 1906, as Army Chief of Staff. He served the last two years of the Civil War as aide-de-camp to the Commanding General of the Army of the Potomac. He also commanded Bates' Independent Brigade at the opening of the Spanish-American War and commanded the Third Division of the Fifth Army Corps in the Philippines at war's end. Bates' efforts would go a long way toward increasing international competition and civilian interest in NRA.

The First of the Police Matches

Police competition as an annual event did not begin until the 1920s, but the first police revolver match occurred more than a decade earlier at the 1910 Annual Matches. Though the tournament attracted only a small number of entries, it was an important step forward. Like marksmanship in the Army before 1870, the ability of all policemen to shoot was taken for granted. Some men were chosen as city police officers because they had

a reputation as marksmen, but the majority were selected because they were large enough to command respect or because they stood well with local political bosses. Few had any marksmanship training, and most never fired a shot until they were called upon to use a revolver in the line of duty. The results could be disastrous.

Before he left office, Drain suggested that NRA schedule a police revolver match as part of its Camp Perry program. "These men ought, every one of them, to be expert shots with the revolver," he said. Thus NRA held its first police revolver match in August 1910. It was won by the Chicago Police Department. Two years later, K. K. V. Casey published a comprehensive course of rifle and revolver practice for police in the May 30, 1912, issue of *Arms and the Man*.

Arms to Men

Early in 1910, Congressman John Albert Tiffin Hull of Iowa, the Chairman of the Committee on Military Affairs, introduced a bill authorizing the

---

General John C. Bates succeeded Drain as NRA President, serving from 1910 to 1913. Bates had a distinguished Civil War record and was former Army Chief of Staff.

In 1912 the U.S. rifle team (above) won the Palma Trophy Match after the Canadian team gave the Americans their heaviest competition in years. The following year introduced the first Individual Palma Match, which was won by a Canadian. The individual Palma Trophy (right) was presented by the National Guard Association.

War Department to issue free rifles and ammunition to rifle clubs "under such regulations as the Secretary of War may prescribe." When this bill later became law, the National Board for the Promotion of Rifle Practice was charged with distributing the free matériel. Affiliation with NRA became a prerequisite for qualification.

Meantime the War Department found itself with a surplus of Krag rifles after adopting the Model 1903 Springfield as the official infantry arm. On November 3, 1910, Secretary of War Dickinson authorized the Chief of Ordnance to set aside a supply of Krag rifles to sell to NRA members at $10 each plus costs with the stipulation that they could not acquire the rifles to resell them.

International Competition

Both Drain and Bates used their influence to step up the tempo of international competition. So when the Republic of Argentina announced an elaborate Pan-American Exposition in connection with its 1912 centennial that included an inter-American shooting tournament, NRA readily accepted an invitation to compete. This would be the first opportunity American marksmen had to compete against riflemen south of the border.

The Pan-American International Rifle Match involved unfamiliar rules for the American team, but in spite of that handicap, the U.S. shooters outmatched the South American marksmen in every phase. The final scores were United States, 4,722; Argentina, 4,597; Chile, 4,122; Peru, 3,912; Brazil, 3,876; and Uruguay, 3,460.

That summer, 10 national rifle teams were on the field at Stockholm, Sweden, for the Olympic Games. Although the Americans had felt some dismay when they learned there would be no events involving ranges over 600 meters, where American marksmen were at their best, they took home a total of eight gold medals for individual and team events, including one for the important military team match.

The most popular marksman in the American ranks that year was Arthur P. Lane of New York City, a dapper but modest young man of 20 who had been shooting only two years. Shooting in starched collar and business suit, the "boy wonder of Manhattan" swept the revolver matches and led the American pistol team to an overwhelming

THE '03 SPRINGFIELD: THE RIFLEMAN'S FAVORITE

THE U.S. MODEL OF 1903 SPRINGFIELD rifle was adopted in that year as America's first clip-loading magazine rifle, replacing the .30-40 Krag-Jorgensen series of rifles and carbines. Chambered initially for the .30-'03 round-nosed cartridge, the Army adopted a then-new spitzer bullet in 1906 and changed the designation to .30-'06. The M1903 was the first U.S. military arm that remained the same as issued to both the Cavalry and the Infantry. It was a bolt-action repeater with two front-locking lugs, a large claw extractor on the bolt's right side, and an internal five-round capacity magazine fed by five-round stripper clips. The rifle was heavily based on the Mauser Model 1898, although only a royalty on the stripper clips was paid to Mauser. The M1903 had a precisely adjustable open rear sight and a fine blade front,

both of which were well suited to accurate shooting. As the M1903 was the primary issue rifle of the U.S. Army and Marine Corps at the start of World War I, it saw combat in the trenches of France, where it was dubbed by some "the most accurate rifle on the battlefield."

The Model 1903 proved to be an incredibly accurate rifle, especially after accurizing by a competent gunsmith, and was for decades the favorite arm of military and civilian shooters alike at Camp Perry. From 1921 to 1928, Springfield Armory manufactured a special National Match version with "star gauge" barrels and a host of other improvements that aided match shooting. Then when the M1903A1 "C" or pistol grip stock was introduced, a National Match version of it was made from 1928 until 1940. Several other target shooting versions, including the Model 1903 NRA Sporter, were also made.

victory. Lane himself won three gold medals: for the duel-shooting match at 30 meters, the 50-meter championship match, and for the highest individual score in the team match.

The final international match in 1912 was the Palma Match, held at Canada's Rockcliffe range on September 14. The Canadian team, shooting improved Enfield rifles, gave the Americans the heaviest competition they had faced in years, but the Americans won by eight points with a final score of 1,720 to 1,712.

The 1913 competition was even more spectacular than the previous year's. Events at Camp Perry that summer included NRA's Annual Matches, the Palma Match, the Pan-American rifle and pistol competitions, the International Shooting Union's

(ISU) rifle and pistol competitions, the Ohio State Rifle Association's matches, and the NBPRP's National Matches. Truly Camp Perry had become the axis of the shooting world.

NRA's push into international shooting was so rewarding that it decided to send a Palma team to Canada in 1914 and accepted an invitation from the National Rifle Association of Peru to organize a team for the Pan-American matches in Lima. The Association also agreed to enter the Sixth Olympiad in Berlin in 1916—as long as the German Olympic Committee rescinded its insistence that all teams compete with German military Mausers. But all of these fine plans crashed to earth a few months later when the Kaiser's hordes swarmed into Belgium and lit the powder keg of World War I.

More Civilian Interest

General Bates had asked that he not be nominated for reelection and was replaced as President in 1913 by Brigadier General Charles D. Gaither, a Commander of the Maryland National Guard.

Gaither's first year as President showed a substantial growth in civilian interest in NRA. In the last two months of 1913, 40 civilian rifle clubs, most of them representing schools, colleges, and other youth groups, applied for affiliation with NRA.

That year NRA oversaw tournaments from 28 civilian rifle clubs, 34 colleges, and 18 military schools. For several months during 1914, targets poured into the NRA offices at a rate of 2,200 a week. Each had to be marked, scored, and recorded—a meticulous activity that cramped the limited office space and taxed the resources of the little office staff. That spring NRA moved into more spacious quarters in the Woodward Building on Fifteenth Street in Washington, D.C.

The NRA tournaments were developing some phenomenal marksmen. The top man in the 1914 interclub league was T. K. "Tackhole" Lee of the Birmingham Alabama Athletic Club. Lee ran up an amazing record of 1,999 out of a possible 2,000. In the Dewar Match that year, he shot a possible 500 against the British and then continued shooting for a score of 999 out of 1,000. In 1915, he made it 2,250 out of 2,250. In 1918, Lee would be chosen as one of the first rifle instructors at the new Small Arms Firing School.

Brigadier General Charles D. Gaither succeeded Bates as NRA President in 1913. During his two-year tenure, there was a substantial rise in civilian interest in NRA.

Above: Colonel Peter S. Bomus founded the Boy Scouts of the United States. He was also the Executive Officer of the first National Matches at Sea Girt.

Right: Colonel William Libbey served as NRA President from 1915 to 1921, leading NRA through its war preparedness and postwar programs.

Boy Scouts and NRA

NRA's involvement with the Boy Scouts was the next step in its campaign to teach the country's youth about gun safety, respect and responsibility toward firearms, marksmanship, and the pure enjoyment surrounding the shooting sports.

The Boy Scouts originated in Great Britain in 1908 with Major General Sir Robert S. Smyth Baden-Powell and spread rapidly around the world. Baden-Powell, a leader of the British forces in the Boer War, had been disturbed by the lack of basic field skill in the soldiers of his command. His soldiers were as brave and staunch as any in the world. But send one of them alone to scout the enemy and he might never return. City-bred and city-oriented, they knew nothing of reading compasses and maps or living off the land. It was, in part, to instill these skills in young Britons that Baden-Powell formed the Boy Scouts.

The Boy Scout movement reached the United States in several separate forms. One was the Boy Scouts of America, which was incorporated early in 1910. Another, with a rather close affinity to the National Rifle Association, was the Boy Scouts of the United States, organized by Colonel Peter S. Bomus. The Boy Scouts of America was an extension of the Sons of Daniel Boone, or Boy Pioneers, organized early in the century by naturalist-author Daniel Carter Beard.

Bomus founded his Boy Scouts of the United States without knowing that another organization was already on the scene, and his ideas differed considerably from Beard's. In October 1910, the Boy Scouts of the United States, Dan Beard's Boy Pioneers, and Ernest Thompson Seton's

Woodcraft Indians formally merged under the National Council of the Boy Scouts of America. Early in 1911, the group held its first annual meeting at a banquet attended by President William Taft. Seton became Chief Scout, while Beard, William Verbeck, and Colonel Bomus became National Scout Commissioners.

The first *Boy Scout Handbook*, printed in 1910, contained specifications for a badge in marks-

manship that closely followed the NRA junior marksmanship course. The second edition, released in 1911, made qualification in the NRA junior marksmanship program a prerequisite to obtaining a merit badge in marksmanship.

In 1914, with war raging in Europe and Mexican unrest threatening to spill over the Rio Grande, marksmanship training among America's youth was suddenly tinged with urgency. NRA,

RESTRICTIONS IN NEW YORK: THE SULLIVAN LAW

UNTIL 1911, THERE WERE FEW RESTRICtions on the gun owner other than a rather general prohibition in some states against carrying concealed firearms. The right of the citizen to carry firearms openly or to keep them in the home or place of business without restriction was accepted almost universally by state law, and the federal government found no reason to enter the regulatory picture.

In the state of New York, that traditional freedom changed on May 25, 1911, when the New York legislature passed Timothy D. Sullivan's "Act to Amend the Penal Laws in Relation to the Sale and Carrying of Dangerous Weapons." The Sullivan Law, as it was called, was the parting gesture of a machine politician in the final plunge of his decline from power. Only months after he introduced the bill, and hounded by charges of corruption, Sullivan was committed to an institution for the insane. He was killed by a railroad train on September 1, 1913, after escaping from custody.

Under the Sullivan Law, nearly everyone in the state who wished to legally possess a firearm that could be concealed on the body had to first obtain a license issued by a court or the police. The process for obtaining the license required an intense, complicated, and expensive investigation of both the applicant and the intended purpose of the firearm. Most applicants were denied.

Proponents of the law reasoned that the way to eliminate crime was to remove the instruments used by criminals; thus the police of New York City made it almost impossible for anyone to own or to purchase a handgun, regardless of his or her need. As opponents of the law predicted, crime rates in New York continued to rise as rapidly as before and more rapidly than in many jurisdictions where no restrictions prevailed. Within the first year of its enactment, murders increased 18 percent in New York state. As a May 24, 1913, editorial in the *New York Times* noted, "The concealed weapon law has not worked as well as was expected by those of us who commended it. This is an act too obvious for denial. Criminals are as well armed as ever, in spite of the sternness with which the law has been applied to a few of them."

Supporters of the Sullivan Law responded by tacking on new amendments—67 over the next 52 years—all designed to make the law even more restrictive. Those who wanted to acquire a pistol for illegal purposes, of course, paid no attention to the Sullivan Law and purchased their guns through other means. But those who wished to defend themselves against robbers, rapists, or prowlers were told that they should leave police matters to the police and were denied permits.

through its national offices and affiliated clubs, cooperated closely with the Boy Scouts, offering its ranges for practice and providing coaches and supervisors. In October 1915, the Executive Committee created a new class of NRA membership of affiliated Boy Scout troops.

Shadows of War

By the time Colonel William Libbey succeeded Gaither as President in 1915, the mood across the country was tense and watchful. The assassination of Archduke Ferdinand in June 1914 had touched off a series of delicately balanced alliances, plunging parts of Europe and Asia deep into war. Germany, Austria-Hungary, and Turkey had squared off against the combined might of the Allied powers of France, Great Britain, Japan, and Russia.

The United States was ill prepared for conflict on the scale of that in Europe. As soon as it appeared that America could become involved in the war, the federal government initiated a recruiting campaign for the armed services and stepped up the production of firearms. Living in the shadow of war, many who had regarded the National Rifle Association as an organization for sport or play changed their opinion and saw how vitally important the Association was.

The value of NRA's work had already been dramatized at Vera Cruz in April 1914. When the Atlantic Fleet landed its Marines, Ensign W. A. Lee, who as a Midshipman had starred in the Matches of 1907, was in charge of one of the landing boats. When small-arms fire from the shore pinned down the men on his barge, he borrowed a rifle from a Marine and with amazing marksmanship picked off three of the enemy snipers.

NRA was the only nonmilitary organization in the United States designed to teach men to shoot. As such, it was creating a reserve of trained civilian riflemen who could carry their skill into the services whenever the Army, Marine Corps, or Navy needed them.

1916: Congress passes the National Defense Act to promote civilian marksmanship, naming NRA as the liaison between the Army and the civilian reserve.

1917: America enters World War I; NRA opens all its ranges to recruits and launches a smallbore qualification course to aid their training. It also works with Congress to form a Small Arms Firing School, which opens the following year.

1934: Congress passes the National Firearms Act; NRA launches a new Legislative Division and helps defeat California's Alco Bill, which proposed to outlaw all concealable firearms.

1916: NRA buys its first official publication, *Arms and the Man,* for one dollar. In 1923, the name changes to the *American Rifleman.*

1926: NRA blends its own youth training with the Winchester Junior Rifle Corps, forming a stronger junior marksmanship training program.

1927: NRA forms a Police Division to reflect its growing emphasis on police training programs.

PART TWO

SUPPORTING SOLDIERS AND CIVILIANS

B Y THE START OF WORLD WAR I, THE United States was on top of the shooting world and was prepared to defend it from tyranny, thanks in large part to the National Rifle Association of America. NRA's inexhaustible efforts during this trying era were nothing short of remarkable.

While NRA expanded its programs for civilians, the matches at Camp Perry grew progressively larger, despite fluctuating government funding. Meanwhile, NRA attended hearings in the 1930s involving the first federal firearms laws. More restrictive firearms legislation during the 1960s would have a lasting influence on NRA's direction, but during the first two-thirds of the century, its activities focused mainly on competitive shooting and civilian programs such as police training, youth activities, safety education, and programs for hunters.

1941: America enters World War II; NRA develops a preinduction smallbore service course, opens its ranges to the federal government, and forms a training program for the Home Guard.

1949: NRA launches its hunter safety program in New York, drastically reducing the number of hunting accidents.

1963: NRA launches a home firearms safety course designed to educate people on how to avoid unsafe conditions related to keeping firearms in the home.

1941–1945: Throughout the war, NRA publishes training manuals on everything from pistol shooting to handloading for plant guards. By the time the war ends, NRA members had taught 1.75 million students the correct use of small arms.

1960: NRA begins certifying police firearms instructors and begins working with wildlife conservation organizations.

1938: The Federal Firearms Act is passed, which imposes heavy penalties for the criminal misuse of firearms.

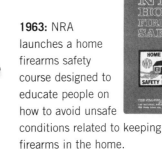

The Springfield Armory M1911 (top) and the Remington-UMC M1911 (bottom) were made under contract for the U.S. military. *(Pistols courtesy National Firearms Museum)*

CHAPTER SEVEN

PATRIOTISM AND PREPAREDNESS

1915–1918

No time should be wasted. . . . The fact now stands out clear and plain that our men must be taught to shoot.

—*Arms and the Man*, October 1917

AS THE UNITED STATES ASSUMED a position of war preparedness, the training program available through the National Rifle Association became more important than ever.

On July 29, 1915, NRA launched an intensive drive, which in three months brought in 15,000 new annual members. Many prominent military and civilian figures, among them Thomas Edison, lent their support by becoming Life Members. The Association earmarked all Life Membership dues received during these years to a special trust fund for promoting rifle practice. It also started a drive to organize rifle clubs at industrial firms and various government agencies. At the end of 1915, NRA had thriving civilian clubs in the various plants of General Electric, Goodyear Rubber, Willys-Overland, Jordan Marsh Company, Petroleum Iron Works, and Hydraulic Pressed Steel.

Assistant Secretary of War Henry Breckinridge encouraged NRA's civilian program and spread his enthusiastic support to others within the War Department. At NRA's Board of Directors meeting in July 1915, Breckinridge announced that the War Department was furnishing trophies and medals for teams from civilian rifle clubs in a national competition.

NRA also participated in the October 1915 Conference of National Defense. This meeting was attended by the leaders of the more prominent veterans' organizations, the National Defense League, the Navy League, and the Army and Navy Union. By unanimous vote, the conference endorsed NRA President William Libbey's proposal for a national shooting academy to train civilian rifle instructors in the event of war.

This idea, too, had originated with Breckenridge. During the 1915 National Matches, Breckenridge advocated constructing a series of government rifle ranges throughout the United States that would be open to all civilian rifle clubs affiliated with NRA. He also encouraged NRA to expand as fully as possible its civilian training program as a contribution to the defense effort. Breckinridge's ideas, although they reached fruition after he left government service, formed the foundation of Section 113 of the National Defense Act of 1916.

Shortly after NRA's first 1916 board meeting, General James Drain decided to retire from the publishing business to devote his full time to law practice. Though *Arms and the Man* had become the leading magazine of its kind in America, it was no gold mine. Drain sold the magazine to the

Senator Smith Brookhart of Iowa, while commissioned a Major, was chief instructor at the Small Arms Firing School in 1918.

National Rifle Association for the price of one dollar, giving NRA its first official periodical. Drain's association with NRA had been so close that the content of the old and the new magazine was almost identical. Seven years later, with the June 1923 issue, the magazine's name was changed to the *American Rifleman,* and it has been published continuously by that name ever since.

Skilled Civilians

Under the increasingly tense international situation, a close relationship sprang up between military and civilian rifle clubs. It started under a program sponsored by NRA at the Marine Corps range near Winthrop, Maryland. Since 1913, the Winthrop range had been open to NRA members as well as civilian teams.

The relationship between civilian and military rifle clubs grew even tighter when Congress passed the National Defense Act on June 3, 1916, which expanded the standing Army from 90,000 to 175,000 and allowed for its gradual enlargement

Above: Major William C. Harllee of the U.S. Marine Corps was an NRA Vice President and a member of the NBPRP. Harllee promoted civilian rifle practice by permitting NRA-affiliated civilian rifle clubs to use the Marine Corps' Winthrop range for training during World War I.

Left: In 1916, James Drain sold *Arms and the Man* to NRA for one dollar, giving the Association its first official magazine. Shown here is the premiere issue as an NRA publication.

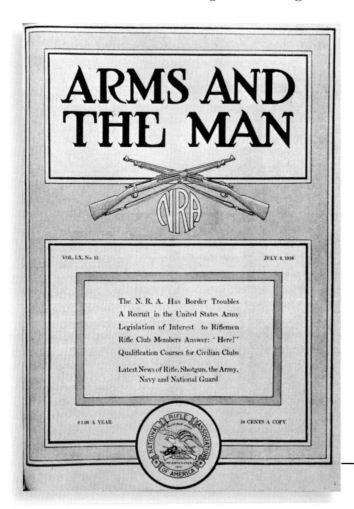

to 223,000. The act also enabled a National Guard of 440,000.

The National Defense Act was a milestone in NRA's development, for it incorporated into government policy many of the ideas that NRA had advocated for years. For starters, the act earmarked $300,000 to promote civilian marksmanship training and authorized the War Department to distribute appropriate arms and ammunition to organized civilian rifle clubs, under rules established by the National Board for the Promotion of

Rifle Practice. In addition, the act provided funds for government rifle ranges and transportation of military instructors to assist civilian rifle clubs. It opened all military rifle ranges to civilian shooters and provided $60,000 to transport civilian teams to the National Matches. Finally, it created the office of the Director of Civilian Marksmanship under the NBPRP. Congress specifically named the National Rifle Association of America as the liaison between the regular Army and the civilian reserve.

Colonel Samuel W. Miller, the Executive Officer of the 1916 National Matches, was appointed the first Director of Civilian Marksmanship, or DCM. He served only six months, however, before being called back to service when America entered World War I. His replacement was Major Edwin V. Bookmiller.

Not surprisingly given NRA's recent focus, civilians did remarkably well in their first appearance in the National Matches, held in conjunction with the 1916 NRA Matches.

Doing Its Part

When America entered World War I on April 6, 1917, its arsenals contained only 800,000 Model 1903 Springfield rifles. Under a normal, eight-hour production cycle the country could produce 200,000 rifles a year; at capacity, production could be increased to 500,000—still far short of the need. Moreover, the Springfield rifle did not lend itself to mass production at other plants without complete retooling.

Fortunately, three private plants in the United States—Winchester, Eddystone, and Remington—had been tooled up to produce .303 British caliber Pattern 1914 Enfield rifles under contract from Great Britain. On May 11, 1917, the Ordnance Department accepted the Enfield, modified to chamber the M1906 cartridge, as an American service rifle. Before the war was over, American plants produced nearly 4 million of the Model 1917 Enfield rifles.

The Model 1917 was a sound and reliable rifle, but the adoption of a "foreign rifle" caused grumblings that grew into ugly rumors. Word soon spread that the M1917 Enfield was totally inaccurate and unsafe to shoot. NRA helped dispel these rumors after General George Wingate, known as the father of American rifle practice, was assigned to test it. In a series of articles published in *Arms and the Man,* he supplied a reassuring report— that the Enfield in many respects was as good as the Model 1903 and totally reliable under battle conditions. By burying the rumors quickly and decisively, NRA improved the morale of many Americans who found themselves carrying Enfield rifles into France.

World War I had an immediate and heavy impact on the National Rifle Association. The rifle shortage led the NBPRP to suspend issuing or selling rifles and ammunition to civilian clubs for the duration of the war. Moreover, many of the Association's more prominent members were National Guardsmen who were ordered immediately to the colors, and men from affiliated clubs volunteered *en masse* for active service.

Eager to do its part for the war effort, NRA began encouraging members of affiliated clubs to volunteer for the Home Guard. One of the first clubs to respond to the call was the Home Club Target Association from the Department of the Interior.

As a wartime measure, approximately 2.5 million of these Model 1917 Enfield rifles in .30-06 caliber were produced in U.S. arms manufacturing plants.

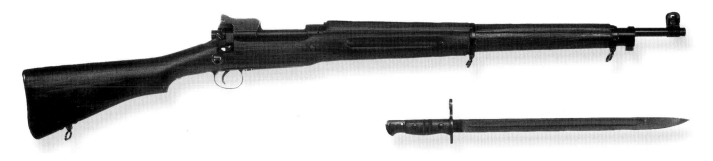

Armed with antiquated .45-70 Springfields, its members walked sentry duty before public buildings in Washington. Later, NRA succeeded in having the Home Guard armed with shotguns, which were more practical for potential street warfare.

Discovering that the Reserve Officers Training School at Fort Myer, Virginia, had no rifle range, NRA opened all of its local ranges to trainees and succeeded in putting 2,500 men through a 40-shot qualification course. With .30 caliber ammunition almost impossible to obtain, NRA launched a smallbore qualification course based on a reduced version of the regular military course. NRA's course used scale-model targets to be shot at with .22 caliber rifles. Affiliated rifle clubs throughout the United States built similar ranges, and thousands of prospective soldiers were able to familiarize themselves with conditions comparable to those on military rifle ranges. As the war effort intensified, some soldiers had to depend almost entirely on the rifle training they had received on NRA ranges.

Learning the Art of War

In September 1917, the War Department announced that it was bringing to America some British and French instructors to teach American recruits the art of war. The new program included a series of schools in musketry that would be directed by foreign officers.

NRA protested this decision, for many of the Allied officers who were assigned to training duty in the United States had already expressed prejudices against the rifle. Although the British considered skill in marksmanship a useful quality in a soldier, some also believed that training marksmen was too time consuming to be practical in time of war. The French view of the rifle was even dimmer. Several high-ranking French officers had

publicly stated that a rifle was merely a useful handle for a bayonet. Soldiers, they claimed, could never be trained to shoot straight in the heat of battle. French soldiers were taught to close with the enemy using grenades and bayonets.

Within a few days of the War Department's announcement, NRA's position received indirect but powerful endorsement. In France, General John J. Pershing had become exasperated by the poor marksmanship among his recruits. Some had never fired their rifles, and many had never had a rifle in their hands before entering military service. Valuable time and energy had to be spent in retraining them overseas—and wartime France had few places where adequate rifle ranges could be established without endangering civilians or the millions of Allied soldiers who crowded the territory behind the lines. The demands of war often made it necessary for Pershing to assign

While in France during World War I, General John J. Pershing had been troubled by the lack of marksmanship training among recruits. He became a strong advocate of marksmanship training and was a loyal supporter of NRA programs. Pershing donated the Pershing Trophy for smallbore competition between the United States and Great Britain.

"NRA" M1911

PERHAPS THE BEST-KNOWN MILITARY service pistol of all time is the "U.S. Pistol, Model of 1911, Caliber .45," invented by John M. Browning and developed by Colt Patent Firearms Manufacturing. The approximately 100 NRA-marked pistols that were manufactured prior to World War I and that were for sale through the Director of Civilian Marksmanship represented an interesting and rare variant of the Springfield-made pistols. "N.R.A." was stamped on the right side of the frame below the pistol's serial number. Very few original NRA-stamped M1911s still exist.

Pistol courtesy National Firearms Museum

green troops to frontline duty before they had learned more than the rudiments of shooting.

Pershing's view of the rifle was quite different from those of the French and British, and he stated it unequivocally to Secretary of War Newton D. Baker in October 1917: "You must not forget that the rifle is distinctively an American weapon. I want to see it employed. . . . Long experience with conditions in France confirms my opinion that it is highly important that infantry soldiers should be excellent shots. . . . I, therefore, strongly renew my previous recommendations that all troops be given a complete course in rifle practice prescribed in our firing manual before leaving the United States."

Two weeks later, on October 20, NRA renewed its earlier plea for action in *Arms and the Man*, asking the War Department to establish a school of musketry.

Section 113

The pleas of Pershing and NRA did not fall on deaf ears. The National Board for the Promotion of Rifle Practice met in Washington on January 8, 1918, and recommended unanimously that a "central school of musketry for the Army, Navy and Marine Corps" be established at the earliest pos-

sible date. In coming to the decision, the NBPRP cited Section 113 of the National Defense Act of June 3, 1916:

The Secretary of War shall . . . submit to Congress . . . a comprehensive plan [that] will ultimately result in providing adequate facilities for rifle practice in all sections of the country. . . . [A]ll ranges so established. . . shall be open to use by those in any branch of the military or naval services of the United States, and by all able-bodied males capable of bearing arms, under reasonable regulations to be prescribed by the Secretary of War.

The National Defense Act of 1916 was one of the most sweeping military laws ever enacted by Congress. It paved the way for the conscription of any able-bodied male citizen between 21 and 30 (later, from 18 to 45), increased the size of the regular Army, and provided for a College Reserve Officers Training Corps and a Federal Officers Reserve Corps. It was a long and complex act, and for a time Section 113 had been all but overlooked. But read in the light of General Pershing's urgent appeals for trained manpower, Section 113 was a tacit endorsement of what the National Rifle Association had been advocating since the start of the war. Clear legal authority for the establishment of a small arms firing school did exist; the War Department had only to implement it.

The Small Arms Firing School

Spurred by Pershing's appeals, the Secretary of War endorsed the recommendations of the NBPRP almost as soon as he received them. On April 15, 1918, the Chief of Staff of the U.S. Army, General Peyton C. Marsh, signed orders authorizing establishment of "the Small Arms Firing School for the Instruction of Officers and Enlisted Men in Rifle and Pistol Shooting" at Camp Perry, Ohio. A companion order assigned Lieutenant Colonel Morton Mumma as Commandant and charged him with establishing the new school; Major Smith Brookhart of Iowa was chosen as chief instructor.

The right men had been put in the right jobs. Mumma was probably the most experienced rifleman in the regular Army, with a career that had started with a borrowed rifle when he was nine years old. He had won Distinguished Marksmanship rank with rifle and pistol and was a top man with a shotgun. He had been a high-scoring member of the Cavalry rifle and Army pistol teams and had won many individual honors both in the National and NRA Matches. He won the Marine Corps Cup twice and placed second in the President's Match. He had been Adjutant of the Palma team of 1912 and Captain of the team of 1913. While on assignment with the State University of Iowa as an instructor of military science, he had consistently turned out championship rifle teams in the NRA intercollegiate matches.

Brookhart, like Mumma, was a member of NRA's Executive Committee and of the National Board for the Promotion of Rifle Practice. Though he was not an outstanding marksman himself, he was a builder of marksmen. He had captained the high-scoring Iowa team in nine National Matches and the 1912 Palma team. At the time of his appointment he was a captain in the Army Ordnance Department.

The Small Arms Firing School opened in May 1918. Colonel Mumma assured the first class of officers and enlisted men that hereafter the American soldier would be taught to place his shots. The American soldier was to be shown how he

might become an accomplished "bullet placer"— and at the same time be best prepared to protect his own life.

Under a plan devised by Mumma, the school's primary objective was to train instructors rather than expert riflemen. Each student, without regard for rank, was selected for his ability to teach. On returning to his regiment, he was qualified to pass his new knowledge to the men in the ranks.

Each trainee at Camp Perry underwent approximately a month of intensive training and shooting under the guidance of the best riflemen in the world. The staff, personally selected by Mumma and Brookhart from the best contemporary marksmen, were men who were well known in national and international competition. Among them were T. K. "Tackhole" Lee, one of the greatest smallbore riflemen in the world, and William Libbey, President of the National Rifle Association.

Colonel Morton C. Mumma (below) was responsible for organizing the new Small Arms Firing School at Camp Perry (opposite) in 1918. Mumma was arguably the most experienced rifleman in the U.S. Army and had a gift for turning out championship rifle teams.

Civilian Inclusion

The NBPRP decided to resume the National Matches in the fall of 1918, deeming them important to the "existing emergency . . . not only as an incentive to those already in the service, but as a medium for the development of competent coaches."

Under regulations adopted just before America entered the war, each state was entitled to send only one civilian team to the National Matches. But conditions had changed with passage of the Defense Act of 1916. Under the act, most civilian male citizens were subject to military service, and it was logical that their usefulness would be enhanced by prior training with the standard infantry rifle. Since all Model 1917 rifles were going directly to military units, few civilians were familiar with their construction or qualities.

Colonel Mumma strongly endorsed opening the National Matches to civilians. "It appears to me," Mumma stated, "that great good could be accomplished if a plan were perfected whereby members of civilian rifle clubs could receive training at the Camp Perry school in connection with the National Matches. . . . There are plenty of men who will gladly take advantage of such an opportunity."

The War Department then decided to form a marksmen school for civilian rifle teams that would prepare civilians for the 1918 National Matches. Although only one civilian team from each state could travel to the National Matches at federal expense, the War Department opened the Matches and the Small Arms Firing School to all civilian or school teams that traveled to Camp Perry at their own expense.

The Infantry School of Arms

Both the War Department and Congress recognized the success of the Small Arms Firing School in producing outstanding military marksmen. In October 1918, Congress appropriated $10 million for an expanded version of the Camp Perry model to be built on the banks of the Chattahoochee River near Columbus, Georgia. Its 120,000 acres accommodated 12,000 student officers in a single class, or 144,000 in one year. This was the Infantry School of Arms, later named Fort Benning. Originally it combined the old School of Musketry from Fort Sill, the Small Arms Firing School from Camp Perry, an experimental section, a trench warfare section under foreign officers, and an automatic weapons section.

The Infantry School of Arms was based on an idea that NRA had been advocating since the beginning of the war. The school was formed too late to play a significant role in the war effort; Colonel Mumma and his staff arrived there in early October 1918, only a few weeks before the armistice was signed. But it developed into one of the most important Army training complexes in America, and it was an important tribute to the programs so diligently pursued by NRA.

Before he was President of the United States, Franklin Delano Roosevelt was Assistant Secretary of the Navy and chaired the National Board for the Promotion of Rifle Practice.

CHAPTER EIGHT

THE SOARING TWENTIES

1918–1925

. . . [T]he National Rifle Association of America is the average rifle-man—no more, no less.

—NRA Executive Committee, 1925

NOVEMBER 11, 1918, MARKED the end of World War I. As the United States demobilized, the War Department continued its interest in marksmanship training, as Richard D. LaGarde, a Captain in the U.S. Army, became Director of Civilian Marksmanship. At the same time, the National Board for the Promotion of Rifle Practice was reorganized to comprise 12 members who were "thoroughly informed of marksmanship." Franklin Delano Roosevelt, who at the time was Assistant Secretary of the Navy, was appointed Chairman. Several prominent NRA officers sat on the NBPRP, including Colonel Morton Mumma, Lieutenant Colonel William Harllee, Colonel William Libbey, Lieutenant Colonel Smith Brookhart, Brigadier General Fred Phillips Jr., and Lieutenant Colonel Townsend Whelen.

The new NBPRP went to work early in 1919, voting to restore the purchase privileges of arms and ammunition to civilian rifle clubs. It also adopted tentative changes in regulations governing the free issue of arms and ammunition, giving NRA-affiliated rifle clubs access to modern military firearms and increased allowances of ball cartridges.

Championing the .22

Because of the shortage of .30 caliber ammunition during the war, many affiliated clubs of NRA had practiced with the .22, and more than a few members had grown to like it. Unfortunately, there was no magazine-equipped bolt-action .22 rifle in production at the time. Springfield and Krag rifles had been adapted to the .22 caliber by plugging the magazine and inserting auxiliary barrels. These, however, were makeshifts with poor accuracy beyond 75 feet, and they had to be loaded singly.

Early in 1919, the United States Cartridge Company developed a new .22 cartridge especially for NRA's smallbore program. A few months later, the Savage Arms Company produced its .22 NRA bolt-action rifle. Winchester followed six weeks later with its "experimental target rifle," the forerunner of its famous Model 52. Both rifles loaded from detachable magazines, were well stocked, and had pinpoint accuracy. Two years later, the federal government unveiled the first model of the Springfield rifle specifically designed for .22 caliber shooting.

The .22 rifles were very popular with young shooters, but at its 1919 annual meeting the NBPRP debated whether the National Defense Act of 1916 imposed an age limit on civilians eligible to shoot

Senator Francis W. Warren of Wyoming served as NRA President from 1925 to 1927.

at government rifle ranges. Many base and post Commanders had barred shooters below the age of 18 and above 45 on the grounds that they were not eligible for military service.

The 1920 Army Appropriations Bill clarified the matter. It authorized the expenditure of $10,000 "to establish and maintain indoor and outdoor rifle ranges for the use of all able-bodied males capable of bearing arms under reasonable regulations prescribed by the National Board for the Promotion of Rifle Practice and approved by the Secretary of War." Further, the NBPRP appropriated $300,000 for the promotion of small-arms target practice on military ranges and authorized "such ranges and galleries to be open as far as practicable to the National Guard and organized rifle clubs under regulations prescribed by the Secretary of War."

The NBPRP also decided that the National Matches of 1919 should be held at the new, sprawling Navy rifle range near Caldwell, New Jersey. This was the newest and largest range in America and was only an hour from New York City. Its "Century Butt" held 100 targets, and there was ample room for 150 more.

William Harllee, First Vice President of NRA, had helped plan and build the Caldwell range and was named Executive Officer of the National Matches. Captain Edward C. Crossman, one of the most enthusiastic smallbore shooters in the country, was in charge of the miniature rifle range.

Edward Crossman threw himself into the task of devising a unique smallbore program. "There ought," he wrote on April 5, 1919, "to be nothing under 50 yards and there ought to be events out

MODEL 1903 SPRINGFIELD SPORTER, STYLE NRA

IN 1924, THE SPRINGFIELD ARMORY BEGAN production on a .30-'06-caliber Model 1903 Springfield rifle for sale to NRA members. At the time, commercial sporting rifles appropriate for high power matches were not readily available. The rifle was based on Springfield's M2 .22 LR rifle in general lines: it had a pistol grip and half-stock sporter style stock and could be fitted with a Lyman 48 aperture rear sight. Full-length stocks were also available. The 24" barrels were star-gauged and chambered to National Match specifications. The rifle, also called the "DCM Sporter" was discontinued in 1933 because several arms makers were offering comparable .30-caliber rifles commercially.

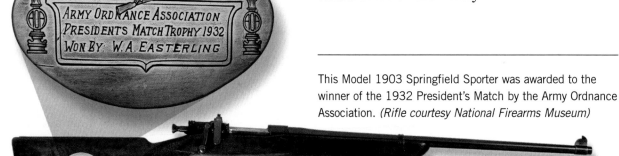

This Model 1903 Springfield Sporter was awarded to the winner of the 1932 President's Match by the Army Ordnance Association. *(Rifle courtesy National Firearms Museum)*

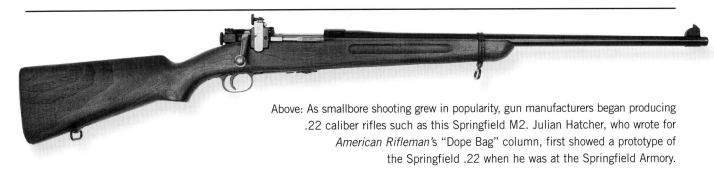

Above: As smallbore shooting grew in popularity, gun manufacturers began producing .22 caliber rifles such as this Springfield M2. Julian Hatcher, who wrote for *American Rifleman*'s "Dope Bag" column, first showed a prototype of the Springfield .22 when he was at the Springfield Armory.

Below: The Navy's range near Caldwell, New Jersey, was the site of the 1919 National Matches. The tent city on the left was dubbed "Commercial Row" because various manufacturers and dealers displayed guns and accessories there.

to 200 yards." Such distances with .22 caliber rimfire rifles had been considered impractical, but Crossman had tested the new rifles and cartridges and found them to be adequate. The .22 was new in the National Rifle Association's Annual Matches, and Crossman—the rifle's most ardent advocate—was determined to make it an outstanding success.

The First Postwar Match

Just as the first teams arrived at Caldwell, however, disaster struck. Heavy rains battered New Jersey for nearly a week in mid-July. On July 23, as the Passaic River turned into a torrent, a dam on one of its tributaries near Morristown let go. A sheet of water rolled over the Caldwell range, turning it into a shambles. Tents were flooded; the boardwalks floated through the camp like battering rams; and Crossman's wooden smallbore butts piled into the Century Butt nearly a quarter of a mile away. Sailors and Marines worked around the clock to tow floating material back into position.

It was a credit to the U.S. Navy and the Marine Corps that the Matches were held that year. But Harllee was a stubborn Marine with a reputation as a drop-of-the-hat fighter. Everything was back in place by the day of the Matches. Little sign of

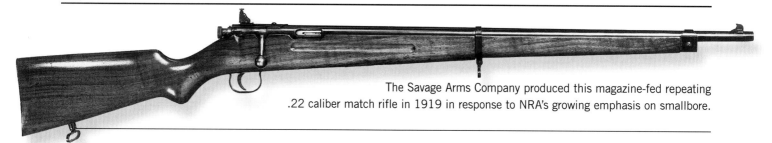

The Savage Arms Company produced this magazine-fed repeating .22 caliber match rifle in 1919 in response to NRA's growing emphasis on smallbore.

the disaster was apparent except for puddles and pools of water that dotted the landscape.

By 1919, NRA was putting greater emphasis on the pistol. Young Arthur Lane added the first-prize medal of the NRA Individual Pistol Match to his many national and international honors. There were other new features, including a Trapshooting Match and a Police Revolver Team Match. The NRA Annual Matches that year were the largest held to that time. Seventy-two teams were on the field, and hundreds entered the individual events.

The smallbore matches were popular with everyone; nearly all of the .30 caliber shooters tried their hands with the .22s. In the Dewar International Smallbore Match, which hadn't been held since the outbreak of war, the American team turned in a record performance, scoring 7,617 out of a possible 8,000 points. The British shot on their home range across the Atlantic and scored 7,523.

Olympic Competition

In 1920, the Board of Directors voted a new class of membership to accommodate veterans' organizations and such organizations as the American Trapshooting Association and the United States Revolver Association. It also endorsed American participation in the shooting phases of the seventh Olympic Games, which were to be held in Antwerp, Belgium, that summer.

The selected members of the U.S. Olympic rifle team, captained by Lieutenant Colonel George Shaw, included 10 marksmen from the Army, four from the Marine Corps, two from the Navy, and two civilians. The Army provided the team's transportation to Antwerp, marking the first time the government helped finance the travel of an Olympic shooting team.

The American pistol team for the Olympics included some of the long-famous names in handgun shooting—Arthur Lane, Dr. H. A. Bayles, and Dr. J. H. Snook. But its roster also contained a new-

comer to international shooting, a tall, handsome New York attorney named Karl T. Frederick, who in the trial matches seesawed with Lane as the winner and second-place man in every event.

The Americans performed well in the military matches. In the team rifle match, the United States placed second to Denmark among a field of 15, while in the individual military match, Commander Carl T. Osburn of the U.S. Navy picked up the first gold medal for the United States. After that, the Americans began to sweep the field, winning both the team and individual matches in the miniature rifle events. They took gold medals in the 300-meter

and 600-meter prone team matches, the 300-meter free-rifle team event, and the individual free-rifle match. In winning the free-rifle events, the Americans used "as-issued" Springfield rifles. Nearly all of the other teams shot special rifles equipped with set triggers and custom stocks.

In the four pistol matches, the American team picked up three gold, one silver, and two bronze medals. Frederick won the 50-meter individual match and placed third in the 30-meter individual match, which was won by a Brazilian. American trapshooters also turned in outstanding performances, sweeping both the team and individual championships.

All in all, the Olympic Games of 1920 placed the United States solidly on top of the shooting world. Once the Americans returned home, they, along with other American marksmen, began planning for the big National Matches to be held that August in Camp Perry.

Enjoying Success

Most of the civilian marksmen at the 1920 Matches were dressed in the new khaki NRA official uniform—riding breeches, wraparound puttees, and pleated shooting jacket topped by a wide-brimmed ANZAC-style hat. Camp Perry had been refurbished and expanded and now boasted 50 targets for 200 yards and 100 each for 600-yard and 1,000-yard shooting. For the first time, the clubhouse at Camp Perry was operated as a hotel and restaurant by the state of Ohio. That year also premiered what was known as the "Squaw Camp"

Above: Lieutenant Colonel Smith W. Brookhart, a former Senator and Inspector of Small Arms Rifle Practice of Iowa, served as NRA President from 1921 to 1925. He was also chief instructor at the Small Arms Firing School in 1918 and served on the NBPRP after World War I.

Left: Camp Perry's so-called "Squaw Camp" was created in 1920 to house married couples, women shooters, and women spectators.

for visiting ladies, married couples, and a scattering of female shooters.

Edward Crossman was again in charge of the smallbore range and added a few new events to those he had devised at Caldwell. Several were for juvenile shooters. One 13-year-old girl, Marjorie Kinder, fired more than 500 shots every day in the Junior Reentry Match "C" to place among the winners. Marjorie had been at Caldwell the year before and had been an attentive student at the Small Arms Firing School, a lone girl among dozens of male shooters.

With the successful Olympic matches and reactivation of the National Matches at Camp Perry, 1920 was a far better year than many had expected, and NRA headed into the new year with high hopes for the future. Colonel Libbey, after ably guiding the Association for five years, stepped down as President at the Annual Meeting in January 1921. His successor was Smith Brookhart.

NRA's growing programs kept its staff busy, and the months passed quickly until the next Camp Perry gathering of the nation's top shooters. Shortly

before the Matches were scheduled to open, the National Rifle Association sent a team to represent the United States in the 1921 International Shooting Union matches at Lyons, France. Although they had almost no time to practice, the Americans turned in remarkable performances, with a record score in the team match. They beat the second-place Swiss by 82 points and France, Italy, and Holland by from 400 to nearly 1,000 points.

Less than two weeks later, the combined NRA Annual Matches and NBPRP National Matches of 1921 got underway. The newly expanded NRA pistol program attracted many participants that year. It also lured some of the country's top shooters like Arthur Lane and Karl Frederick. Public interest in the smallbore matches was also high, with nearly all of the prominent firearms and ammunition manufacturers offering trophies or prizes for matches featuring the .22. There were so many first-class smallbore shooters at Camp Perry that year that NRA officials made no effort to hold tryouts for the Dewar International Smallbore Match. They merely selected the most likely prospects

Above: Despite the federal government's spending cut for the National Matches, the United States was able to produce a winning 1922 international team, which competed in the ISU matches in Milan, Italy. Sitting from left: Major J. K. Boles, Major L. W. T. Waller Jr., and Lieutenant Commander C. T. Osburn. Standing from left: Captain Joseph Jackson, Lieutenant Commander A. D. Denny, Lawrence Nuesslein, and Sergeant Morris Fisher.

Left: Many of the arms manufacturers and powder and ammunition companies offered trophies for the 1923 National Matches. From left: the Peters Cartridge Company Trophy, the U.S. Cartridge Company Trophy, the Western Cartridge Company Trophy, the Winchester "Plainsman" Trophy, and the Hercules Powder Company Trophy.

from among those competing in the NRA events. On September 18, 1921, this American pickup team soundly beat the best marksmen in Great Britain by more than 100 points and the Canadians by more than 400.

By early 1922, the National Rifle Association was finding many new and previously unexplored avenues to interest its expanding membership. The pages of *Arms and the Man,* which had recently gained Thomas G. Samworth as a second Associate Editor, now included articles on hunting, shotgunning, handguns, ballistics, and new shooting products. Many articles dealt with the conversion of American and foreign military rifles to sporters. And regular notices of action by the DCM appeared for the first time.

United We Stand

With the lessons of World War I still fresh, Congress had generously supported the marksmanship training program. But by 1922, the lessons had begun to fade. Congress was looking for ways to cut the budget, and with the "war to end all wars" already fought, where better to cut expenses than in the military? That year Congress and the Harding Administration eliminated the appropriation that provided federal assistance to the states for sending National Guard teams to the National Matches. And no civilians were to travel at government expense. There had been 150 such civilians at the 1921 Matches.

The spending slash upset the shooting program and led to speculation that there would be no National Matches in 1922 except among teams representing the regular services. The Dewar Match, which was scheduled to be held on September 24, seemed doomed to cancellation.

As it turned out, these predictions proved overly pessimistic. The National Rifle Association immediately canvassed the adjutants general of the various states, urging them to send representative teams to the Matches that summer. The response was spectacular. Thirty states sent National Guard teams at their own expense, and the Militia Bureau managed to dredge up enough funds to finance the travel of one civilian team from each of the nine Army Corps areas. The uncertainty that prevailed almost up to the time of the Matches cut atten-

dance and caused some losses of affiliated clubs who felt that the economy drive had doomed NRA's shooting program. What it actually did was prove that the NRA program had matured enough to stand on its own legs. Most of the clubs that strayed away soon drifted back to the fold.

Major changes in scoring procedure were introduced that year. So many bullseyes had been made in the previous year that ties were commonplace. To separate the near-perfect shooters from run-of-the-mill experts, the NBPRP, at its meeting in January 1922, adopted the "nickel" target, featuring a 12-inch inner V-ring in the bullseye of the B target and a 20-inch V-ring in the C target. From that point, the overall score and the number of shots in the inner rings determined the winner.

Kernel Mumma's Amatures

The new system proved valuable during NRA's Herrick Match. Under the Herrick Match

rules, only one team from each of the regular services and one National Guard and a civilian team from each state could shoot for record. The 29 official teams were required to use the service rifle with issue sights, but the six unofficial teams were allowed to use any special equipment they wished—the same conditions as for the Palma Match.

Five of these unofficial teams were second teams of the regular services or National Guard, but one, known as "KMA," for "Kernel Mumma's Amatures," was a pickup group organized by Mumma. Among its members were Lieutenant Colonel Mumma's son, Midshipman Morton C. Mumma Jr. With the exception of the young Mumma, the team members all had competed regularly in national events.

Midshipman Mumma had not won a place in this elite company purely through parental indulgence. Although he was an unknown to most of the spectators, he had fired on the Iowa civilian team

in 1919–1920 and had won the NRA high school championship in 1921. In the opening phase at 800 yards, the KMA team, shooting scope-sighted experimental models of the Model 54 Winchester, missed a perfect score by only four points, a new world record for the distance. Midshipman Mumma was one of the five who finished with a perfect score. The record stood only five minutes, however, before the official Massachusetts National Guard team, using issue sights on regulation rifles, broke it by a single point. Then this record, too, toppled as the unofficial Infantry team turned in a clean score for the distance.

Of the 150 shots fired by KMA and the unofficial Infantry teams, 146 were in the bullseye and 112 of these were in the new scoring system's V-ring. To cap this remarkable shooting performance, the official Marine Corps team, placing second to Massachusetts, equaled the previous world record. Young Mumma continued his perfect performance at 900 yards, and then at 1,000, to finish the course with the first perfect score. In the official scoring, the Massachusetts National Guard took the Herrick Trophy from the Marines for the first time in nearly 10 years.

Despite the federal cuts to military spending, NRA's program fared well in 1922, and the NRA board was optimistic when it met in February 1923. The Secretary's report showed a gain of 5,000 individual members over the 13,000 in 1922 and an aggregate membership of 150,000 in affiliated clubs.

Refined Words

In June 1923, the name of NRA's *Arms and the Man* magazine officially changed its name to the *American Rifleman.* Later in the year, Charles Dunn was hired as the magazine's first Art Editor. The scope of the magazine's coverage expanded too, thanks in large part to four men who joined the pub-

At the 1922 Matches, a pickup team called "Kernel Mumma's Amatures," led by Executive Officer Morton Mumma, proved its professional talent by making a world record during the Herrick Match. Colonel M. C. Mumma and his son Midshipman M. C. Mumma Jr. are standing at far left.

lication's staff that year and whose long careers with NRA were just beginning. Major Julian S. Hatcher, who had served on the staff at the Springfield Armory and was already a leading authority on small arms and ballistics, wrote a regular column called "Dope Bag," which dealt with technical aspects of firearms and shooting. A column covering shotgun and field shooting was written by Captain Charles Askins Sr., the leading authority in his field. Townsend Whelen, one of the leading target shots in the United States who had spent years exploring and hunting in the wilder portions of the world, wrote "Rifles and Big Game Hunting." C. B. Lister, who had worked for the Du Pont Powder Company, contributed "NRA Notes," which covered the programs and activities of affiliated clubs and headquarters affairs. In addition, "DCM News," written by DCM Colonel Stodter, appeared in every issue. And

for collectors, *American Rifleman* featured "Firearms of Yesterday."

Always on Top

The National Rifle Association of America continued to grow in spite of recurring governmental economies and cutbacks that often made it touch and go whether the National Matches would be held. The National Matches of 1923 had both bright spots and disappointments. Retrenchments in federal spending were more stringent in 1923 than in previous years, and no civilian teams traveled to Camp Perry at government expense. NRA, however, persuaded the major railroads to offer half-fare rates to civilian shooters traveling to the range at personal expense. In spite of the federal austerity program, more than 100 civilian shooters attended,

The National Matches of the National Board for the Promotion of Rifle Practice and the Annual Matches of NRA had become closely associated. Camp Perry was large enough to host both events and was even large enough to include, in 1920, an Airplane Match, in which crews fired machine guns at ground targets on the 1,000-yard range. The winning team flew a deHavilland and scored 295 direct hits for a total score of 906.

and the state and federal services turned out more than 1,000 marksmen.

In 1923, Captain John G. Dillin of Pennsylvania brought a historical, muzzleloading Kentucky rifle to the Matches that sparked a separate competition—later called the Davy Crockett Match—in which competitors fired the antique rifle at one of the traditional X-targets. Dillin later wrote a book called *The Kentucky Rifle,* which was published by NRA under a cooperative arrangement with the author. The book did much to stimulate gun collecting in America and to revive interest in muzzle-loading guns of the past.

Major General George C. Richards, Chief of the Militia Bureau, was instrumental in reinstating the policy of sending civilian teams to Camp Perry at government expense. As a result, the 1924 Matches attracted more shooters than ever. That year the

American team won the Dewar Cup for the sixth consecutive year and broke the world record too.

The Dewar Match wasn't the only international competition the Americans dominated. The 1924 Olympic rifle team, which was financed entirely by public subscription through NRA, easily took home the gold for the Olympic team match, and Sergeant Morris Fisher of the Marine Corps took the gold in the Olympic individual match. Major J. K. Boles won the single-shot individual Running Deer match for another gold medal, and the American trapshooting team won against a field of 12 opposing teams.

Also in 1924, NRA agreed to join with the National Board for the Promotion of Rifle Practice in organizing, equipping, and financing a team to compete in the Pan-American matches in Lima, Peru. The U.S. team swept the rifle matches, smashing all

records by 100 or more points and winning the Argentine Cup in a commanding victory over Cuba, Argentina, and Peru. Sergeant Morris Fisher won the Visitors Cup, and Lieutenant Sidney Hinds won the individual championship. The Americans also won the match for the Peruvian Trophy.

All in all, the United States finished 1924 as champions of the world in nearly every form of shooting used in international competition, including several specialties that until then had been considered European.

Police Training

Closer to home, police teams, after several years of lukewarm interest, were at last beginning to show interest in the Matches at Camp Perry. The Delaware and Hudson Railroad Police sent teams to the 1923 Matches, as did the police departments of Toledo, Buffalo, Portland, and New Orleans.

After a major outbreak of mail train robberies, in 1923 Colonel Mumma took it upon himself to develop a course in shooting for railroad mail clerks. Practically all of the country's 10,000 mail clerks were armed, but few had any training in the use of their firearms. The program was closely connected to the NRA police training program at the Small Arms Firing School.

More police departments were also realizing the need for firearms training. In November 1923, the Denver Police Department staged a turkey shoot at a police benefit program. The city's Director of Public Safety was so appalled by the poor quality of the officers' marksmanship that he immediately ordered all patrolmen and detectives to undergo a thorough course in marksmanship training. The course was based largely on that developed by NRA.

In 1922, the entire New Jersey State Police force had affiliated with the National Rifle Association. Several years later, Chief of Police R. Lee Heath of the Los Angeles Police Department decided to do something about the shooting inadequacies of his force and asked Captain Edward Crossman to help. The city ended up building a modern pistol range designed by Crossman. Before the end of the year, 20 Los Angeles police teams were competing regularly on the range, and nearly all of the Los Angeles police became NRA members.

We, the People

Thus far, the 1920s had been kind to the National Rifle Association, and at the first 1925 NRA board meeting in February, there was no inkling of the internal problems that lay ahead. Senator Francis W. Warren of Wyoming was elected the new NRA President, and the business of the meeting centered principally on plans for sending an American team to St. Gall, Switzerland, to shoot in the ISU matches in the coming summer. The first indication that anything was amiss came in March 1925, when the National Board for the Promotion of Rifle Practice moved its offices from the Woodward Building and relieved NRA Secretary Fred Phillips Jr. of his duties as Executive Officer and Recorder of the board.

Ever since the War Department had created the NBPRP, it had shared offices with NRA, and the NRA Secretary had traditionally served as the Recorder of the NBPRP. The move by the War Department was not alarming, but the manner in which it was done caused some apprehension among members of the Executive Committee and the Board of Directors. NRA, therefore, formed a subcommittee to investigate.

Its investigation focused sharply on Phillips, who had served as Secretary for several years. During his term, NRA had enjoyed good growth, but the importance, responsibility, and power of his position had expanded significantly. Instead of serving as custodian of a few trophies and accounts ranging into a few hundred dollars, as in the days of Albert Jones, the Secretary in 1925 dealt with accounts ranging into hundreds of thousands of dollars and supervised a salaried staff of nearly 20 people. He also had one-man control over a national magazine.

The subcommittee voted that Phillips be replaced. After extensive study and debate, the board terminated Phillips's connection with NRA. His role as Secretary was temporarily filled by C. B. Lister, and his role as Editor of *American Rifleman* was filled by Thomas Samworth.

Before adjourning, NRA's board voted to continue studying the Association's legal framework, which led to tremendous organizational improvement. Legal counsel reviewed its bylaws, and an auditing committee was appointed. With the coun-

COLONEL TOWNSEND WHELEN

"**O**NLY ACCURATE RIFLES ARE INTEResting," wrote Colonel Townsend Whelen, namesake of the .35 Whelen cartridge and the man considered to be the dean of American gunwriters for the first half of the 20th century. Whelen's affiliation with *American Rifleman* is long and storied. Beginning in 1923, he wrote hundreds of articles and columns for the magazine. His presence in *American Rifleman* continued into the 21st century through the "Dope Bag" data and comment section found in every issue. Whelen also wrote "Rifles and Big Game Hunting" and a "Loads and Reloads" column.

sel's recommendation, in September NRA voted to change the bylaws to make the Board of Directors a body of 60 Life Members divided into three classes of 20 each, with the classes to serve staggered terms of three years.

The following year, the board allocated the administrative affairs of NRA to a Secretary who would be directly responsible to the Executive Committee. Brigadier General Milton A. Reckord was elected to the post. General Reckord had a distinguished career as a soldier and businessman. He had risen through the ranks of the Maryland National Guard and was a Major in the First Maryland Infantry. During World War I, he led the 115th Infantry as a Colonel. After fighting in the Battle of Meuse-Argonne, he won both the Distinguished Service Medal and the Croix de Guerre with Palm. When he was elected Secretary of NRA, he was Adjutant General of Maryland and a former President of the National Guard Association.

By the end of 1925, NRA's annual membership had risen from 15,173 to 22,054, and Life Members increased from 245 to more than 1,500. Because the National Rifle Association had taken steps to cure its own hidden weaknesses, in 1925 it was able to state without fear of rebuttal a description of itself that would hold true for decades to come:

In the final analysis, the National Rifle Association of America is the average rifleman— no more, no less. The Association is not a mystical organization of a few individuals and a few officers in Washington. . . . It is rather an organization of everyday citizens who believe in the rifle as a means of recreation and national defense, banded together for the purpose of advancing the sport, and, in a sense, pooling their resources in order to accomplish a most worthy end.

The Minuteman Trophy captured the spirit of nationalism that the National Matches represented. It was selected by the NBPRP in 1925 as a trophy to be awarded to the high ROTC or service academy team in the National Trophy Rifle Team Match. Daniel Chester French's life-sized statue of the "Minuteman of Concord," from which this bronze statuette was replicated, stands in Concord, Massachusetts.

CHAPTER NINE

STRONG LEADERSHIP, STRONG SUPPORT

1926–1931

[T]here shall be held an annual competition known as the National Matches. . . . [T]he sum necessary for the above named purposes is hereby authorized to be appropriated annually as part of the total sum appropriated for national defense.

—amendment to Section 113 of the National
Defense Act, May 28, 1928

GENERAL MILTON A. RECKORD brought to the National Rifle Association a zeal for work, a great personal prestige, and an impeccable reputation. He was known and widely respected by the leaders of the veterans' organizations and the military and political leaders of the state and federal governments. Reckord gave NRA precisely the quality of leadership it needed to overcome any problems it faced and emerge stronger than ever.

To Better Protect, to Better Serve

As soon as he became Secretary, General Reckord expanded the police program, announcing an entirely new incentive to familiarize police officers with their firearms. He initiated two pistol tournaments, open only to members of law enforcement agencies. These tournaments operated under a postal system that permitted the officers to shoot on their home ranges. In addition to medals and qualification decorations, NRA offered cash prizes to the winning teams and leading individuals in the two tournaments. Los Angeles, which had been among the first cities to develop a police marksmanship training program, adopted the NRA-based program immediately and was the first city to offer increased pay to policemen who qualified as experts with the pistol.

Charles Gaither, the former NRA President, had begun a similar program in Baltimore, Maryland, after his appointment as Commissioner of Police. On his first inspection tour, General Gaither was horrified at the quality of the handguns carried by his men. They were required to purchase their own handguns, but there were no standards. Many had purchased secondhand pistols of ancient vintage, inadequate power, and poor accuracy.

General Gaither, himself a crack shot, quickly changed all this. He required every man on the force to buy a new handgun of standardized caliber and to learn to use it. He set up a target range on city land and ordered every man on the force to spend several hours each week in practice. By 1926, Baltimore had one of the best-trained police departments in the United States.

NRA's police training program was directly responsible for elevating the standards of the American police forces. In 1920, after conducting a poll of all cities with at least 25,000 inhabitants,

The United States Coast Guard Trophy, awarded for annual competition in the Coast Guard Rapid-Fire Match, depicts Alexander Hamilton.

Above: During his long tenure as an executive officer at NRA, Major General Milton A. Reckord built up the Association's strength in a number of ways, which included expanding the police and youth programs, increasing membership, and influencing Congress to include a mandatory annual appropriation for the National Matches in the budget of the War Department.

NRA had found only three definite police marksmanship training programs in the entire country. In 1926, NRA established its police marksmanship qualification course at the Small Arms Firing School, and though it attracted some immediate interest, it wasn't until 1927 that police departments all over the country began to see marksmanship as a necessary part of police training. That year more than 2,000 policemen from all over the United States qualified in the course, and several police departments sent officers to Camp Perry to train as instructors. From that time on, police marksmen were always among the leading contenders in the annual NRA pistol matches.

Also in 1927, NRA established a Police Division, directed by Eugene F. Mitchell, who joined the NRA

staff from Colt's Patent Firearms Manufacturing Company. Mitchell supervised the tournaments and traveled extensively to attend police conventions and meetings of civic groups. He also edited police tournament news for *American Rifleman* and contributed a regular police column.

The Winchester Junior Rifle Corps

A short time before General Reckord became Secretary, the Executive Committee had unanimously voted to accept responsibility for managing the Winchester Junior Rifle Corps (WJRC). This organization of school-age shooters had been created in 1917 by the Winchester Repeating Arms Company primarily as a promotional program. From the beginning, it overlapped NRA's youth program, after which it was loosely patterned, but it possessed a few unique features that made it appealing to young people. The NRA junior marksmanship program required participants to shoot on a formal range. Members of the WJRC, however, could qualify anywhere, provided the shooter could obtain adult witnesses to authenticate his targets. Moreover, the

WJRC featured a series of qualification courses through which individual participants moved by stages as their skill increased. Medals and other prizes recognized each stage of proficiency as the shooter moved toward expert status.

The Winchester Junior Rifle Corps was a huge success. By the time NRA took it over, it had qualified 135,000 boys and girls who had been organized in 3,000 clubs and supervised by more than 500 volunteer instructors.

Although there were differences between the WJRC's and NRA's junior marksmanship programs, both were organized on a postal basis, with targets scored at a central office. NRA combined the two programs into one that included the best features of each.

New Business

During their September 1926 meeting at Sea Girt, the NRA Board of Directors voted to promote General Reckord from Secretary

to Executive Vice President. C. B. Lister was promoted to the dual office of Secretary-Treasurer. Lieutenant Colonel F. M. Waterbury, who had been the First Vice President, was promoted to President. Waterbury had been Ordnance Officer of the New York National Guard and had been acting President since July 1926, when Senator Francis Warren resigned due to the press of his official duties.

That year the board rewrote the bylaws to establish a more orderly method of succession to the presidency. The President was selected from the slate of Vice Presidents but could serve only two one-year terms. Usually this honor went to the First Vice President, while the two remaining Vice Presidents moved up in rank and a new Third Vice President was elected. Meanwhile, the Executive Vice President and Secretary-Treasurer provided continuity to the administration.

Renewed Support

The National Matches of 1926 promised to be much smaller than in previous years, for the economy-minded War Department had eliminated funds for the Matches from its budget. But those who believed in NRA's program quickly pooled their resources. On behalf of the New Jersey National Guard, Bird Spencer, the former NRA President, offered the use of the Sea Girt range. Then Major L. W. T. Waller Jr. and Colonel A. J. Macnab, who had been Executive Officer of the Matches of 1925 and General Pershing's

Above: NRA's youth program grew steadily during the late 1920s and early 1930s. The Whistler Boy Trophy was one of two identical trophies for junior shooters in the age 12 to 14 class and the 15 to 18 class. It was presented to NRA in 1931 by Grover A. Hughes.

Left: Smallbore competition gained more prevalence at NRA after the organization took over the Winchester Junior Rifle Corps and established a Junior Division in 1925.

Instructor of Rifle Practice overseas, convinced the Commandant of the Marine Corps to assign Marines as support personnel. General Spencer served as Commandant of the Matches. This was the last of his many contributions to NRA. A few years later, on July 28, 1930, he died in the clubhouse of the rifle range to which he had devoted so much of his life.

A number of other prestigious organizations avidly supported NRA's work, including the Reserve Officers Association, the National Guard Association, and the American Legion, which established local rifle clubs throughout the country. The widespread support for NRA's objectives resulted in renewed federal funding for the 1927 National Matches and free ammunition to clubs affiliated with NRA.

The Leading Authority

Beginning January 1, 1927, the National Rifle Association began sending *American Rifleman* to all annual members, whereas previously it had been mailed without charge only to Life Members and to the secretaries of affiliated clubs. This new policy broadened the magazine's appeal to advertisers, and for the first time provided a direct liaison between the offices of the Association and all the members.

By that time, *American Rifleman* was being published monthly instead of semimonthly, and it

Left: Lieutenant Colonel Fred M. Waterbury served as NRA President from 1927 to 1928. He was also one of the first four members of the Executive Council, which NRA created in 1937.

Below: Though the War Department eliminated funds for the 1926 National Matches, that year's shooting events were held at the Sea Girt range in New Jersey, thanks to the generosity of Bird Spencer and the New Jersey National Guard.

had been overhauled and expanded. Thomas Samworth had resigned as Editor in 1926 to devote full time to his book publishing business. A new Editor, L. J. Hathaway, joined the staff in June 1927. By this time the magazine had become self-supporting. It boasted a circulation of 30,000 and a substantial list of paying advertisers.

The expert staff of the "Dope Bag"—Charles Askins, Julian Hatcher, and Townsend Whelen—quickly became the last word on technical shooting questions. In 1928 alone, the "Dope Bag" staff processed more than 5,000 letters on hunting equipment, ballistics, reloading, and the selection of arms and equipment for special tasks.

In an effort to reach a wider audience beyond members, NRA launched a Publicity Bureau in 1929 under the direction of C. B. Baker. Through a newsletter to newspapers and magazines, the Publicity Bureau gave national publicity to recreational shooting for the first time. Many of its news items featured the junior marksmanship program, which had a broad appeal to newspaper editors. The junior rifle club program then had more than 3,000 individual members in 540 separate clubs scattered all over America.

Lieutenant Colonel Lewis M. Rumsey Jr. was NRA President from 1928 to 1930. He joined NRA's Executive Council in 1937.

The NRA Service Company

With all of the new and expanding activities, it soon became necessary for NRA to seek more office space. In November 1927, NRA moved to the Barr Building on NW K Street off Farragut Square, in what was then one of the newest office buildings in Washington, D.C. The NRA suite of 15 offices occupied 4,650 square feet of the eighth floor, while additional space in the basement housed the NRA Service Company.

The NRA Service Company was created in 1927 to supply targets, target rifles, shooting accessories, and match ammunition to NRA members at moderate prices. At that time, only a few manufacturers produced quality material suitable for target shooting, and the equipment was not readily available. During its first few years, the Service Company was a relatively simple operation handled by C. B. Lister in his capacity as Secretary-Treasurer. But as more manufacturers entered the market with products designed for the target shooter, the operation became more complex. By

1928, General Reckord found it necessary to employ a full-time director of the retail outlet. In that year alone, the Service Company sold more than 3 million targets.

At the height of the operation, in early 1929, the NRA Service Company offered all forms of target shooting equipment, including quality rifles and ammunition, special sights, slings, and shooting jackets. After five years of operation, however, the company was drastically curtailed by other suppliers.

Winning Support

Lieutenant Colonel Lewis M. Rumsey Jr. was elected President of the National Rifle Association of America in January 1928. At the meeting of the National Board for the Promotion of Rifle Practice that year, it was still uncertain whether the National Matches would be held, for the War

United States Dewar Team - Nati

Department again had knocked funds for them from its budget.

General Reckord was determined to do something about this on-again, off-again official attitude. At his request, Congressman John C. Speaks of Ohio introduced an amendment to Section 113 of the National Defense Act making it mandatory that an annual appropriation for the National Matches be included in the War Department's budget. This first attempt failed, but Speaks then introduced an amendment to the Army Appropriations Bill, which provided $500,000 to support the 1928 Matches and military members of the American international free-rifle team. This bill passed on March 20, 1928.

Shortly thereafter, Congressman Speaks reintroduced his earlier amendment to the National Defense Act. This time the effort proved successful, and President Calvin Coolidge signed the bill into law on May 28, 1928.

The amendment was a coup for the National Board for the Promotion of Rifle Practice and for NRA. It mandated that the Secretary of War would regulate "an annual competition known as the National Matches, for the purpose of competing for a national trophy, medals and other prizes." It also authorized that the National Matches be open to all U.S. military branches, including the National Guard and organized militia, as well as civilian military training camps, rifle clubs, and

al Matches - Camp Perry Ohio. 1929.

Photo by Dick Dreyer

civilians. The Matches would be connected with the Small Arms Firing School and the competitions in which NRA provided trophies and medals. Furthermore, the cost of the National Matches, including expenses of the NBPRP, would be appropriated annually in the national defense budget.

The U.S. Dewar Team at Camp Perry on the eve of the Great Depression. That year the Americans topped the British by 106 points, shattering both the record set by their own shooters in 1928 and that of the British in 1927. On the team was Mary Ward (front row, fifth from left). At age 19, she was the second woman in history to qualify as a member of an international rifle team.

The Uniform Firearms Act

While the amendment to the National Defense Act was a triumph to NRA, the Association was also facing tighter regulation of the sale and use of firearms. Before World War I, crime had been largely a state or local matter, except in cases of robberies of the mails or other felonies involving interference with interstate commerce. But Prohibition had spawned an entirely new breed of criminal, ones that were highly mobile and backed by a staff of well-organized specialists. The automobile had bred another—the freewheeling desperadoes who

THE 1932 LOS ANGELES OLYMPIC GAMES FIASCO

AFTER THE OLYMPIC GAMES OF 1924, the International Olympic Committee had eliminated all sports not of major spectator interest and those that it called "mass athletics." Among those events dropped under this ruling was shooting. The National Rifle Association and the International Shooting Union protested this decision and conducted an ongoing campaign to have rifle and pistol shooting reinstated, but their efforts remained unsuccessful until 1931, when the NRA Board of Directors appointed an Olympic Rifle Committee chaired by Milton Reckord and an Olympic Pistol Committee headed by Karl Frederick.

That same year, the International Olympic Committee ruled that it would bar from competition anyone who had accepted a cash prize or who had competed in a contest in which a cash prize had been offered. By the 1930s, cash prizes, though small, were still being issued for shooting competitions, and there was scarcely a single experienced target shooter in America or in the world who could meet the committee's standards. Both of NRA's Olympic committees were forced to draw upon unknown shooters of little competitive experience to build their teams.

The International Olympic Games Committee did not consult NRA's Olympic committees on the arrangements of the shooting match or on the construction of the shooting facilities. This slight was further complicated when the International Olympic Games Committee announced that the Sergeant of the Los Angeles Police Department would be "in charge of shooting" at the Olympic Games in Los Angeles—despite the same committee having invited NRA and the United States Revolver Association (USRA) to assume some charge of the shooting facilities.

The result was a fiasco. Although fine for police practice, the Los Angeles Police range was neither designed nor built for formal competitive shooting. When NRA's Olympic Rifle Committee reached Los Angeles, they found that the shooting house was several yards too near the 50-meter targets and out of parallel with the line of the targets. To attain 50 meters, the shooters had to press back against the rear wall so that men moving from one point to another did not interfere with those who were shooting. When the foreign teams arrived, most of them flatly refused to shoot until the range was rebuilt.

Although the Americans had bent over backwards to abide by the rules of amateurism, they soon found that their competitors had taken the rules more lightly. General Reckord and Karl Frederick had been associated with international shooting long enough to recognize men who had been shooting in international circles for years. Frederick had competed personally for cash prizes against a number of them. If they had protested, however, the entire shooting program would have been eliminated, so they decided to make the most of a bad situation.

The shooting events were a major disappointment. But at least to the shooting world, the events were better than no participation at all, and they provided a basis on which future competition could be built.

Gale Evans (left) and L. A. Wilkens (right) were two of the youngest members of the first annual shoulder-to-shoulder international smallbore match against the British. The match was held at Bisley, England, in July 1931.

specialized in hit-and-run bank holdups that were often accompanied by violence. The operations of these criminals were so flagrant that many states organized vigilante groups to help capture bank robbers. Los Angeles even placed police-trained citizens under arms with special permits allowing them to carry concealed pistols. This approach, diametrically opposite to that taken in New York City after passage of the Sullivan Act, brought an immediate drop in the rate of violent crimes and robberies.

Although most of the pressure during the 1920s was for stricter control of firearms by the states, there was growing agitation for some form of federal regulation. This led in 1927 to the enactment of the federal law prohibiting the shipment of pistols through the mail except to officers of the law or to military personnel. President Calvin Coolidge actively discouraged the enactment of more rigid firearms restrictions on the grounds that he doubted their value in disarming the criminal.

In 1923, a special committee of the National Conference of Commissioners on Uniform State Laws (under which future NRA President Karl Frederick served as a special consultant) had begun deliberating for a uniform state law for firearms legislation. Three years later, in 1926, the conference adopted the Uniform Firearms Act, which required handgun dealers to obtain licenses and forbade them to sell to people who had criminal records, drug addiction, alcoholism, or mental defects. It also required a permit to carry a handgun outside the home or business. New York City's Commissioner of Police immediately wrote a strong letter of dissent to the conference, charging that the proposed law would hamper law enforcement and open the doors to unrestricted traffic in firearms by criminals. In August 1930, after further consideration, the National Conference of Commissioners approved the model act for the second time.

The Uniform Firearms Act had a significant influence on the thinking of lawmakers wrestling with firearms legislation during the next decade. During the 1930s, it was adopted in part or in full by some states, and it formed the basis of the law adopted by Congress for the District of Columbia.

With the impending firearms legislation in the background, NRA continued with its central activity of the time—that of competitive shooting. Thanks in part to the secure funding by the War Department, there were 17,521 individual entries at the 1929 Matches, compared to 13,619 in 1928. Police officers won most of the pistol events, a far cry from the situation that had prevailed only five years earlier.

The "Roaring Twenties" ended on a healthy note for NRA's marksmanship program. But that optimism was soon shattered by the unstable conditions brought on by the Great Depression.

In 1939, NRA moved into its new headquarters, a townhouse at 1600 Rhode Island Avenue, NW, in Washington, D.C.

CHAPTER TEN

FROM DEPRESSION TO WAR

1932–1939

[W]e emphatically condemn all efforts to place upon the ballot, or to secure the enactment of . . . drastic anti-firearm laws and denounce such legislation as impractical and un-American. . . .

—California State Peace Officers Association, 1935

THE FULL IMPACT OF THE Great Depression hit the National Rifle Association of America in the early 1930s. By 1932, there was little room in the federal budget for more than the barest essentials, and the appropriations for the National Matches were an early casualty. NRA, which had been collecting contributions to help send a team of riflemen to England in an effort to retrieve the Pershing Trophy, deposited $1,500 in a savings account to send a team to Bisley in better times.

NRA's program suffered further in 1933, when, by coincidence, the federal government leased office space for its National Industrial Recovery Administration in the Barr Building, which already housed the offices of the National Rifle Association. Then the administration abbreviated its name to the National Recovery Administration and emblazoned its blue eagle and the initials "NRA" on placards, posters, and stationery. The National Rifle Association, which for more than half a century had been *the* NRA, strongly protested the infringement of its trademark. More seriously, the identity of initials and addresses often caused delays in the delivery of mail. The problem was not fully solved until May 12, 1935, when the Supreme Court voided the National Industry Recovery Act.

Smallbore Success

The Great Depression didn't affect smallbore shooting as seriously as it did NRA's .30 caliber program. Riflemen who could not afford the 10-cents-a-shot luxury of .30 caliber shooting could still scrape up a penny a shot for the .22. Clubs that found the construction of a .30 caliber range beyond their means could still improvise a 50- or 100-yard smallbore range.

In 1932, largely through interest in .22 caliber shooting, 361 clubs became newly affiliated with NRA. Many of these clubs were in public schools, but a substantial number were in Boy Scout troops, boys' clubs, and local YMCA organizations. The American Legion was extremely active in promoting school clubs.

The success of the smallbore program permitted NRA to expand into other fields. In 1933, it initiated a new outdoor pistol league, and in 1934 it issued the first of its 16-millimeter films designed to promote shooting safety. The next year, it launched an all-risk insurance policy program for

NRA presented the first Critchfield-Herrick Trophy in 1938 to the team with the highest score in the Herrick Trophy Match.

members in cooperation with the Fireman's Fund Insurance Company of Chicago.

One casualty of this period was the NRA Service Company, which had become a liability rather than an asset. In 1932, NRA operated at a deficit for the first time since its early years. Part of the drain was traceable to the Service Company, and the Board of Directors voted to eliminate the sale of firearms and accessories and to confine its operation to the sale of official targets. Three years later, the NRA Service Company was eliminated entirely and the target business transferred under a franchise to the National Target Supply Company.

The National Firearms Act

In the midst of the Depression came a major infringement of Second Amendment rights. The National Council for the Prevention of War, which believed that war and the causes of war could be eliminated if weapons of warfare could be eliminated, had developed in 1922 out of the ashes of World War I. With a budget that in spite of the Depression increased from $150,000 in 1929 to $200,000 in 1930, it threw its full resources behind the anti-firearms fight. While most of the existing laws sought to restrict the use of firearms, the bills proposed by the National Council for the Prevention of War sought to abolish firearms along with all instruments of war. Its legacy, and that of counterpart pacifist groups in other countries, was the series of disarmament conferences of the 1920s and early 1930s. The National Council picked up some important allies in state legislatures and in Congress, and much of NRA's energy at this time was devoted to keeping track of new firearms bills and reporting them to members through *American Rifleman.*

As the number of firearms proposals increased, usual channels of communication became too slow. Lags between the introduction of a bill and its publication in *American Rifleman* often prevented the Association from alerting its members in time for them to take effective action. As a result, in 1934 NRA launched its Legislative Division under the direction of C. B. Lister. When action was needed, the affected members were notified by mail and advised of the provisions of the proposed bills. At that time, NRA did not employ anyone to lobby

for or against legislation. It merely provided the facts and an appraisal of the bill in question and left further action up to the discretion of individual members.

In the opening days of the Seventy-third Congress, there were seven bills dealing with firearms in the House and five in the Senate. The House Ways and Means Committee devoted a full executive session to the discussion of firearms control. The result of these efforts was the enactment on June 26, 1934, of the National Firearms Act.

The original version of this act, favored by Attorney General Homer S. Cummings, imposed unduly severe conditions on all firearms, a move that was vigorously opposed by members of the

During the lean years of the Great Depression, smallbore shooting became more popular because .22 caliber ammunition and ranges were less expensive than for .30 caliber shooting. NRA began running regional smallbore tournaments at various ranges including Maryland's Camp Ritchie (pictured). Milton Reckord had planned and built the Camp Ritchie range while he was Adjutant General of Maryland.

National Rifle Association. General Reckord, Karl Frederick, and other NRA officers were engaged in multiple hearings before various congressional committees. They were supported by Charles V. Imlay of the National Conference of Commissioners on Uniform State Laws; Colonel John Thomas Taylor, legislative representative of the American Legion; and Seth Gordon, Secretary of the American Game Association, representing the hunting sportsmen of America.

The drive for a highly restrictive gun law was led by an intemperate Special Assistant to Attorney General Cummings, who stated flatly that small arms training for civilians was of little importance and that neither the foot soldier nor the battleship would be of any value in the next war. In the end, Congress adopted the recommendations of NRA and the other respected organizations who shared similar views.

The National Firearms Act imposed taxes and registration on fully automatic firearms, short-barreled shotguns and rifles, and silencers. It also required all dealers, importers, and pawnbrokers handling these types of firearms to pay an occupational tax.

The National Firearms Act, however, was not regarded as adequate by Homer Cummings, and he began an immediate campaign to pass more restrictive anti-firearms laws. One of Cummings' assistants, Director of Prisons Julian H. Alco, offered the Alco Crime Prevention Bill of California as an amendment to the National Firearms Act.

The Alco Bill of California proposed to outlaw the possession of any firearm "of any description and by whatever name known, which is capable of being concealed upon the person," and provided for indeterminate sentences to all violators. As such it went far beyond New York's Sullivan Act. Alco's proposal brought him publicity and formed the basic pattern for proposals advanced by the office of Attorney General Cummings.

NRA carried several full-page editorials against the Alco Bill and otherwise supported the thousands of citizens who fought to defeat the bill. It also did some quiet digging into the background of the sponsors. It discovered, among many other damaging factors, that the Publicity Chairman of Alco's "Crime Prevention Committee" had a police record dating back five years with six arrests on various charges in four years. NRA then published the record in full in an editorial in the November 1934 issue of *American Rifleman*. Little was heard from Alco from that time on. His bill received its *coup de grace* early in 1935 after the convention of the California State Peace Officers Association passed this resolution:

Now therefore be it resolved that we emphatically condemn all efforts to place upon the ballot, or to secure the enactment of the so-called Alco Crime Prevention Law or any other similar drastic anti-firearm laws and denounce such legislation as impractical and un-American, and as an encouragement of rather than as a means of preventing crimes and criminality, as a positive menace to the safety and defense of the lives and property of law-abiding citizens, and as opposed to every tradition of a hardy and red-blooded, self-reliant, and law-abiding race of Californians and Americans.

Wary and Waiting

By 1935, America was recovering from the Great Depression and moving toward the precipice of World War II. Gradually, the United States took a

more critical analysis of its military preparedness. President Roosevelt signed a bill authorizing the National Matches of 1935, and the War Department appropriations bill for that year provided $350,000 for the National Matches and for use by the NBPRP. That September, the Small Arms Firing School was able to open the first full-scale marksmanship program in four years.

Although overshadowed again by the reinstated .30 caliber devotees, the smallbore shooters turned out for the 1935 Camp Perry Matches in larger numbers than ever before. They also again clinched the domination of the United States in the international smallbore field. The American team defeated Great Britain in the Dewar Match by 18 points and easily outshot teams representing Australia, Canada, South Africa, and India. In the Rhenish-Westphalian (RWS) Match, a team captained by Dr. Emmet O. Swanson soundly trounced the Germans and retained for the United States the handsome RWS Challenge Cup.

Olympic Controversy

By this time, most of the leading marksmen were looking forward to the Olympic Games of 1936. The National Rifle Association again accepted an invitation to organize a team of American riflemen to participate in Berlin and appointed General Reckord as Chairman and C. B. Lister as Secretary of the Olympic Rifle Committee. Other members included Karl Frederick, who by then had become President of NRA; Julian Hatcher; Gustavus D. Pope, the NRA Vice President; Major L. W. T. Waller Jr.; and Russell Wiles. Frederick doubled as a member of the Olympic Pistol Committee, organized by the United States Revolver Association.

American shooters had been chafing at the bit since the disappointing Olympic fiasco in Los Angeles in 1932. Since then the National Rifle Association of America, its counterparts in other

Karl T. Frederick was NRA President from 1934 to 1936. He and General Reckord spoke at numerous congressional hearings before enactment of the National Firearms Act of 1934 that helped remove some of the bill's undesirable provisions.

Above: Gustavus D. Pope served as NRA President from 1937 to 1939. He was also a member of the 1936 American Olympic Rifle Committee.

Right: After Frederick's presidential term ended, NRA deviated from its set pattern to appoint Ammon Critchfield as President in 1936. The father of Camp Perry had been honored in 1934 when the riflemen of Ohio commemorated the Critchfield Trophy (pictured) to be awarded to the national smallbore rifle champion.

assure that the United States would be represented in Berlin by its best riflemen.

Then the International Olympic Committee announced the rifle shooting program—a single event with miniature rifles, identical to that held in Los Angeles in 1932, instead of the hoped-for military rifle matches. The Olympic Rifle Committee protested in vain and ultimately voted not to participate in the event. In his report, General Reckord called the program "totally inadequate and in no sense designed to meet the requirements of amateur rifle competition."

The NRA Board of Directors backed this decision with a resolution stating, "Solely because of the inadequate rifle shooting program for such Olympic competition, the Association does not approve the sending of a rifle team to such Olympic Games."

Recovery

By 1936, the National Matches and high power rifle shooting in general had been restored to a normal schedule. During the second week of the Matches, NRA officials, shooters from all over America, and the Ohio National Guard joined in a tribute to Brigadier General Ammon Critchfield for his devoted service to marksmanship and national defense. Critchfield was honored with a bronze plaque, which adorned the mall in front of the headquarters building at Camp Perry.

countries, and the International Shooting Union had persuaded the International Olympic Committee to relax its rigid rules of amateurism. Under the new rules, anyone was eligible to compete if he or she had not accepted a money prize between August 1, 1934, and the opening of the Olympic Games. Since nearly all the shooters aspiring to enter the 11th Olympiad had abstained from collecting prize money, the change seemed to

By 1937, NRA had survived the worst of the Depression and was able to send a rifle team (above) to Bisley for the smallbore match against the British. The match was held at Bisley's Petersham range (left).

Below: General John J. Pershing, who avidly supported NRA's marksmanship program during World War I, presented NRA with the Pershing International Team Match Trophy in 1931.

Under the revised bylaws, the leadership of the National Rifle Association continued to follow a stable pattern of succession. NRA's activities were carried on by the Executive Director with the assistance of the Secretary, whose offices were in the national headquarters. The President customarily served for two one-year terms, and the First Vice President then moved into the leading office. In 1934, at the close of Frederick's term as President, the board deviated from its set pattern for one year by appointing General Critchfield as its leading officer in recognition of his long services to the organization.

This was the same meeting at which the board amended the bylaws to create an Executive Council. The four most recent past Presidents—Fred Waterbury, Lewis Rumsey Jr., Karl Frederick, and Ammon Critchfield—were elected as the first members of the Executive Council.

It seemed that the National Rifle Association had weathered the worst of the Great Depression. The board unanimously approved sending a team to Bisley, England, to compete for the Pershing Trophy in July 1937. It also adopted a resolution to introduce rifle practice to the Civilian Conservation Corps and voted to urge the Works Progress Administration to construct rifle and pistol ranges.

By that time, circulation of *American Rifleman* had

climbed to 56,000, and the magazine had a healthy list of paying advertisers. In February 1937, it carried its first full-color advertisement— a four-page spread purchased by the Packard Motor Car Company.

With the recovery of the American economy, the shooting program returned to its pre-Depression level. Thanks to increased support from the administration and Congress, the shooting programs of 1937 and 1938 were the most comprehensive held since the 1920s. There were only 36 registered tournaments in 1936 but nearly 100 in 1938.

As the international conflict that would lead to world war worsened, support for the National Matches increased. In 1938, the Budget Bureau tried to reduce funds for the National Matches, but the House of Representatives stopped the move.

The last peacetime Matches before the outbreak of World War II in Europe were hailed as "the best ever held." Certainly, they produced some of the most spectacular shooting that had ever been seen. The Dewar Match was highlighted by four perfect individual scores by American shooters, who defeated the British with a near-record score and brought the historic cup back to the United States. Americans swept the smallbore field in the international events, winning the RWS, Railwaymen's, and Fidac matches by some of the highest scores ever recorded. In the individual events, William Woodring became the first man in history to win the National Smallbore Championship for three consecutive years.

Sparked by such all-time great marksmen as Harry Reeves and Alfred Hemming, the Detroit police team set three world records and ran up a total of 11 victories. Reeves and Hemming broke the two-man team record three times in 1938, raising the top score by 35 points. Police teams from all over the nation attended the National Matches that year and were strong contenders or winners in all events open to them.

The Federal Firearms Act

The Roosevelt Administration's request for more constraints devoted to unlawful use of firearms led to the adoption in 1938 of the Federal Firearms Act. The 1938 act made it a federal offense

for anyone who was under indictment or who had been convicted of a felony to transport, ship, receive, or carry firearms or handgun ammunition across interstate or international borders; it made punishable the theft or possession of stolen firearms or ammunition while moving in or part of interstate or foreign commerce; and it made it illegal to receive, possess, or dispose of any firearm from which the serial number had been obliterated, removed, or altered.

Though it had opposed such restrictive legislation as the Sullivan Law and the Alco Crime Prevention Bill, NRA supported certain provisions of the Federal Firearms Act. Homer Cummings, with apparently little support from President Roosevelt, still was not satisfied and did all within his power to impose a firearms registration bill. His National Firearms Registration Bill never came to a vote in Congress.

Healthy Growth

In the last years of the Great Depression, NRA continued to grow and expand. In addition to the Legislative Division headed by C. B. Lister, by 1939 NRA had five other divisions, each headed by a staff member responsible to General Reckord and Lister. As of January 1939, Frank Wyman was in charge of Competitions; F. M. Hakenjos headed the Extension Division; L. Q. Bradley oversaw Membership; William Shadel was head of Public Relations; and Herbert Goebel took care of Club Services and the Junior Rifle Program. Each of these members also served as editors for *American Rifleman*, which by then had expanded from 38 to 72 pages and was being printed on higher-quality paper.

Office space in the Barr Building, which a scant 10 years before had seemed commodious, now became cramped. In 1938, the Executive Committee had authorized management to purchase a building of its own, and in January 1939 the National Rifle Association moved into its new quarters, an old mansion in what was then one of the most exclusive neighborhoods in Washington. Located at 1600 Rhode Island Avenue at Scott Circle on the edge of the embassy district, the building and land cost $63,743.05. The Association borrowed most of this amount but paid off the mortgage two years later.

THE M1 RIFLE AND A QUIET GENIUS

"THE GREATEST BATTLE IMPLEMENT ever devised." These words are high praise indeed, and they came from General George S. Patton on the "U.S. Rifle Cal. .30, M1"—otherwise simply known by the name of its inventor, Garand.

Canadian-born John Cantius Garand moved to the United States when he was nine. He became an avid shooter and rabbit hunter and developed an early interest in all things mechanical. During World War I, the U.S. Army Ordnance Department was searching for a reliable machine gun design, and in a week's time young Garand, wondering what all the fuss was about, drew up plans for a primer-actuated one. That got the fourth-grade-educated Garand a job at the Bureau of Standards, and in 1919 he was assigned to the U.S. Springfield Armory as an ordnance engineer. He would spend the next 17 years refining and developing his ideas into a semi-automatic service rifle.

The rifle was gas-operated and fed from an en-bloc clip that held 10 rounds of .276 ammunition. But when U.S. Army Chief of Staff General Douglas MacArthur disapproved the adoption of the new cartridge, Garand redesigned the rifle to accommodate eight rounds of .30-'06 in an en bloc clip.

The M1 Garand was adopted by the Army in January 1936, and production began 15 months later. Initially the Garand had some teething troubles, including the early "gas trap" system as opposed to the later "gas spline" system. Those early troubles—and the Army Ordnance's arrogant attitude—brought criticism of the early M1s from civilian shooters and some NRA staff at the 1938 National Matches.

Eventually a controversy involving the Garand rifle and one developed by Melvin C. Johnson ensued. By the time America entered World War II, the bugs had been worked out, and G.I.s and Marines were equipped with the finest, most reliable semi-automatic rifle of its day. Nearly five and a half million M1s were made by the Springfield Armory, Winchester, Harrington and Richardson, and International Harvester. It was the principal rifle of American troops in both World War II and Korea. In later years, it became the king of Camp Perry's ranges, especially in its National Match configuration. Even into the 21st century, the Civilian Marksmanship Program's John C. Garand Match, in which shooters can use only the Garand, continued to be the most popular event at the National Matches.

Many years after he developed it, Garand, a quiet and humble man, said of his invention, "It is a pretty good gun, I think. I have letters from soldiers who used it in the war. They said it did a lot of good, and that is enough for me."

By 1939, the National Rifle Association was offering its members a full line of books and manuals on shooting and firearms at bargain prices. *The Handloader's Manual* by Major Earl Naramore was one of the first publications on handloading in the United States.

Littleton W. T. Waller Jr. was elected NRA President in 1939. He held numerous honors as a military officer and had been involved with NRA for decades.

Although NRA for years had promoted firearms safety through news items and publicity releases, it did not yet have a centralized program built around safety. It was during the NRA meeting in February 1938 that a firearms safety program began to take shape, chaired by Edwin Pugsley, Chairman of the Safety Committee of the Sporting Arms and Ammunition Manufacturers' Institute. Fred C. Mills, National Safety Director of the Boy Scouts of America, and Seth Gordon, Chairman of the Board of Game Commissioners of Pennsylvania and former Secretary of the American Game Association, were also on the panel. By 1939, the roundtable's suggestions had begun to gain momentum, but full development of the safety program had to be postponed until after the war.

As approaching war clouds grew increasingly darker, the 1939 board meeting convened in the new national headquarters. The directors elected Colonel Waller to succeed retiring President Gustavus Pope, who became a member of the Executive Council. Colonel Waller had been active in the National Rifle Association since long before World War I.

Throughout World War II, *American Rifleman* helped keep Americans informed about guns, troops, and training.

CHAPTER ELEVEN

THE WORLD AT WAR

1939–1945

We, too, born to freedom, and believing in freedom, are willing to fight to maintain freedom. We, and all others who believe as deeply as we do, would rather die on our feet than live on our knees.

—Franklin Delano Roosevelt, June 19, 1941

AFTER GREAT BRITAIN AND France declared war on Germany, President Franklin Roosevelt called a special session of Congress to amend the Neutrality Act, for which Roosevelt admitted, "I regret . . . Congress passed the Act. I regret equally that I signed the Act." Under the amended act, the United States could sell arms to Allies for cash, but the Allies had to take the matériel away in their own ships, as American ships were excluded from war zones. On September 9, President Roosevelt signed an order declaring a limited national emergency.

Closer to War

Though the United States had yet to become directly involved in the war, the conflict brought many changes in the program and personnel of the National Rifle Association, as it did in all American organizations and institutions. "Preparedness" and "defense," rather than neutrality and noninvolvement, became the watchwords of America. When NRA met in Washington on February 2, 1940, the Board of Directors and 225 members heard Assistant Secretary of War Louis Johnson and Chief of Staff General George C. Marshall endorse the National Rifle Association as a major force in preparing the United States to meet threatened dangers.

The last full-schedule National Matches before America entered World War II were held in 1940. The Matches probably would have been canceled if not for the intercession of George Marshall, who was not swayed by arguments that the role of the rifleman had been totally eclipsed by the long-range bomber and the armored tank.

Although attendance was smaller than usual, the participants of the National Matches made up in serious dedication what they lacked in numbers. The only international event at Camp Perry in 1940 was a two-way competition with the Canadians in the Dewar Match. Great Britain did not participate, for England was reeling under the German Blitz and facing triumphant German armies across the narrow moat of the English Channel.

Helping Hands Donate Arms

After Dunkirk, only the British Navy, a pitifully outnumbered RAF, and 21 miles of water

This V for Victory appeared on NRA's "Plan for Approved Small Arms Firing Schools," one of the Association's many efforts to help the Allies win the war and to protect American civilians in the case of invasion.

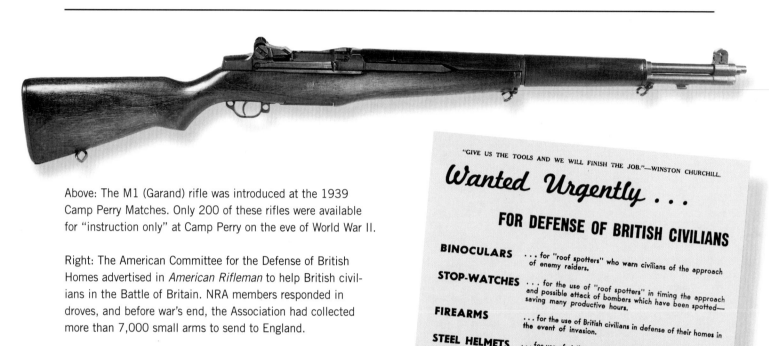

Above: The M1 (Garand) rifle was introduced at the 1939 Camp Perry Matches. Only 200 of these rifles were available for "instruction only" at Camp Perry on the eve of World War II.

Right: The American Committee for the Defense of British Homes advertised in *American Rifleman* to help British civilians in the Battle of Britain. NRA members responded in droves, and before war's end, the Association had collected more than 7,000 small arms to send to England.

"GIVE US THE TOOLS AND WE WILL FINISH THE JOB."—WINSTON CHURCHILL.

Wanted Urgently . . .

FOR DEFENSE OF BRITISH CIVILIANS

BINOCULARS . . . for "roof spotters" who warn civilians of the approach of enemy raiders.

STOP-WATCHES . . . for the use of "roof spotters" in timing the approach and possible attack of bombers which have been spotted— saving many productive hours.

FIREARMS . . . for the use of British civilians in defense of their homes in the event of invasion.

STEEL HELMETS . . . for use of civilians as a protection against bomb splinters, falling shrapnel, and falling masonry during air raids.

British civilians, undergoing nightly air raids, are in desperate need of

Firearms – Binoculars – Steel Helmets
Stop-Watches – Ammunition
(None of this material is procurable for civilians in England now)

IF YOU POSSESS ANY OF THESE ARTICLES
You Can Aid in The Battle of Britain

BY SENDING THIS MATERIAL TO

American Committee for Defense of British Homes
C. SUYDAM CUTTING, Chairman   10 WARREN STREET, NEW YORK, N. Y.

(Firearms and Ammunition may be shipped by express, freight or truck but NOT by mail)

All Materials Are Shipped Immediately by the American Committee for Defense of British Homes to

CIVILIAN COMMITTEE for DEFENSE of HOMES
WICKHAM STEED, Chairman

BIRMINGHAM, ENGLAND

---

separated Great Britain from defeat. Practically all of the arms and equipment of the British Expeditionary Force had been destroyed or abandoned at Dunkirk. Although the "Miracle of Dunkirk" had snatched 338,000 troops from the jaws of Hitler's panzers, most of the survivors disembarked without even their rifles.

Every usable gun, regardless of its age or condition, had been collected for the defense of British soil. Shotguns, sporting rifles, and pocket pistols were the standard armament of many Home Guard units assigned to frontline duty along the English Channel. Even these firearms were in short supply, for anti-firearms regulations adopted before World War I had all but disarmed the British civilian.

At the height of this threat, a group of American citizens headed by C. Suydam Cutting of New York City established the American Committee for the Defense of British Homes. Its most conspicuous advertisement was a full-page notice in the November 1940 issue of *American Rifleman* requesting all NRA members to send pistols, rifles, shotguns, and binoculars to the embattled British. "Send a gun to defend a British home," the notice urged in bold type. "British civilians, faced with the threat of invasion, desperately need arms for the defense of their homes." The grim plight of the British was emphasized by a direct appeal to NRA members by

a British military spokesman: "Send us anything that shoots," he pleaded.

By the end of the following December, the American Committee for the Defense of British Homes had collected more than 1,500 rifles and pistols and 100,000 rounds of ammunition, mostly from NRA members. Before the emergency passed, the National Rifle Association alone collected more than 7,000 small arms for shipment to England to rearm the police and Home Guard units of the embattled kingdom. All of this equipment was given to Britain without compensation.

Winston Churchill underscored the urgency and value of the small arms shipments to his beleaguered country:

"THE RETURN OF THIS RIFLE…WOULD BE GREATLY APPRECIATED"

IN THE DARK DAYS OF WORLD WAR II, when Great Britain faced alone the might of Hitler's war machine, the American Committee for the Defense of British Homes sent out a desperate appeal to Americans for arms for British civilians to use to defend their homeland. Between World War I and World War II, Britain's increasingly strong gun control laws had left her people virtually disarmed.

Tens of thousands of pistols, rifles, revolvers, shotguns, and binoculars were collected from individual Americans and sent to England. One such gun was a .30-'06 Model 1903 target rifle owned by Major John W. Hession. Hession was one of the pre-eminent high power rifle target shooters of his day, and he used this very rifle to win Olympic gold at Bisley Camp in England in 1908 and to set a world record at Camp Perry in 1909, among many other impressive marksmanship accomplishments. The rifle, equipped with a Winchester A-5 riflescope, bears a plaque that reads: "FOR OBVIOUS REASONS THE RETURN OF THIS RIFLE AFTER GERMANY IS DEFEATED WOULD BE DEEPLY APPRECIATED." Unlike the majority of the rifles sent to Great Britain, Hession's rifle was returned and is now an important part of the National Firearms Muscum collection.

Rifle courtesy National Firearms Museum

When the ships from America approached our shores with their priceless arms, special trains were waiting in all the ports to receive their cargoes. The Home Guard in every country, in every town, in every village, sat up all through the nights to receive them. Men and women worked day and night making them fit for use. By the end of July we were an armed nation, so far as parachute or airborne landings were concerned. We had become a "hornet's nest." Anyhow, if we had to go down fighting (which I did not anticipate), a lot of our men and some women had weapons in their hands. . . .

As the United States drew closer to war, young men and women gave serious attention to instruction in handling firearms. Here a crowd of young people gather at Camp Perry's Junior Smallbore Rifle School during the 1940 National Matches.

Business Not As Usual

The war hung heavily over the deliberations of the NRA board meeting in February 1941. Colonel Waller was absent on foreign duty with the Marine Corps, and General Reckord had asked that he be relieved of his duties as Executive Vice President, since he had been ordered to active duty as Commanding General of the Twenty-ninth Division at Fort George G. Meade, Maryland. At this meeting Colonel Nathaniel C. Nash Jr., an officer of the Massachusetts National Guard and for many years a leader of the very active Massachusetts State Rifle Association, succeeded Colonel Waller as President. At the request of General Reckord, the Board of Directors gave C. B. Lister the necessary executive powers to carry on in the absence of the Executive Vice President.

Before adjourning, the board voted to offer to the federal government free and unrestricted use

of 3,500 rifle and pistol ranges owned or controlled by its affiliate clubs. By that time, the national emergency had curtailed much of the NRA shooting program. Sale of surplus military firearms had been suspended and the issue of ammunition by the DCM cut off.

By the end of 1941, nearly half of the NRA staff members were on leave of absence or preparing to leave for duty with the armed services. In April, L. J. Hathaway, who had served as Editor of *American Rifleman* for 14 years, resigned for reasons of health, and William Shadel, head of the Publicity Bureau, became the new Editor.

NRA Preparedness

As America drifted closer to war, the National Rifle Association continued to play a part in the nation's preparedness, first by developing a series of 16-millimeter films on small-arms marksmanship. Master prints of the films were later made available to the Army Service Forces, Army Air Force, Navy, and Coast Guard, from which hundreds of prints were made for distribution to training centers. NRA's film on pistol marksmanship

was the only one of its kind available during World War II.

Anticipating the national need for trained riflemen, NRA developed a preinduction smallbore service course based on the .22 caliber rifle. The targets followed the standard military qualification course with the 200-yard, .30 caliber targets reduced to a 50-foot scale. By the end of the war, NRA had conducted 2,862 preinduction training classes in 1,278 communities, providing training for 158,956 men.

In addition to providing valuable training, NRA evoked a spirit of nationalism through its Camp Perry Matches. Though the .30 caliber championship had to be cancelled altogether because military ammu-

Left: Colonel N. C. Nash was NRA President from 1941 to 1942. He was an old-time rifleman and a leader of the Massachusetts State Rifle Association for many years.

Below: As Executive Vice President, General Reckord (shaking hands, center) was involved in all aspects of NRA activities, including activities at Camp Perry. In 1941, he left for active duty as Commanding General of the Twenty-ninth Division at Fort George G. Meade, Maryland. In his absence, NRA was led by C. B. Lister.

nition was being reserved for troops in training, the 1941 National Matches did have federal support. Colonel F. C. Endicott, Executive Officer of the NBPRP, urged the federal government to help defray the expenses of two high-scoring members from each of the state organizations affiliated with NRA.

At its Annual Members Meeting in September 1941, just a few months before the United States entered the war, NRA formally offered its services to the nation. Director of Civilian Defense Fiorello H. LaGuardia suggested that members could "contribute substantially by enrolling and participat-

Right: NRA staff artist Jim Berryman drew this cover for the July 1943 *American Rifleman* to depict two wartime goals: teaching Americans to shoot and the destruction of Hitler's war machine. The work of this Pulitzer Prize winner graced the pages of *American Rifleman* throughout the war years.

Below: General Holcomb, Commandant of the U.S. Marine Corps during the war, was an expert rifleman and had been actively involved with NRA since the turn of the century.

ing in the auxiliary police and other civilian defense forces now being established by the local and state governments." NRA immediately launched a training program for the Home Guards, which the states were organizing to replace National Guard units that had been ordered into federal service.

Invaluable Aid

By the time the United States joined World War II, the National Rifle Association was already geared to the national emergency. It sent a letter to the Chairman of each state civilian defense agency offering the services and facilities of its state affiliates. It also launched a training program geared to teach marksmanship to 1 million men.

Demand for NRA's services was higher than ever, and the NRA staff worked unceasingly to carry out its mission. Many of the country's manufacturing plants had been converted for wartime production, and it was vitally important that such plants be protected should the war eventually spread to U.S. soil.

NRA developed a pistol training manual for use by plant guards and auxiliary policemen. It also published manuals on plant protection and the use of shotguns for guard duty, both of which were distributed through civilian defense offices throughout the war years. As part of its preinduction training program, NRA printed and donated 20,000 manuals on instruction in small-arms marksmanship.

In May 1942, NRA launched a campaign to collect serviceable M1917 and M1903 rifles from its members and other citizens for donation or resale at cost to the Army. Through its affiliated clubs, NRA established 200 offices where the arms could be inspected. Late in 1942, NRA offered the services of its members and affiliated clubs in handloading ammunition for use by plant guards. On November 23, 1942, the Provost Marshal General issued to managers of war plants a special circular, which noted that "It may be possible for plants to make arrangements for reloading by members of the

THE GENERAL'S U.S. M1903

GENERAL DOUGLAS MACARTHUR, BORN in 1880, was one of America's greatest generals. He served in the Spanish-American War and during World War I rose to the rank of Brigadier General. From 1919 to 1922, General MacArthur served as the Superintendent of the U.S. Military Academy at West Point. After serving as the U.S. Army's Chief of Staff, MacArthur became a military advisor to the President of the Philippines and was recalled to the colors in July 1941. Ordered to evacuate the Philippines by President Franklin Delano Roosevelt in March 1942, he promised "I shall return." He made good on that promise in 1945 when the Philippines was liberated by Allied forces. He led the Allied war effort in the defeat of Japan and was Supreme Allied Commander of occupation forces in Japan.

While serving at West Point, General MacArthur was presented with this Colt Model 1903 .32 ACP Model 1903 pistol, serial number 372130. The John Browning–designed Model 1903 was produced from 1903 until 1946 with 4" barrels and an eight-round magazine capacity. MacArthur's pistol bears the hard rubber stocks used before 1924. *(Pistol courtesy National Firearms Museum)*

A PRESIDENTIAL M1911A1

GENERAL DWIGHT D. EISENHOWER was given this Colt-made U.S. Model 1911A1, serial number 834128, by British Admiral Sir A. B. Cunningham of the Royal Navy in November 1942 during Operation Torch, the Allied invasion of North Africa. The .45 ACP M1911A1 was an improved version of the John M. Browning–designed .45 ACP U.S. Model of 1911 pistol adopted by the U.S. military in 1911.

Pistol courtesy National Firearms Museum

National Rifle Association. Inquiries on available facilities should be directed to the National Rifle Association. . . ."

NRA provided the country with an invaluable source for shooting instructors. During the span of the war, in fact, NRA members were responsible for teaching 1.75 million students the correct use of small arms. Thurman Randle, NRA Vice President, entered the Navy with the rank of Lieutenant Commander in 1942 and was assigned to duty at the Sachuest Range of the Newport Naval Training Station with a staff of junior officers under his command. All were NRA members. They were among 300 key small-arms instructors recruited from NRA during the war by the Army Service Forces, Navy, and the Army Air Force. Both Randle and Colonel Francis W. Parker Jr., who became National Rifle Association President and Vice President, respec-

tively, for 1944 and 1945, served out their terms on active service.

Hard Times for All

In these years the National Rifle Association was devoted almost entirely to the war effort. Eleven of the officers and staff members had entered the armed services by the spring of 1944, when the Allies stood poised for their leap across the English Channel. Then William Shadel, Editor of *American Rifleman,* received his credentials as a war correspondent for CBS and shipped to England to cover the invasion. His duties as Editor were assumed by Associate Editors C. M. Palmer Jr. and E. B. Mann. *American Rifleman* featured articles by Shadel, based on personal experiences and interviews, up until the end of the war.

Pulitzer Prize winner James T. Berryman joined the staff as Art Director in January 1943, and the pages of *American Rifleman* sparkled with his animated drawings for many years. The articles reflected the nature of the times and were mostly devoted to discussions of American and foreign ordnance, narratives of the frontline fighting in Europe by William Shadel, letters from servicemen, and interviews with or articles by prominent soldiers. The latter included an exclusive interview with General Alexander A. Vandergrift, Commandant of the United States Marine Corps, in the January 1944 issue.

Other members of the remaining NRA staff furnished range construction plans to contractors for the armed forces, camp commanders, and station commanders. The staff and affiliated clubs in the Washington area conducted special small-arms instruction classes for more than 700 Army and Navy reserve officers and served as technical advisors to the War Production Board on small arms and ammunition.

General Reckord, meanwhile, had become the first National Guard officer to be appointed a Commander of an Army Corps area. He served as Commanding General of the Third Corps Area for two years and then was ordered to Great Britain and assigned to the staff of the Supreme Headquarters of the Army Expeditionary Force. During the war he won his second and third Distinguished Service Medals; his second Croix de Guerre with Palm; a Bronze Star; the British decoration, Knight Commander of the Order of the Bath; and the French Legion of Honor.

War's End

Demobilization came quickly after Germany and Japan surrendered in 1945. At one point during the war, the armed forces had numbered 12 million. By 1947, that number had dropped to 1.5 million, and in 1950, the Army had dwindled to only 600,000.

Gradually, the staff members, officers, and directors of the National Rifle Association who had seen active military service began to filter back to reclaim their civilian duties. Many had attained high ranks and won distinguished honors. And though organizations do not receive medals, the work of NRA during World War II was recognized by the highest government office—the President of the United States. On November 14, 1945, President Harry S. Truman sent this letter of praise to the National Rifle Association:

. . . During the war just ended, the contributions of the [National Rifle] [A]ssociation in the matter of small-arms training aids, the nation-wide preinduction training program, the recruiting of experienced small-arms instructors for all branches of the armed services, and technical advice and assistance to Government civilian agencies aiding in the prosecution of the war—all contributed freely and without expense to the Government—have materially aided our war effort.

I hope that the splendid program which the National Rifle Association has followed during the past three-quarters of a century will be continued. It is a program that is good for a free America.

Similar letters of commendation came from Chief of Staff George Marshall and Fleet Admiral Ernest J. King, Chief of Naval Operations. Without a doubt, the National Rifle Association of America had proven successful in its mission to improve national defense.

After the war ended, President Harry S. Truman sent a letter of commendation to NRA, applauding the organization for its many contributions to the war effort.

Both World War II and the Korean War had made it difficult to continue the National Matches at Camp Perry, but by the mid-1950s, Camp Perry had once again become the biggest name in shooting.

CHAPTER TWELVE

POSTWAR PENETRATION

1946–1955

An organization such as the National Rifle Association of America, utterly selfless in its aims, can do more than any other single group in achieving the cooperation we need [to maintain world peace].

—Dwight D. Eisenhower, February 1946

BY THE EARLY MONTHS OF 1946, nearly all of the staff members on active service during the war had reported back for duty. Major General Reckord reassumed his duties as Executive Vice President in December 1945.

The 75th Annual Meeting held in February 1946 was the organization's first peacetime meeting in four years. The banquet was attended by 34 general officers of the Army and Marine Corps, by many Admirals, and a large representation from both houses of Congress. General Dwight D. Eisenhower was the principal speaker. He heaped great praise on NRA, saying, "An organization such as the National Rifle Association of America, utterly selfless in its aims, can do more than any other single group in achieving the cooperation we need [to maintain world peace]."

That year the board elected Colonel Francis Parker Jr., a patent lawyer in Chicago, as President. Julian Hatcher resigned from the board to become head of an enlarged Technical Division at NRA. General Hatcher had retired as Chief of Field Service of the Army Ordnance Department and had served as Coeditor of the "Dope Bag" in *American Rifleman* from 1922 to 1931. Hatcher was a leading authority on small arms in the United States, and as Walter Howe, Editor of *American Rifleman* from 1953 to 1964, pointed

out, "he was a giant among gun writers of his time."

Making Adjustments

The postwar growth of the National Rifle Association was nothing short of phenomenal. In August 1945, NRA had 86,000 members. One year later the membership totaled 155,000, and by 1947 membership had passed the quarter-million mark and affiliated clubs totaled 4,800.

NRA's shooting program quickly picked up momentum once the production of sporting arms and ammunition had been restored. More than 700 competitors from every state were at Camp Perry for the National Matches in August 1947.

In 1948, Dr. Emmet O. Swanson of Minneapolis, at age 42, became the youngest President in the history of NRA to that time. Swanson was a dentist by profession and was one of the ranking smallbore marksmen in the world. One of NRA's most important decisions that year was to revise the procedure for future meetings. Until that time,

NRA's hunter safety program helped reduce hunting accidents through education and hands-on instruction. This badge was one of numerous ones that NRA produced to recognize shooters who completed hunter safety courses.

Above: Though Camp Perry events were slow in reviving after the war, the United States continued to prove its merit in international competition. At the 1949 ISU World Championships, Arthur Jackson won the gold medal for his best score in the Prone Championship Match.

Right: NRA's recently enacted annual conventions were lively affairs, where gun enthusiasts could come together to share their hobby. This program for the Second Annual Convention in Denver aptly noted that "the greatest dividend that anyone receives out of an investment in the shooting game is good fellowship."

pistol shooters. Camp Perry was still unavailable for full-scale Matches as late as 1949, and the pistol and smallbore events were held that year at separate locations—smallbore at Camp Dodge, Iowa, and pistol at Fort Sheridan, Illinois.

New Bylaws

NRA's Second Annual Convention was held in Denver, Colorado, in October 1949. General Merritt Edson, who had become the Director of Public Safety of Vermont, became the new NRA President. Harry Linn became Vice President, and Alice Bull of Seattle, Washington, became the first woman ever elected to the Board of Directors. Maryann Carter—who in 1953 married Harlon Carter, one of NRA's most memorable officers—used to attend board meetings with her husband in the early 1950s, when Alice Bull was the only female board member. "Women were just not seen very much in these meetings," she said, remembering how the President's wife took her under her wing. "That was very nice because then, of

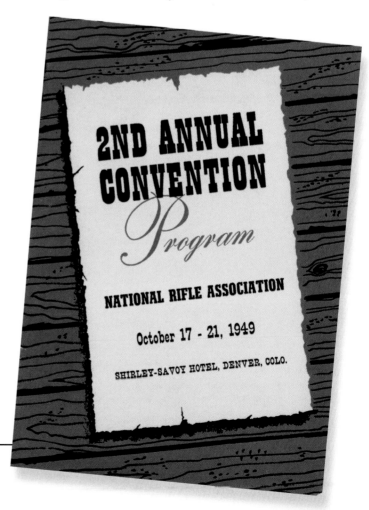

2ND ANNUAL CONVENTION *Program*

NATIONAL RIFLE ASSOCIATION

October 17 - 21, 1949

SHIRLEY-SAVOY HOTEL, DENVER, COLO.

the Annual Meeting of the Board of Directors had been held, according to the bylaws, in February, in Washington, D.C. The Members Meeting was held at Camp Perry in conjunction with the National Matches, but many members, particularly the growing number in the western and southern states, found it difficult or impossible to attend. From then on, the business meetings were to be held in conjunction with an annual convention, meeting at various locations throughout the country as determined by the Board of Directors.

Despite postwar enthusiasm for the shooting sports, .30 caliber shooting was slow to recover after being disrupted by the war. Between 1945 and 1950, the spotlight was on the smallbore and

In 1949, Executive Director C. B. Lister congratulated Alice Bull on being the first woman elected to NRA's Board of Directors.

course, I became the one who would take someone under my wing when the women started coming in."

Milton Reckord retired as Executive Vice President in 1949. Except for his absence during the war, Reckord had guided NRA continually since 1926. By his energy, courage, and executive ability, he had been a dominant force in building NRA into a dynamic and influential organization. C. B. Lister became the new Executive Vice President, retaining his position as Executive Director and Editor of *American Rifleman*.

By this time, NRA's leaders were realizing the need to rewrite the organization's bylaws. The original bylaws had been written in 1871 and were last overhauled fully in 1926, when the Association had a relatively simple program, a small staff, and comparatively uncomplicated administrative problems. They had been drafted for an organization quite different from that which now existed. Thus in 1949, the Executive Committee appointed a Bylaws Revision Committee under the chairmanship of Francis Parker.

Adopted in 1950, the modernized bylaws more clearly defined the obligations and privileges of individual members and affiliated organizations. For starters, special meetings could be called by the President, Board of Directors, Executive Committee, or no less than 5 percent of the Life and Endowment Members. In addition, *American Rifleman* was to publish all names of nominees to the Board of Directors at least 30 days before the Annual Meeting. Elections would be done by secret ballot by those attending the Annual Meeting. (The mail ballot was not established for another two years.)

The new bylaws also made room for special standing committees that were appointed as the

Above: George Whittington (left), for whom the Whittington Center was later named, and Thurman Randle pose for a photo in March 1949.

Right: Dr. Emmet O. Swanson, shown here at practice, was the ranking smallbore marksman in the world when he became NRA President in 1948. At age 42, he was also the youngest President in NRA's history.

Cold War Beginnings

The American economy, meanwhile, was booming. Federal expenditures built up during World War II had pulled the United States out of the Great Depression, and those influences continued to drive the economy in postwar America. At the same time, Americans were wary of having their freedoms infringed upon. In 1949, more than 1,000 delegates and guests, the largest number ever recorded at an NRA social function, heard Lieutenant General Robert L. Eichelberger, who had commanded the Eighth Army in the Pacific, speak out against firearms registration at the annual banquet. Spoken on the eve of the Korean War, his words, in hindsight, seem prophetic:

Some well-meaning people have urged the general registration with the police of all privately owned firearms as a means of curbing crime and

need arose. The committees conducted continuing studies of the rules, regulations, and programs pertaining to their respective fields. Each was charged with examining the effectiveness of the organization's activities in its field and with determining ways to promote greater public participation by members and by the public at large. Each also acted as a direct link between the general membership and the Board of Directors.

Finally, the 1950 bylaws established Junior Patrols—groups of from three to nine youngsters who were under the supervision of an adult instructor. In this way, rural communities where there was an insufficient number of boys or girls to form full-fledged junior clubs could still form shooting groups that were affiliated with NRA.

A FITTING START FOR A GREAT GUNMAKER

WILLIAM B. RUGER AND HIS FRIEND Alexander M. Sturm formed a partnership in January 1949 to make a new .22 semi-automatic pistol of Ruger's own design. The first advertisement for a Ruger firearm appeared in the August 1949 issue of *American Rifleman.* In November 1949, Technical Editor Major General Julian S. Hatcher reviewed the new pistol in the "Dope Bag" column of *American Rifleman* and found a lot to like about it.

Ruger's design has since become one of the most successful pistol designs of all time. Likewise, Sturm, Ruger & Company is one of America's greatest gunmakers and manufactures a full line of rifles, handguns, and shotguns. More than 2 million Ruger .22 pistols have been made since 1949. The Ruger .22 with serial number 1,000,000 resides in the National Firearms Museum. Ruger's support of NRA—in particular to the National Firearms Museum—has continued into the 21st century.

Above: The Sturm, Ruger & Company Standard Pistol Serial Number 1,000,000

Below: In 1949, Major General Julian S. Hatcher, Technical Editor for *American Rifleman*, gave a favorable review to the Ruger .22 Standard Pistol. The design represented the first overall improvement in automatic pistol design since the Browning patent of 1905. *(Photo courtesy Don Findley)*

fifth column activities. These people are poor students of history. . . . In spite of strict government control of the manufacture, distribution and possession of firearms, the fifth column groups made sure they were powerfully, although illegally armed. It is my hope that this will never happen here. . . . If war starts today, we are going to have a lot of boys lying in the mud with rifles.

As a result of the Korean War, the Annual Meetings, Annual Convention, and National Matches of 1950 were canceled. NRA reactivated

---

Bottom left: C. B. Lister handled numerous jobs in the administrative work of NRA and helped to keep the organization moving during difficult times. He died on May 14, 1951.

Bottom right: Major General Merritt A. Edson of the U.S. Marine Corps was NRA President from 1949 to 1951 and served as Executive Director after Lister's death. During his tenure, NRA revised its bylaws to include committees devoted to the organization's various programs. Edson also boosted high power shooting, and his influence helped renew federal funding for the NBPRP.

its preinduction training program, which during World War II had graduated more than 1.75 million trainees in basic military marksmanship. By February 1951, 87 training schools were being run by NRA-affiliated clubs, which also schooled civil defense workers in basic pistol marksmanship in cooperation with police departments, plant protection, and civil-defense organizations. Many of the nation's best-known tournament shooters devoted much of their time to this work.

Change of Leadership

During 1951, NRA saw many changes in its programs and staff, some the result of growth, others due to unexpected circumstances. Five members of the staff, including John Scofield, Managing Editor of *American Rifleman,* were called to active service with the outbreak of the Korean War. Then NRA suffered a tragic loss with the death of C. B. Lister on May 14, 1951.

Lister's career with the Association began in 1921 as Advertising and Promotion Manager. He was Reckord's right-hand man during the General's long tenure from 1926 to 1949. Even before 1926, Lister had played a vital role in tripling the mem-

Harry Linn was President of NRA from 1951 to 1953. He was also on the committee that modernized NRA's bylaws in 1950.

bership of the organization by broadening its appeal to civilian shooters. He was a leader in the fight to preserve the rights of Americans to keep and bear arms. He was also largely responsible for the development of the youth program through a genuine interest in youngsters. He was a member of the National Council of the Boy Scouts of America, a director of the Boys Club of Washington, and had been active in many other civic organizations. NRA's important contribution to the war effort had been accomplished under his guidance.

After Lister's death, the Executive Committee met to select his successor as Executive Director, a man who would be capable of wearing Lister's many administrative and leadership hats. Effective June 15, 1951, Merritt Edson resigned his posts as NRA President and Commissioner of Safety of Vermont to accept the position. Edson had retired from the Marine Corps in 1947. In World War II, he had seen 44 months of continuous active service in the Pacific. He was an outstanding rifle-

man, having served as a firing member, coach, or captain of a dozen or more Marine Corps teams. As a leader and organizer of the First Marine Raider Battalion and Commanding Officer of the Second Battalion, Fifth Marines, he was one of the first in the American land forces to take the offensive against the Japanese. Edson's personal gallantry in action had won him the Medal of Honor.

Harry Linn became the new President of the National Rifle Association. Linn was the former Secretary of Agriculture of Iowa, a past President of the Iowa State Rifle Association, and the former National Marksmanship Chairman of the American Legion.

Under General Edson's leadership, NRA made some changes to its programs. Big bore shooting had never fully recovered after World War II, and the Korean conflict set it back further. Suitable ranges were scarce in a nation rapidly shifting to an urbanized society, and the expansion of suburbia was robbing many local clubs of their shooting facilities. The intermittent loss of Camp Perry had forced NRA to farm out its Matches to scattered military posts instead of holding them at a centralized location each year. At the same time, the influence of the National Board for the Promotion of Rifle Practice had decreased for lack of appropriations. General Edson corrected all of these deficiencies in a personal campaign.

Programs for Hunters

By the time Edson took over as Executive Director, NRA had already begun placing more emphasis on developing programs for hunters. Early in 1947, Julian Hatcher's Technical Division began collecting information from hunters to determine the most efficient deer rifle and load and the most effective placement of the shot. More than 4,500 deer hunters returned reports that included anatomical diagrams of deer. An analysis showed that the .30-'06 with 180-grain loads was being used by more deer hunters than all other cartridges combined.

Under General Edson's urging, hunters received even more attention, and with more hunters in the field hunter safety became a major concern for NRA. During the 1940s, New York, Michigan,

Minnesota, and Pennsylvania had been conducting statewide surveys of hunting accidents, but there was no uniform system of gathering facts on a national scale. In most states, hunting accidents were considered entirely in the province of state or local police. Many newspaper reports included death from heart disease and en route traffic accidents as "hunting fatalities."

Thus NRA began a uniform hunter casualty report. Lister had conceived the idea in 1945 and presented it to the North American Wildlife Conference in 1946. By then NRA had begun to gather facts with which to develop a uniform system of reporting. In 1950, the International Association of Game, Fish and Conservation Commissioners adopted the NRA standards and urged its members to cooperate with NRA in gathering the necessary details. In the first year of the program, 30 states and two Canadian provinces participated. In subsequent years, most of the states and several Canadian provinces contributed annual reports to the program.

The idea of training youngsters for hunting had been proposed well before World War II by Seth Gordon, then Secretary of the American Game Association. His idea was adopted on a local scale by various clubs affiliated with NRA. Then in July 1949, in compliance with a newly enacted law, the New York State Conservation Department ruled that no hunter below the age of 17 who had not held a license before could hunt until he had received instruction in safe gun handling from a state game protector. This put an enormous workload on already overworked game protectors, and the Conservation Department asked NRA to take over some of the responsibilities. On February 10, 1950, the New York State legislature passed a bill authorizing qualified NRA members to serve as instructors in the junior hunting program. The New York program was so successful in reducing hunting accidents that in 1952 NRA expanded it to a national program.

In 1950, NRA initiated a 15-foot air gun program in which youngsters could qualify for medals with BB guns under qualified supervision. These programs were designed to train boys and girls in the safe handling of arms where ranges for powder guns were not available. In 1951, the

By 1951, the 25th anniversary of NRA's junior program, there were more than 3,000 NRA-affiliated junior clubs in schools and organizations such as FFA, 4-H, and Boy Scouts of America.

25th anniversary of the NRA junior program, more than 200,000 boys and girls participated in the junior activities. There were more than 3,000 junior clubs in local schools or at installations maintained by cooperating organizations. These included Future Farmers of America, 4-H clubs, the Boy Scouts of America, Veterans of Foreign Wars, the American Legion, and high schools and colleges.

Gaining Specialties

By the time the Korean War ended in July 1953, NRA had become increasingly involved in all aspects of peacetime shooting. Through the new standing committees, which acted as direct representatives of the membership and handled many details formerly assigned to the overworked Executive Committee, NRA was able to become more involved in all aspects of firearms, shooting, and the laws and restrictions governing the Association's programs.

But rising costs were beginning to catch up with the organization. For the second time in three years, the financial report showed a deficit. To help offset these costs, the Board of Directors

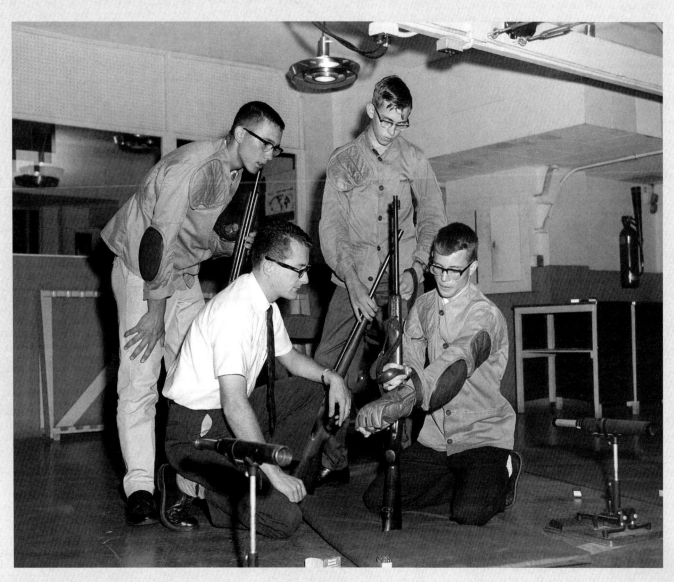

BILL JORDAN:
A LIFELONG NRA SUPPORTER

LIKELY ONE OF THE GREATEST HAND-gunners of the 20th century, Bill Jordan, who served with the U.S. Border Patrol before going on to second and third careers as an NRA Field Representative and as a gun-writer, respectively, was a stalwart supporter of NRA for his entire life. He even made a movie for NRA in the 1960s in which he demonstrated his incredible skill: using wax bullets, he shot aspirin tablets off a table from across the room.

Jordan's writing on personal protection, including the very influential book *No Second Place Winner,* changed the way many law enforcement officers looked at handgunning. Jordan was a shooter of incredible skill whether it was with a rifle, shotgun, or handgun.

The March 1954 *American Rifleman* featured Bill Jordan on the cover with a turkey he took with a drilling.

police firearms instructors. Thousands of police officers had graduated from NRA marksmanship courses.

Preservation and Conservation

In addition to the legal aspects of shooting and gun ownership and hunting and range safety, NRA became more active in wildlife conservation and the development and preservation of shooting opportunities.

Modern scientific wildlife management, administered by the Bureau of Sport Fisheries and Wildlife and the various state fish and game agencies, had greatly increased the supply of game while also increasing opportunities for sportsmen to enjoy it by developing public hunting grounds and liberalizing hunting seasons where possible.

To further the aims of wildlife conservation and management, in 1960 NRA began working closely with the International Association of Game, Fish and Conservation Commissioners; the Wildlife Management Institute; the National Wildlife Federation; and the Izaak Walton League of America.

NRA also sought to improve relationships between landowners and sportsmen. In 1961, it developed a code of hunting ethics to which members could subscribe. This code was printed on a wallet-sized card that could be presented to farmers or landowners when asking permission to hunt on their lands.

More Places to Shoot

The rapid population growth of the United States, accompanied by urbanization and suburban development, brought problems not only to the hunter but to the target shooter. By the 1950s, many rural rifle ranges that formerly could accommodate high power rifle shooting had become hemmed in with apartment buildings, shopping centers, and highways.

To help shooters find suitable ranges, in September 1957 *American Rifleman* began a new column called "A Place to Shoot," which described various rifle ranges developed by member clubs or other organizations to make target shooting compatible with growing urbanization. NRA also developed plans for all types of range facilities, and a model indoor pistol and smallbore rifle range was incorporated in the plans for the NRA headquarters building.

At its Annual Meeting in 1963, the Board of Directors earmarked $100,000 to build a proto-type outdoor safety range. The following year, the organization purchased a tract of 97 acres in Prince Georges County, Maryland, only 25 miles from the center of the nation's capital. On this land it began developing a 40-acre shooting area that would accommodate all types of shooting, including high power rifle, out to 300 meters. Safety walls and baffles eliminated all danger of stray shots and reduced noise to a minimum.

The Dodd Bills

American shooters may have proven them-selves superior in the international arena, but closer to home, their right to bear arms was being increas-ingly challenged by a determined faction of politi-cians. Through it all, NRA led the fight to keep firearms legislation free of loopholes so as not to repeat occurrences like the ATTD's 1957 attempt to impose arbitrary regulations.

Of the many proposed federal firearms bills in the 1960s, the "Dodd Bills" received the greatest attention from the public. Beginning in 1961, NRA staff members met with the Senate Subcommittee on Juvenile Delinquency chaired by Senator Thomas Dodd to discuss various legislative drafts concerning firearms.

Following these conferences, a bill to amend the Federal Firearms Act known as S-1975 was introduced on August 2, 1963. NRA supported this bill, which sought to prevent delivery of hand-guns to unsupervised juveniles, criminals, nar-cotics addicts, and adjudicated alcoholics, and to prohibit interstate shipment in violation of state or local laws.

In the emotion-charged atmosphere following the death of President Kennedy in November 1963, many people lashed out in anti-firearms cam-paigns that were often unreasonable and intem-perate. Five days after Kennedy's assassination, Senator Dodd introduced a series of amendments to S-1975. For starters, the bill would now apply to all firearms, not just handguns, which had been the focus of Dodd's investigation on juvenile delinquency. The amended bill also proposed enormous restrictions on any law-abiding citizen who wanted to purchase a firearm outside his home state.

More than three months before the shocking tragedy in Dallas, NRA had stated its concern about mail-order guns. Noting that a few unscrupu-

Judge Bartlett Rummel served as NRA President from 1963 to 1965 and wrote a column for *American Rifleman* titled "A Court Case of Consequence."

lous merchants were creating a situation in need of prompt correction, an editorial in *American Rifleman* flatly stated, "Steps must be taken to stop the traffic of mail-order guns into unauthorized hands."

At the same time, the editorial reminded people that, in moving against the misuse of firearms, due caution should be exercised so that law-abiding citizens would not be severely penalized or deprived of their individual rights.

Despite some media reports to the contrary, the National Rifle Association was deeply concerned with crime and had supported many measures to prevent and punish the criminal misuse of firearms. In 1965, NRA made a major contribution toward reduction of crime by sponsoring an independent Law-and-Order Committee. While this 20-man committee was chaired by former NRA President Hilliard Comstock and included several other NRA members, it was composed primarily of unaffiliated, eminent leaders in the fields of law, penology, sociology, communications, the military, and other vital segments of American society.

The committee's studies contemplated the use of firearms in crime; the laws designed to cope with violence; and the history, character, and varying conditions of violence. It also dealt with the private ownership of firearms. Moreover, the committee made recommendations as to how NRA could make further contributions in support of law and order.

In 1966, NRA reaffirmed its desire to maintain law and order by supporting a number of policies: a legislative program that would impose mandatory prison terms for those who committed specified criminal acts while armed with a firearm; an amendment to the Federal Firearms Act making it a federal offense for a federally licensed dealer or manufacturer to ship a firearm in interstate or foreign commerce in contravention of a state law; and an amendment to the National Firearms Act to make subject to that act the sale or transfer of certain items of military ordnance (such as bazookas).

Studies showed that disarming the public to prevent criminal misuse of firearms would not lower the rates on violent crime but would, instead, hinder Americans' ability to protect themselves. Still, cries for reformed legislation to disarm Americans and place unreasonable and illogical restraints on their right to own firearms became more and more frequent.

In the later years of the 1960s, NRA focused more and more on fighting to ensure that Second Amendment rights were not infringed upon. On September 1, 1966, Ashley Halsey Jr. was named Editor of *American Rifleman* and Director of the NRA Editorial-Technical Division, following a long career at the *Saturday Evening Post*. Over the next decade, the Charleston, South Carolina, native became the dominant voice for Second Amendment rights in America in ringing monthly *Rifleman* editorials and investigative articles.

This editorial by Halsey, titled "Washington, Lincoln and Firearms," was written for the February 1967 *American Rifleman* and illustrates his love of American history.

President John F. Kennedy, shown here with rifle champion Gary Anderson and Executive Vice President Franklin Orth, was a firm believer in Second Amendment rights.

February marks the birth anniversaries of two of America's greatest Presidents, George Washington and Abraham Lincoln.

Both of these titanic leaders reached their zenith of greatness while guiding our country through wars which could have killed off the nation at birth or before maturity. Both knew firearms, for military and for sporting purposes.

George Washington spent nearly a quarter of his life under arms. When he died at 67, he had soldiered for 15½ years. When peace and leisure permitted, he hunted constantly. Hunting was perhaps the favorite and foremost recreation of the Father of His Country.

Abraham Lincoln's numerous biographies note that he "hunted," that he "shot wild turkey," and that he served in the militia in the Black Hawk War. His interest in firearms, especially in military weapons efficient enough to shorten the Civil War, led him personally to test-fire and approve the Spencer repeater, the first magazine cartridge arm extensively used by U.S. Forces.

Lincoln as commander-in-chief directed probably the biggest rifleman's war in the Western hemisphere, in which by far the highest percentage of casualties were caused by infantry bullets. Like Washington, he fully recognized the role of firearms. For one man, they created a new nation. For the other, they held it together.

So America was fortunate that both of these heroic wartime leaders of classic stature had a thorough grasp and understanding of firearms.

But the wars themselves, in 1775 and 1861, what did they start over?

In 1775, was it the Stamp Tax, the quartering of British regulars in the homes of American colonials, "taxation without representation," or what?

In 1861, was it the Fugitive Slave Act, "Bleeding Kansas," the tariff issue between industrial North and agricultural South, or what?

What actually turned each clash of words into a "shooting war"?

The answer in both instances is very nearly the same.

In 1775 the shooting began when the British, after methodically disarming every individual

Ashley Halsey Jr.'s love of American history was often apparent in the editorials he wrote for more than a decade.

American who left Boston, marched a column of redcoats from Boston to Concord, Mass., to seize the arms of American militia stored there.

In 1861, the first shots were fired over whether a fort in the harbor of Charleston, S.C., should be evacuated and in effect disarmed.

Both wars, then, sprang in their full-blown form from efforts to disarm Americans who would not be disarmed.

Whenever anyone stops to ask himself what will make Americans fighting mad, he might do well to consider 1775 and 1861.

Perhaps, on the anniversaries of Washington and Lincoln, that is as timely a thought as any.

1968: The U.S. Congress passes the Gun Control Act, and NRA membership reaches the 1 million mark, a compelling testament to concern for Second Amendment rights.

1975: To fight against growing anti-gun legislation, NRA's Board of Directors forms the Institute for Legislative Action (ILA) led by Harlon B. Carter.

1982: NRA's concerted education campaign sees a landslide victory when most California voters say "no" to a referendum issue that would stop handgun sales and initiate gun registration.

1970: Army Captain Margaret Thompson Murdock made shooting history at the 40th World Shooting Championships, which NRA hosted on behalf of the United States.

1977: Members revolt at the Annual Meeting, demanding changes in the bylaws and a new focus on protecting Second Amendment rights. Harlon Carter is voted Executive Vice President.

1986: NRA's work with Senator James A. McClure and Representative Harold Volkmer leads to congressional passage of the Firearms Owners Protection Act.

PART THREE

PROTECTING FREEDOM

A NUMBER OF FACTORS SPURRED AN onslaught of anti-gun legislation like never before. For a decade, NRA wavered between establishing itself as a lobbying force to protect Second Amendment rights or becoming an organization whose primary focus was on supporting ancillary shooting activities. The members' revolt in 1977 decided the issue, and NRA gradually became one of the nation's most powerful lobbying forces, fighting to preserve Americans' right to bear arms. Even as NRA—its leaders and its members—battled against anti-gun legislation, the organization's programs became increasingly more focused. Today, the National Rifle Association offers something for everyone—programs for hunters, marksmen, military, police, women, and youth. At the same time, its safety and anti-crime programs underscore its commitment to protecting American liberties while making America a better place to enjoy them.

1988: NRA debuts its award-winning Eddie Eagle GunSafe® Program for children, developed through the guiding force of Marion P. Hammer, who would become NRA's first woman president in 1995.

1994: NRA moves its headquarters from Washington, D.C., to a new complex in Fairfax, Virginia, that would feature a state-of-the-art range and National Firearms Museum.

2000: NRA membership crosses the 4.3 million mark heading into the victorious grassroots effort to elect George W. Bush as U.S. President.

1991: Ushering in "the New NRA," Wayne R. LaPierre is elected Executive Vice President, while James J. Baker becomes Executive Director of ILA. New initiatives promise to give NRA a powerful presence nationwide.

1998: Screen legend Charlton Heston is elected NRA President. He would serve an unprecedented five terms in office.

Standing just behind President Lyndon B. Johnson as he signs the Gun Control Act of 1968 on October 22 were (from left) Senator Joseph Tydings (D-Maryland), Senator Thomas J. Dodd (D-Connecticut), Representative Emanuel Celler (D-New York), and James V. Bennett, Department of Justice consultant. Attorney General Ramsey Clark can just be seen standing between Tydings and Dodd.

CHAPTER FOURTEEN

NRA's Darkest Days

1967–1969

Many young men today in Vietnam have been trained with the Service rifle at NRA Clubs under the [NBPRP] program, largely at NRA expense. . . . I have recently asked some prominent Americans this question: "Who is NRA's enemy? Who is intent on destroying it, and who would be best served by doing so?" Certainly not the American people.

—Franklin L. Orth, 1969

STANDING FIRM

AGAINST EFFORTS TO DISARM AMERICAN SPORTSMEN BY RESTRICTIVE LEGISLATION

NATIONAL RIFLE ASSOCIATION

IN THE LATE 1950S AND EARLY 1960s, every threat to the right to keep and bear arms on Capitol Hill or with the White House had been braved, forestalled, or defeated in large measure through the personal efforts of one man—Franklin L. Orth, the NRA Executive Vice President who came to office in 1959. Orth's influence on behalf of NRA was carried out one-on-one with key players in Congress. For his era—for the pre-'60s cultural-revolution days—he was part of the inside dynamic of power in the national capital. With Orth, the organization had survived demands for new federal gun controls in the emotional frenzy following the November 1963 assassination of President John F. Kennedy, himself an NRA Life Member and supporter of the Second Amendment. But those media-driven demands were mounting yearly. Ultimately they would overwhelm Franklin Orth's personal skill and influence.

NRA's very existence was to become a major public issue. The organization, in the mid-1960s, still considered itself a gun club. It was the hub of organized shooting in America, the keeper of national records, the trainer of Olympians, the guardian of gun safety, a mentoring organization to millions of youngsters, and a deeply patriotic Association. In the 1960s culture, for the media

elite, patriotism was not a virtue. Those who didn't know the truth about NRA—a growing segment of American society that was exposed only to the image of the Association painted by the media—saw it as they were conditioned to see it: as something sinister: the "gun lobby."

Lyndon Johnson's Media-Driven Gun Control Schemes

By 1967, President Lyndon B. Johnson's leadership was undergoing a political death of a thousand cuts, with virtually all of his policies—from the conduct of the war in Vietnam to his much vaunted war on poverty—either failed or tainted. Johnson needed a diversion. He found it in gun control. In addition to putting the full weight of his administration behind congressional efforts to enact a national system of centralized gun owner registration and licensing, Johnson went on the attack through the executive branch.

As threats to disarm Americans mounted, NRA increased its efforts to "stand firm" against restrictive gun legislation for law-abiding citizens.

Above: Warren L. Cheek began working in NRA's training department in the early 1960s. He was Director of Training for 10 years and served as NRA's Secretary for 17 years before joining the organization's Executive Council. He also wrote a number of training manuals and directed NRA Police Instructor Schools. In 1996, he began volunteering at Camp Perry.

Below: When the Army withdrew its support of the National Matches, that support was replaced by the "can do" spirit of some 225 volunteers and a handful of NRA staff who—with the financial backing of 1,847 contributors—joined forces to make the 1968 NRA National Rifle and Pistol Championships one of the smoothest run events of its kind.

In 1967, the Department of Defense and the Department of the Army abruptly ended its historic long-standing support for the National Matches at Camp Perry. It was a blow meant to put a stake in the heart of NRA's most traditional competitions. Instead, it awakened the power of the Association: grassroots volunteers. Warren L. Cheek, who served in the Competitions and Training Division at the time, remembered the remarkable outpouring of volunteer spirit and enthusiasm that kept the Matches alive after all. "We advertised in our magazine for volunteers to assist in running the Matches, and the very next year we were able to run them with hundreds of volunteers. They came from every walk of life." Cheek himself continued volunteering as Match Director for the pistol competition long after he retired as NRA Secretary in 1994.

NRA's Military Ties Stay Strong

While military support was withdrawn from Camp Perry, NRA's support of the military remained high. Following sensational congressional hearings investigating the M16 rifle being used by troops in Vietnam, *American Rifleman*'s Senior Technical Advisor, Colonel E. H. Harrison, wrote a two-part "special report" that covered 15 pages in the January and February 1968 issues. Colonel Harrison's expert conclusions about the M16 were based on 26 years' experience as an Army ordnance officer and familiarity with the rifle dating back to 1962 when his testing found the rifle to be inaccurate due to low projectile stability from the 14" rifling twist. A faster 12" twist was soon adopted.

A HIGH-FLYING BERETTA

O N OCTOBER 14, 1947, U.S. ARMY AIR Force Captain Chuck Yeager became the first man to crack the sound barrier. He was flying the Bell X-1. Yeager was born in Myra, West Virginia, on February 13, 1923. He enlisted in the U.S. Army Air Corps in November 1941 and eventually became a fighter pilot. Over the skies of Europe, Yeager shot down 13 German aircraft—five of them on the same day. He flew 64 combat missions and earned the Silver Star and Distinguished Flying Cross for his valor in the air war of Germany.

Yeager became one of America's premiere test pilots and logged more than 19,000 flight hours in 180 different types of aircraft before his retirement at general's rank in 1975. A lifelong hunter and shooter, Chuck Yeager is also a champion of the Second Amendment right to keep and bear arms and proudly participated in the "I'm the NRA" campaign, in which he is shown cradling his favorite muzzleloading rifle.

*Photo courtesy
National Firearms Museum*

This Beretta Model 1935 semi-automatic pistol, serial number 823309, was presented to Brigadier General Chuck Yeager by the Cuban Minister of Defense in 1950. This particular Model 1935 in 7.65 mm is gold-washed and has full coverage scrollwork engraving.

NRA took a prominent role in Inauguration Day ceremonies in January 1969, hosting a reception and banquet at the Washington Hotel for nearly 200 Medal of Honor winners. Included among the honorees was former South Dakota Governor Joe Foss, who, nearly two decades later, would become NRA President. The military background of Executive Vice President Franklin Orth was noted three months later when he was unanimously elected President of the U.S. Olympic Committee. The *New York Times* observed that, "as rugged as his new Olympic job may be, it can't be any tougher than the assignment he volunteered for in World War II," service with Merrill's Marauders behind Japanese lines.

The "Gun Lobby" and the Gun Industry

Gun control gave Lyndon Johnson respite from the media, which openly despised him for the way he managed the Vietnam War. The beleaguered President knew that when he spoke in favor of harsh controls on firearms ownership, he was on the media's wave length and would receive its blessing in print and on the airwaves. As a media target, in editorial cartoons NRA was depicted as a gangster or thug or as a tool of an evil gun industry. In print, the organization was vilified as "the gun lobby."

"Gun industry." Those two words in the media smear always seemed to resonate, at least with the media itself. A few short years of steady vilification tying the words "gun lobby" and "NRA lobby" to "gun industry" gave these phrases a pejorative meaning. There was deep irony in the thrust of these attacks. In the politics of gun control, a gulf exists between the interests of NRA and major segments of the firearms industry. For their part in the equation, NRA members are consumers, whether they are collectors, shooters, hunters, competitors, or simply purchase a firearm for defense of their homes and families against criminal violence. The firearms industry, on the other hand, is made up of profit-making entities, which at times have affected national legislative changes to restrain trade, bolster their profit margins, or outright close down their competitors. The industry's heavy hand in manufacturing gun controls as a means of restraint of trade was one of the great ironies of the whole debate.

If the words "lobby" and "lobbyist" took on a sinister connotation with the unknowing public, those words held the same dark sense within the hierarchy of NRA. Franklin Orth, during a gun control hearing, was challenged by Senator Ted Kennedy as to why the organization was not a registered lobby. His reply: "It is not our principal business to lobby. It is just in recent years that we have had this harassment with respect to some of these legislative problems that we have spent as much time lobbying as we have." NRA members in particular, and all firearms owners in general, were about to become the real losers in the failure of Orth's insider game and in the success of the kill-the-competition game played by the industry. That philosophy would continue for nearly a decade and feed an anger that would culminate in a revolution within NRA.

Assassinations Stun the Nation

The efforts of Franklin Orth's NRA to hold the line against the combined weight of an anti-gun-rights administration and Lyndon Johnson's able allies in the House and Senate might have succeeded had it not been for two seminal events in the turbulent history of the 1960s—events that utterly doomed the gun control fight. On April 4, 1968, civil rights leader Dr. Martin Luther King Jr. was assassinated in Memphis. The nation was stunned and deeply saddened. The urban riots and upheaval that followed were cataclysmic and frightening, and the press for gun control took on a never-spoken but tacit racial overtone. The media frenzy demanded the civil rights leader's murder be avenged by Congress with new gun controls.

In the past, a major element of NRA's legislative defense had been in making compromise. Part of that strategy, mainly for public relations purposes, had been for NRA itself to offer up support for some form of gun control.

In February 1968, NRA President Harold W. Glassen, a distinguished Michigan attorney and a hunter-conservationist of national repute, had attempted to answer media critics by undertaking a marathon television speech tour across the country. President Glassen appeared on television or at press conferences 31 times in nine days, blaming the congressional impasse on gun legislation directly on Senators Robert and Ted Kennedy. "They have shown no effort at compromise, while we have been willing to compromise," he said. NRA had supported bans on mail-order sales of firearms and bans on foreign imports in tune with the industry's song. For its efforts, NRA got virtually zero credit in the media.

Following King's assassination, NRA's friends in the Senate led by Nebraska Republican Roman Hruska attempted a preemptive strike with an NRA-supported bill, which *American Rifleman* said "provided affidavit controls over interstate handgun sales, and barred all interstate firearms sales

Harold W. Glassen, a practicing attorney in Lansing, Michigan, became NRA President in 1967 and represented the Association on numerous national television programs such as the *Tonight Show with Johnny Carson*. He became the 12th NRA Honorary Life Member in 1983.

to persons under 18." It hit the Senate floor on May 16 and failed on a 45–37 vote.

The NRA membership was told that "NRA spokesmen were hopeful that the Hruska program would be substituted and would put an end to the long wrangle over federal controls." It was an utterly vain hope and a terrible strategy. The very notion that NRA was touting itself as being for gun control, in any principle, was confusing to its friends in Congress and even more confusing and disheartening to the NRA membership and gun owners in general who believed the media hype about the uncompromising "gun lobby."

If the shock and reverberations from King's assassination were not enough, New York Senator Robert Kennedy, brother of the martyred President, was murdered during a presidential campaign appearance in Los Angeles on June 5, 1968. His assassin used a handgun. With that event, the media was to generate more mass fear, which was seized and shaped into a campaign for harsh national gun controls. Almost immediately following the Kennedy murder, Congress was flooded with some 62 gun control bills. Anti-handgun measures that had been included in the Senate Judiciary Committee's Omnibus Crime and Safe Streets Act were given a fast track.

In April, the Senate Judiciary Committee had included a series of strictures on handguns as part of its version of the Safe Streets Act. The day following the Kennedy shooting, the House began moving on its version of that legislation, creating major harsh restrictions on commerce in pistols and revolvers including outright import bans. After three years of steady media demands for federal gun control, there was now, seemingly, no stopping the gun control juggernaut—not without a massive and effective NRA grassroots mobilization, and that mechanism simply didn't exist. The will to use all-out people power to fight the battle lay elsewhere—with the opponents of NRA.

Emergency Committee for Gun Control

Following Robert Kennedy's assassination, U.S. Attorney General Ramsey Clark met with the leadership of 38 private advocacy organizations to form an entity called the Emergency Committee for Gun Control. Created as part of the National

New York City attorney Woodson D. Scott assumed NRA's presidency in 1969, 40 years after first joining the Association. A member of numerous state associations and shooting clubs, Scott won Silver and Bronze Stars as an infantry battalion commander in World War II.

Council for a Responsible Firearms Policy, it was a government-endorsed political confederation pledged to assist the Johnson administration's all-out push for "rigid gun control laws." It had support from Madison Avenue advertising firms and free printing. Most importantly, it received unlimited widespread free publicity from media outlets in every corner of the nation. The Emergency Committee was headed by astronaut John Glenn (later a U.S. Senator from Ohio).

The Glenn committee blitzed the American public with ads and staged spot news and canned editorials, all exhorting people to demand action on gun controls by Congress. Among the ad copy was this headline: "We have written a letter to your congressman about gun control. All you have to do is sign it and mail it." Most of the ads had a tag line, "WRITE YOUR SENATOR . . . WHILE YOU STILL HAVE A SENATOR." It was slick and highly effective. Its message saturated the media. The entire effort was an extension of the Johnson administration, in effect, a campaign on behalf of the government.

The perennial and leading opponent of gun rights in the U.S. Senate was Connecticut Democrat Thomas Dodd, who would be the front man for the Johnson administration. He was followed as a close second by Maryland Democrat Joseph Tydings, whose single most important goal was universal, compulsory registration and licensing. Where Dodd was an old warhorse, Tydings was young, the inheritor of an aristocratic family political dynasty in Maryland. His father had also been a U.S. Senator.

Tydings always made a conscious effort to demonize the National Rifle Association and its members. On NRA's staunch public position opposing registration and licensing, Tydings condescendingly said, "It is because their membership has been brainwashed for so long by the national leadership which is principally directed, financed by the munitions industry. They do not have a chance because they never see the facts." In 1967–68, Joe Tydings made gun control the center of his political life, and the media loved him. Everything Tydings said to vilify NRA made news. At one point, Tydings demanded IRS investigations of NRA because it was not registered as a lobbying organization.

"We Contact Only Our Members"

A confrontation between Senator Tydings and NRA President Harold Glassen during a Senate gun control hearing was instructive. Tydings made repeated attempts to tag NRA with the word "lobby." After a question about NRA influencing Congress, Mr. Glassen said, "We contact only our members. I have never gone on national television or any other kind and asked everybody within the sound of my voice to write a letter to his Congressman."

The exchange was interrupted by South Carolina Senator Strom Thurmond, who said he had seen a national telecast just days before "where John Glenn did go on television and asked

ONE WAY TO WEAKEN AMERICA

TOM ☆ ELLINWOOD

This cartoon, first published in the *Arizona Daily Star* before passage of the Gun Control Act of 1968, captures the essence of NRA's stance to protect Second Amendment rights. Before the Members Meeting in 1977, NRA remained divided on how much strength it should devote to legislative battles.

the people to write to the Members of Congress." And there was the rub. While NRA was shying away from reaching out to millions of people who agreed philosophically with its legislative position, the Glenn committee was marshalling its forces. NRA's only connection with the membership was through *American Rifleman,* which required a lead time of several months. No matter how well presented it was, news and information printed in the magazine was always old news. And the instant access afforded the Glenn committee by the news media was either denied to NRA or twisted in its presentation.

John Glenn was indeed heading a grassroots lobby. The Emergency Committee on Gun Control was well disciplined and well financed and had inside connections to the highest reaches of the Johnson administration and the full resources of the national media at its disposal. The Glenn Emergency Committee's only purpose was to lobby, to influence public opinion in order to change the will of Congress. In the end, it won a huge victory.

The Gun Control Act of 1968 would be Lyndon Johnson's only victory in his last months in office. The new law would cast a dark shadow over the lives of millions of peaceable consumers of firearms and related products well into the future. Allan D. Cors, who had served as minority counsel to the House Judiciary Committee and later became a corporate lobbyist, remembered the fight well. He was in the thick of the battle and was among a handful of people fighting hard to prevent a legislative disaster. Recalling the NRA leadership, Cors said, "The atmosphere in the organization was still myopic: 'if we just keep our heads down, maybe we won't be hurt any more.' And my livelihood being a full-time lobbyist, I had a much different perspective on it. I recognized that you don't ever win anything by keeping your head down." Cors, who would become a member of the NRA Board of Directors, would never forget the lessons of 1968. He was destined to become a major quiet force within the Association for moving it to become a truly effective lobbying organization.

Just days after Robert Kennedy's assassination, the House and Senate voted on a final version of the Safe Streets Act, one that contained severe restrictions on lawful commerce in handguns. It was signed into law June 19 by President Johnson and was set to take effect December 16. That legislation banned mail-order sales of handguns, made interstate transfers of handguns illegal, banned importation of military handguns, set the minimum age for purchase of a handgun at 21 years, and banned importation of "non-sporting purpose" handguns.

The Safe Streets Act wasn't enough to satisfy Lyndon Johnson, who wanted full registration and licensing and, at the least, demanded that restrictions on handguns in the Safe Streets Act be extended to all firearms. Johnson was not deterred when Research Associates, Inc. (a private firm

working for the National Commission of the Causes and Prevention of Violence, which Johnson had appointed), determined that a federal registration and licensing system would cost the equivalent of nearly 15 percent of all the funds spent annually on law enforcement. The media and Glenn Committee campaigns against private ownership of firearms continued at a frenetic pace until October, when Congress enacted what would be the Gun Control Act of 1968. Like the Safe Streets Act, it would take effect December 16, 1968.

Johnson Signs Gun Control Act of 1968

The Gun Control Act of 1968 was signed into law by President Johnson on October 22. It wasn't Senator Joe Tydings's be-all, end-all registration and licensing. And it wasn't the ban on handguns sought by the Glenn Committee. National legislative leaders like Michigan Congressman John Dingell prevailed against those extremes, but what remained in the new law was a sad loss for individual NRA members. It was a "first step" in what was planned by the anti-gun movement as a quick two- or three-year fight. Ironically, many normally friendly members of Congress, who were about to vote for the '68 Act and against their constituencies, sought the advice of NRA. They would later complain that they got mixed signals, wrong signals, or no signals at all from the organization. The final vote in the U.S. House of Representatives on what would be the Gun Control Act of 1968 came on October 10 and gave Lyndon Johnson his lame-duck victory by 161 votes to 129, a 32-vote margin.

The real shame of it, the real story, was in another number: the 141 members of the House who didn't vote, who took a walk. Among those legislators were more than sufficient numbers of people who normally would have been staunch supporters of NRA members or who were friends by inclination, Democrats and Republicans, especially those from rural districts. All NRA needed was at least 32 votes from the legislators who didn't vote. All NRA needed to do was what it refused to do: LOBBY—to awaken the millions of fellow citizens the organization could reach through its membership—one on one, family to family, friend to friend.

For the National Rifle Association, the loss created lasting damage. It was devastating on Capitol

Hill, where legislators on both sides of the issue saw NRA as merely a shadow, without force of will or substance. Gun prohibitionist Illinois Congressman Abner Mikva would call NRA a "paper tiger." And for the individual members of NRA, the loss was to fuel a slow and burning anger that wouldn't be assuaged until nearly a decade later, when NRA members would be justly proud to call themselves the best grassroots lobby in the nation.

The immediate and significant fallout from the gun owners' legislative loss came in the November 1968 elections. Many national legislators who had voted for the '68 Act felt the ire of their constituents. Some, like Senate Majority Leader Mike Mansfield of Montana barely won reelection while others, like Pennsylvania U.S. Senator Joseph S. Clark, who held what had been considered a safe seat, were soundly defeated in upsets widely credited to firearms owners and sportsmen. Clark's opponent, Richard Schweiker, a moderate Republican with his political base in the Philadelphia suburbs, welcomed and helped organize an effort to tap the volunteer and voting power of hundreds of thousands of frustrated firearms activists coupled with the state's nearly 1 million hunters and their friends and families. The purely state grassroots effort was spearheaded by the Pennsylvania Rifle and Pistol Association, which organized a political committee called Outdoorsmen for Schweiker. The impressive can-do effort led the way in the future for other states.

Oregon's Wayne Morse, who had been a fixture in the U.S. Senate since 1945, also lost his seat—not because he voted for the '68 Act, but because he didn't vote against it. He was among those who took a walk on final passage. *American Rifleman* explained the elections almost apologetically: "Although the NRA took no position in the election at any level, in line with its fixed policy, there were indications that sportsmen and conservationists in general, and many and perhaps a majority of them entirely unconnected with the NRA, weighed the gun control issue and acted according to their conclusions." The Association, in the same breath, chided the more hard-line segment of its natural constituency: "In several isolated instances, spokesmen for these [political] groups overzealously assailed even lawmakers who had stood for the basic principals of the program of positive gun control legislation because they wanted no new laws whatever." The "program of positive gun control" included NRA's endorsement of bans on imported handguns.

The Gun Control Act Takes Effect

After the election, on December 16, when the provisions of the 1968 Act took effect, the nation's firearms owners discovered how much the new law had changed their lives, especially in what had been normal innocent commerce. All firearms transactions of any kind between private individuals who lived in different states were illegal. For millions of Americans who lived in state border communities of the lower 48, the '68 Act was a rude awakening when they walked into their local bordering state gun store. They all heard the same message, "I can't sell you that gun. You're not a resident." Overnight, even a direct gift of a .22 rifle between a grandfather in Covington, Kentucky, and a grandson in Cincinnati, Ohio—living just a riverbank away—was a federal felony. Firearms pur-

NRA's relationship with America's law enforcement community is an enduring one, and police marksmanship has long been a concern of the Association. NRA held its first National Police Pistol Championships at Indiana University in 1962, and the matches remain an ongoing event.

chasers and sellers were obliged to fill out a new federal form, giving their names and addresses. The dealer had to supply the type and serial number of the firearm involved in the transaction. The only thing that kept this from being a national gun-owner registry was that the federal forms, 4473s, were required by law to be kept in the federally licensed dealers' premises. It was a hard-fought protection against centralized registration.

Overnight, anyone who "engaged in the business" of firearms and ammunition transactions, with sales or purchases, had to be licensed by the federal government or face criminal prosecution. But there was no definition in the law as to how many sales of firearms or ammunition constituted "engaging in the business." And "engaging in the business without a license" constituted a federal crime with federal felony provisions. More than 160,000 individuals and small and large businesses applied and received Federal Firearms Licenses (FFLs). In a flash, the entire range of commercial commerce of firearms and ammunition in America came under the strict control and scrutiny of the federal government, in this case the Alcohol and Tobacco Tax division of the Internal Revenue Service, which was renamed the Alcohol, Tobacco, and Firearms Division. The pedigree of every firearm manufactured or imported from December 16, 1968, would be recorded and tracked through licensed commerce.

Retail licensees were required to keep two separate records of every transaction they made for all firearms and ammunition. In addition to the federal form 4473, they had to keep a bound book with the names and addresses of purchasers or sellers of guns. Much of the initial thrust of the act created a hardship on small business people. Licensed dealers couldn't sell their private guns without committing a crime. The law required that private firearms be kept separately, away from dealer inventory. But a dealer who might occasionally do what other Americans could do legally—sell a private gun to a private individual in the same state—could be accused of selling a firearm "off the books."

The worst part—and this was unique in all federal criminal law—was that there was no scienter; that is, no knowledge of the criminality of an act was required for prosecution. "Knowingly"

or "willfully" breaking the law wasn't an element for prosecution. The only standard was breaking the law, period. The '68 Act was at heart a regulatory scheme with felony consequences for every transgression large or small, intentional or inadvertent. This lack of a standard would be the ultimate weapon used by zealous federal agents to ruin the lives of hundreds of otherwise well-meaning and innocent Americans in a blitz of civil liberties abuses, which would ultimately lead to reform of the law. The no standard of knowledge would allow federal agents to manufacture hundreds of criminal cases against innocent, unwitting Americans and turn them into what they would label as "gun criminals."

There was one section of the law that wasn't part of a scheme to regulate lawful commerce, that in fact actually dealt specifically with real violent street criminals and guns. It was a section most firearms owners would welcome and which has been supported by NRA to this day. It made possession, transportation, and any commerce in firearms or ammunition by convicted felons, fugitives from justice, known drug users, adjudicated lunatics, and illegal aliens criminal acts. If a convicted felon anywhere in the country possessed a gun, it was a crime. But that no-nonsense part of the law would be ignored by federal law enforcement and especially by gun control advocates for years to come.

For those who thought the '68 Act would slow the attack on firearms rights, the words "first step" would take on a critical meaning. Indeed, the real threat was in lesser increments, always called something like "sensible first steps," that would lead to registration and licensing and systematic bans. Senator Ted Kennedy would call a partial ban on handgun ownership a "gentle step." The combination of industry restraint-of-trade and NRA's search for a compromise to keep the wolf at bay created a never-win situation—a sure-fire losing game of attrition with inherent dangers that only a few within the power structure of the Association saw with any clarity.

But the danger of compromise was something that a multitude of grassroots activists and ordinary members understood all too plainly. The wolf would come knocking again soon enough. And as always, he wanted more.

The American flag is raised at the 1970 World Shooting Championships in Phoenix, Arizona, for gold medal riflemen (from left) D. I. Boyd, John Foster, John Writer, and Lones Wigger. These prestigious international matches were hosted by NRA on behalf of the United States of America, and more than 300 NRA members volunteered their time to help make the event a great success.

CHAPTER FIFTEEN

COUNTDOWN TO CRISIS

1970–1975

The Constitution . . . is not adequate to protect the individual against the growing bureaucracy in the Legislative and Executive Branches. . . . [He] is almost certain to be plowed under, unless he has a well-organized active political group to speak for him. . . . But if a powerful sponsor is lacking, individual liberty withers—in spite of glowing opinions and resounding constitutional phrases.

—Justice William O. Douglas, 1968

THE NEW DECADE DAWNED with NRA, on behalf of the United States, hosting the 40th World Shooting Championships. The matches in Phoenix, Arizona, drew shooters from 50 member nations of the International Shooting Union. Operating without the full governmental support customarily given the World Championships in other countries, NRA put out a call for volunteers, and, as always, the call was answered. More than 300 NRA members helped in many phases of match operations, both at Black Canyon Range and the Phoenix Trap & Skeet Range, and insured the successful conduct of what was the largest international shooting match held in the United States since 1923.

While the Soviet team captured the most medals, American marksmen won 12 gold, 14 silver, and eight bronze medals. The highlight of the championships came when Army Captain Margaret Thompson Murdock from Topeka, Kansas, became the first and only woman to win a free-rifle title at a World Championship. She fired 375 out of a possible 400 to capture the 300-meter standing event by three points. Shooting history had also been made earlier that year at Camp Perry, when Navy shooter Thomas N. Treinen shattered the seemingly invincible Wimbledon Cup record set in 1939. Treinen,

using a borrowed rifle chambered in 7 mm Rem. Mag., fired 32 consecutive rounds into the 20" V-ring at 1,000 yards for a history-making score of 100-20V +12V.

NRA Enters Its Second Century

NRA's 1871 founding was celebrated well into 1971, beginning with January's special centennial issue of *American Rifleman*, which, at 168 pages, was easily the largest magazine the Association had ever published. It included the first full-color, full-size photographs of firearms ever printed in the *Rifleman*. Pictured were NRA Centennial Commemorative Daisy air guns, a Colt National Match Gold Cup .45, a Colt Single Action Army, a Winchester sporter styled after the Model 64, and a Winchester musket based on the Model 1895 NRA musket brought out in 1905 for military rifle matches.

NRA held an NRA Centennial Celebration in Washington, D.C., during the first week of April. During the festivities, 12-year-old Michael D. Peterson of Oconto Falls, Wisconsin, was honored

---

The 40th World Shooting Championships were shot in Phoenix and attracted the premier marksmen of 50 nations.

for becoming the 5 millionth graduate of the NRA Hunter Safety Program. At the Members Banquet, Arizona Senator Barry Goldwater delivered a rousing keynote speech, declaring that he found a "marked similarity" in the arguments of some "who shout the loudest for restrictions on the possession of guns by law-abiding Americans" and "people who argue most strenuously for unilateral disarmament of the United States." Senator Goldwater congratulated NRA "for 100 years of distinguished and exemplary service to the United States of America," adding, "I especially want to congratulate the NRA for its dignified and responsible performance in the present era of hysteria and criticism relative to civilian possession of firearms."

But away from the firing lines and birthday celebrations, the depressing realities of the strictures of the 1968 Act were being discovered by individual NRA members. Franklin Orth at last registered as a federal lobbyist. "This action," NRA President Harold Glassen wrote in *American Rifleman*, "constitutes an emphatic answer to

Arizona Senator Barry Goldwater was keynote speaker at NRA's centennial anniversary dinner. The organization hosted a number of special events to celebrate its first 100 years.

any question as to how far the NRA will go in fighting against unfair and harassing legislation." Orth would soon be forced to confront a legislative issue that would haunt NRA well into the 1970s.

"Saturday Night Specials"

That issue—bans on so-called "Saturday Night Specials"—was, ironically, one that the organization's leaders unwittingly had helped create in their search for acceptable "gun controls" designed to

improve NRA's image and assuage the media. In the opening months of 1968, before the traumatic assassinations and media frenzy that would make NRA's guardianship of gun rights virtually impossible, the Association had decided to throw the wolf a bone.

A series of *American Rifleman* editorials appeared, calling for efforts to "shut off importation of tons of cheap foreign pistols." NRA got what it asked for, an import ban, now wrapped in the rest of the strictures of the Gun Control Act. But the issue of banning some handguns was far from over.

Though prohibited from bringing most foreign-made handguns into the country, there was nothing to prevent importers from manufacturing those same guns in the United States using imported parts. A whole new segment of domestic industry grew overnight, and that effort gave birth to a new generic form of anti-firearms legislation: bans on "Saturday Night Specials." The definition "Saturday Night Special" would quickly grow way beyond assembled imported parts and would gobble up virtually the entire product lines of handgun giants like Smith & Wesson and Colt.

WHITTINGTON CENTER DEVELOPMENT

AT THE 1973 ANNUAL MEETINGS IN Washington, D.C., Executive Vice President Maxwell E. Rich announced a possible site location for the long-anticipated NRA national center for the shooting sports and wildlife management. Land outside Raton, New Mexico, owned by Kaiser Steel Corporation, would accommodate high power rifle target ranges up to 1,000 yards, camping and trailer facilities, and a wildlife management and conservation complex.

The NRA board voted to set up an NRA Special Contribution Fund and authorized the loan of up to $2 million to buy the land, subject to a feasibility study. At its next meeting in late September, the board approved purchase of the 32,500-acre site, with NRA holding the mortgage, and transferred the necessary funds to the Special Contribution Fund on a three-year note.

Four years later, the board voted unanimously to name the center the NRA Whittington Center as a tribute to one of its strongest supporters, Honorary Life Member George R. Whittington of Amarillo, Texas. Whittington, a champion rifle shooter and oil company executive, had served as NRA President in 1957–58.

Above: Retired General Maxwell E. Rich was Executive Vice President from 1970 to 1977. Supporters of the Institute for Legislative Action, as well as many members, disagreed with the direction in which Rich was leading NRA.

It was a natural trap, where both gun owners and members of Congress were already confused as to its meaning. "Saturday Night Special" would become an elastic phrase, ever expanding to encompass more and more firearms. And it would be expanded beyond banning the manufacture of a generic class of handguns to the banning of all transfers and eventually banning possession by private individuals.

"Saturday Night Special" bans found a willing champion in U.S. Senator Birch Bayh of Indiana. As Bayh's bill was moving through the Judiciary Committee, NRA Executive Vice President Maxwell E. Rich, an NRA board member and commander of the Utah National Guard, who had taken office after

Franklin Orth had succumbed to a heart attack in January 1970, spoke haltingly in favor of the concept. It was a comment that would cloud the issue for many otherwise pro-firearms rights Senators.

The threat to those rights became more eminent when a crazed assassin wounded Alabama Governor George Wallace during a May presidential campaign stop in Laurel, Maryland. The fact that the shooter was armed with a small, short-barreled revolver gave Bayh and his allies the horsepower to ram Bayh's legislation through the Senate by a 68–25 vote on August 9. A day later, NRA mailed a million-member legislative bulletin that had been approved in mid-July by a deeply fearful NRA Executive Committee. A mailing to the full membership was a massive and expensive undertaking and was cumbersome to get underway. This was the first full-member bulletin since 1965. And it was the first time NRA members received any real detail about legislation that empowered the Secretary of Treasury to decide what handguns the American public could own, in addition to giving the government power to buy banned handguns from individuals. The text of the "bulletin" urged NRA members to contact their members of Congress to stop the legislation in the House of Representatives. The mailing worked wonders. From the grassroots, individual NRA members linked with their friends and neighbors, all of whom worked Congress hard with mail, calls, and visits.

NRA Members Exercise First Amendment Rights

The House version of the Bayh Bill died in the House Judiciary Committee. Congress was swamped with letters, and this time the juggernaut was halted dead in its tracks. It was the work of the real gun lobby—individual NRA members exercising their First Amendment rights. The effect of the massive response from NRA members and gun owners from the grassroots would last for a year and would considerably dampen the ardor of many Senators and U.S. Representatives for gun controls, including a revisiting of the Bayh Bill.

In the fall of 1972, despite the growing Watergate scandal, Richard Nixon won reelection over George McGovern. Early in his second term, Nixon appointed Elliott Richardson as his new Attorney General. Richardson was aggressively

CAT: WHAT GRASSROOTS POLITICS IS ALL ABOUT

A SIGNIFICANT SIDEBAR IN NRA'S POLITical history began in 1971 in Montgomery County, Maryland, when local officials in that Washington, D.C., suburb proposed locally what their U.S. Senator, Joseph Tydings, had failed to garner in Congress: gun registration and licensing.

To face this threat, a wholly independent effort of a handful of organizers and activists in Maryland formed an organization with a singular purpose—defeating Joe Tydings. Their grassroots effort would ultimately lead to a series of events that would change NRA forever.

When Tydings gave personal support to an effort that was set for public hearings at a local school, a local dentist, C. P. "Chic" Chaconas, and a criminal defense attorney, Michael J. Parker, said enough was enough. They rallied firearms owners to attend the hearing.

"Chaconas organized a mob," Parker recalled. "The fire marshal had to close down the school. There were 15,000 to 20,000 people who came to the council meeting. There was a traffic jam on either side of the school for three or four miles."

The hearing was postponed in order to get a larger meeting place at a large high school. "Chaconas mobbed it again," Parker remembered. "There were thousands of people packing the school grounds and the gym. And the county council rapidly got the concept that this was not such a grand idea. Though they scuttled this pro-

posal, they were swept out of office that fall. All of them."

The grassroots action was of little note beyond the county, but it would form the center of a political tidal wave.

In 1969 and 1970, Joe Tydings had made firearms registration and licensing the centerpiece of his personal legislative agenda. As the campaign year 1970 broke, political experts in both parties and the media considered Joe Tydings's reelection a sure bet.

But the experts, least of all the media, did not understand the seething anger of gun owners. And they didn't take into consideration the efforts of Parker and Chaconas and a handful of other activists. Chaconas called a meeting of about 50 organizations, including labor representatives, throughout the state. And out of that grew Citizens Against Tydings (CAT).

Using only a mailing list of combined groups, CAT mobilized angry firearms owners throughout the state with rallies and meetings and fundraisers. Thousands turned out to volunteer.

Parker created a simple slogan, "If Tydings Wins, You Lose." By midsummer, the Tydings campaign had decided the Senator's real opponent was not Republican J. Glen Beall; it was the "gun lobby."

CAT grew exponentially. It printed a newspaper that was delivered to 50,000 households and raised sufficient funds to take out full-page advertisements in the *Baltimore New American* and to buy radio time in small markets. When Tydings responded to the advertising, calling it "political pornography," CAT responded with another ad declaring "the naked truth."

In the end the Tydings campaign bled itself to death. The campaign claimed that its candidate was the victim of a monolithic national gun lobby when in reality he was the target of anger from voters. Every reference to the "gun lobby" made this broad constituent body madder.

When the general election returns were in, Joe Tydings's "totally safe" seat was lost by 30,000 votes. The defeat was a seminal event, one that would all but end any direct effort to create federal gun owner registration and licensing for years to come. In the short term, the success of the CAT campaign chilled any serious congressional interest in the gun control issue for all of 1971.

In the 1970 elections, Tydings was not the only significant congressional figure to lose reelection, and many attributed those empty saddles to voter anger on the gun issue. Connecticut Senator Thomas Dodd, a chief architect of the 1968 Gun Control Act, issued a campaign pamphlet labeling that legislation "The Dodd Gun Rights Act," but voters were not fooled. Dodd, who had been censured by the Senate for misuse of campaign funds, finished a poor third. In Tennessee, three-term Senator Albert Gore Sr., who had voted for gun registration, licensing, and the 1968 Act, was unseated. In New York, Senator Charles Goodell attempted to blur his Gore-like voting record by claiming he stood only for "reasonable control," but he lost a three-way election to the lone pro-gun candidate, James L. Buckley.

Several prominent Senators, including Minority Leader Hugh Scott of Pennsylvania, and William Proxmire of Wisconsin, were reelected after voicing regret for voting for the 1968 Act. Former Vice President Hubert H. Humphrey captured a Minnesota Senate seat after pledging he "would not support any federal legislation that could lead to confiscation." No one immediately stepped in to fill the anti-gun leadership vacuum.

anti-gun. As Attorney General of Massachusetts, he had drafted a model national gun registration and licensing bill. Nixon's appointment of an active enemy of NRA's cause combined with the previous year's huge loss in the form of the Senate Bayh Bill vote was the impetus for the NRA board to finally move the Association into an area it had so long avoided—lobbying.

Dingell Resolution Paves Way for ILA Creation

During the 1973 Annual Meetings, NRA Director and U.S. Congressman John Dingell forced a resolution to create a committee to recommend how an NRA lobbying effort would be organized, with findings reported by a July 1 deadline. Specifically, the committee asked for "a strong Washington lobbying effort" and a "political activism service" to "organize and mobilize sportsmen at the local and state level to lobby in the state capitals and municipal governments."

Perhaps the biggest boost for creation of an NRA lobbying unit came following an Elliott Richardson press conference, which released a

Michigan Congressman John D. Dingell (right) speaks with ILA Director of Federal Affairs Richard L. Corrigan during congressional hearings on sportsmen-supported legislation to establish a federal excise tax on ammunition reloading components. The tax would provide funding for firing range construction.

report by the National Advisory Commission on Criminal Justice Standards and Goals. In its treatment of new gun controls, the commission report, titled "A National Strategy to Reduce Crime," recommended confiscation of all functioning private handguns by 1983. It also recommended that states' stop-and-frisk laws permit police to search for illegal handguns and that states establish their own gun control agencies to purchase all voluntarily surrendered handguns and to register and modify handguns to be retained by private individuals as inoperable curios.

The report's black-and-white reality—paid for with taxpayer dollars and heralded by the U.S. Attorney General—turned out to be a boon to those arguing that all forms of gun control were part of a "slippery slope" toward forced confiscation. In that

sense, it would serve those on the NRA board who were opposed to a ban on any handguns.

In December 1973, NRA members learned of the creation of a separate and distinct Legislative Action Unit. Its primary responsibility would be to address the entire problem of legislative action within Congress and the states. It would be responsible for developing programs to defeat unfavorable legislation and to support legislation helpful to the objectives of the Association.

NRA Board Reverses Compromise Policy

But the biggest turnaround for NRA was yet to come in a total reversal of policy: rejection of any gun controls, including any form of "Saturday Night Special" legislation. On March 24, 1974, NRA's board resolved to oppose "any proposed legislation, at any level of government, which is directed against the inanimate firearm rather than against the criminal misuse of firearms." At that moment the board also erased any confusion about the issue of "Saturday Night Specials." Furthermore, NRA adopted an official position: all attempts to outlaw certain kinds of handguns—whether by legislation or regulation—by employing size, metallurgical, or similar standards or characteristics, would be considered arbitrary and unsound.

Members were told about the action in the September *American Rifleman,* which said, "The decisive action came as the new Office of Legislative Affairs (OLA), the NRA's first lobby and full-fledged liaison with lawmakers, began to make itself felt at both national and local levels."

Among the first hired to staff the new Office of Legislative Affairs was a young grassroots activist named Richard L. Corrigan, who made history by becoming NRA's first full-time registered lobbyist. When NRA announced that a legislative unit was to be created, Corrigan, an Army officer, was just leaving his dual faculty assignment in the Army's Armor

A long-time member of NRA's Board of Directors, legendary handgunner Jeff Cooper served in the Marine Corps during World War II and in Korea. In addition to his wartime service, Colonel Cooper founded the International Practical Shooting Confederation and the American Pistol Institute.

An architect by training, Wisconsin native Fred M. Hakenjos developed the first NRA model range plans. He was elected NRA President in 1971, a year before retiring as an executive with Hercules, Inc., where he developed, produced, and sold small arms propellants.

School at Fort Knox, Kentucky, and at the University of Kentucky Center, where he was teaching political science. Corrigan was a life-long black powder shooter who headed the North-South Skirmish Association (N-SSA), a large history-based national organization of marksmen who compete using original or replica Civil War small arms.

Corrigan was an N-SSA regional leader when the 1968 Gun Control Act was passed, and that's when his opposition to firearms legislation began. The '68 Act was followed in 1970 by the Organized Crime Control Act, which banned the sale of all but minute quantities of black powder to shooting enthusiasts. "I began mobilizing an effort on behalf of N-SSA to deal with the black powder restrictions

that all but made our sport impossible," he said. "NRA had done nothing to protect us." With the support of the N-SSA, Indiana Sportsman's Council, and other groups mobilized by OLA, NRA won its first legislative victory in more than a decade with the enactment of a black powder exemption bill at the close of 1974.

From Congressman John Dingell's unique perspective as a member of the U.S. House of Representatives and an NRA board member, OLA's structure was not strong enough to face future challenges. OLA was still under the control of NRA's Executive Vice President Maxwell E. Rich. "He wanted control of everything," Dingell said, "and he didn't want much of anything to happen. . . . There were a few of us who wanted an independent lobby. I had seen what good lobbies could do in Washington. I also studied how they did it. They have to have a careful mix, an ability to generate a good legislative strategy, an ability to analyze legislation, and an ability to muster the grassroots."

With the help of two other board members—Allan D. Cors, an accomplished Washington lobbyist, and James E. Reinke, Vice President of Government Affairs of Eastern Airlines—Dingell introduced a resolution at NRA's Annual Meetings in San Diego on April 21, 1975, creating an entity called the NRA Institute for Legislative Action (ILA). As accepted, the resolution created an Institute that was to be wholly independent from NRA headquarters, reporting directly to the Board of Directors.

Carter to Head NRA Institute for Legislative Action

Following a series of interviews, an ILA oversight committee hired a former NRA President to be the head of the new organization. His name was Harlon B. Carter. Carter had lived and breathed NRA since he was a young competitor in the 1930s. A Life Member since 1936, Carter held 45 shooting records and was among an elite group classified as both Distinguished Rifle and Distinguished Pistol. He was also a Lifetime Master in several disciplines. With a wide, ready smile and a handshake that enveloped like a catcher's mitt, Carter possessed real charisma. He was a spellbinding orator and had been a hard-line, no-compromise gun writer who had

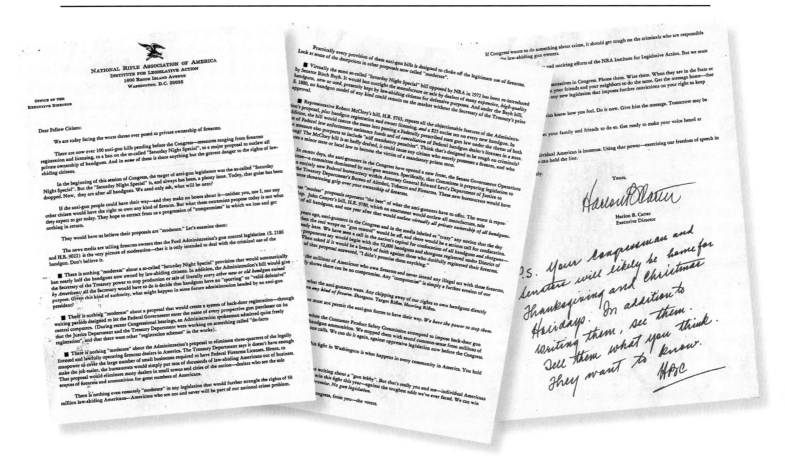

This is a reproduction of a letter written to NRA members by NRA-ILA Executive Director Harlon B. Carter against a major gun control proposal pushed by President Gerald R. Ford in 1975.

been published regularly in *Guns & Ammo,* among other publications. NRA members knew where he stood. Members first heard about Carter's appointment in the June 1975 *American Rifleman,* and for those who had been waiting for someone who would not give an inch, Carter was their man.

Carter, who had served a life-long career in the U.S. Border Patrol, eventually becoming its chief, found little welcome at NRA's headquarters on 1600 Rhode Island Avenue. At 61, he was beginning a new career that would mark him as a gun-rights icon. Carter and his wife Maryann moved to Washington, D.C., on April 28, 1975, and took up residence in suite 606 of the Gramercy Hotel located next door to NRA's headquarters. The Carters lived there for 19 months. Maryann Carter remembered that "Harlon started with nothing. I mean from pen-

cils right up. We paid rent to the Gramercy for a suite of offices because NRA had nothing available. He just got it all started from scratch and even asked me to help find furniture and serve as his secretary until he could find somebody."

Carter Pulls Together a Staff

Carter's first task was to develop a staff. He was looking for people who lived and breathed his cause. He told everyone his final criteria: "This is not a job I'm offering—it's an avocation. I want people who would take any loss personally."

First among the handful of people who would form the nucleus of the Institute was OLA's Richard L. Corrigan, who became the head of Federal Affairs and who would later rise to ILA's Deputy Executive Director. Next Carter brought in Michael J. Parker, the co-architect of the Citizens Against Tydings campaign in Maryland, who had since worked closely with Congressman Dingell on the firearms issues as a member of Republican Representative Harley Staggers' staff. Parker would become ILA's General Counsel.

Critically important among Carter's first hires was ILA's fiscal officer, Hubert K. McGaffin, who had worked with him for years at the Immigration and Naturalization Service. McGaffin was a shrewd self-taught number-cruncher and a talented administrator who knew the kind of lean personnel operation Carter wanted to create.

Carter also brought in Merle Preble, a retired Army Colonel, one-time Director of Civilian Marksmanship, and an NRA board member who had a proven vision of grassroots organizing. Corrigan had met Preble in Kentucky, where Preble had worked with state and local activists to organize a unique grassroots political organization called Unified Sportsmen. It would serve as a model for a series of NRA-seeded independent grassroots entities throughout the nation that had an emphasis on political and legislative activism.

Freshman Idaho Senator Steps Forward

In the first days of ILA's existence, Carter and his staff confronted an issue that would prove Dingell's vision was on the mark. That issue would create a relationship with a U.S. Senator that endured for years through legislative success after legislative success.

The Senator was the freshman Republican from Idaho, James A. McClure, who had served quietly in the House of Representatives for three terms. He was an activist legislator on firearms rights but had been lost in the shuffle of 435 members of the U.S. Congress. In the Senate, McClure would assume amazing depth and power, especially regarding firearms control. McClure believed there could be no com-

---

A bit of shooting history was made at the 1975 Pan American Games in Mexico City before a single round was sent down the range. For the first time, a shooter—rifleman Lones W. Wigger Jr.—was honored to carry the flag for the entire U.S. team at the opening ceremonies.

Above: Harlon B. Carter, Executive Director of the newly formed Institute for Legislative Action, spoke on behalf of NRA at a 1975 Senate hearing regarding restrictive gun legislation.

Right: Best known to friends and associates as "Pink," Dr. C. R. Gutermuth was elected NRA President in 1973. Recognized internationally as a leader in the conservationist movement, Gutermuth served as Vice President of the Wildlife Management Institute from 1946 to 1971.

ammunition. In 1974, however, when Congress enacted the Hazardous Substances Act, to be administered by the CPSC, no such exemption was in place. On February 14, 1975, the CPSC asked for public comments on the proposed ban that were to be put into the record, which would remain open for 60 days. Senator McClure immediately put out a press release attacking the proposed ban, urging firearms owners to make their voices heard by writing to CPSC at the address he provided.

James O. E. Norell, who was the Idaho Senator's press secretary and legislative assistant, said the results were astounding. "The Associated Press picked up the McClure call to action," Norell said. "As a result, every anti-gun media outlet in the nation attacked Jim McClure's release. They universally maligned the Senator's concerns and reprinted the CPSC address, claiming this would be a national referendum on gun control. It was a plebiscite on gun control all right, but it didn't turn out the way the media wanted. The ammo ban folks racked up 400 letters in favor of the ban. Gun owners, on the other hand, provided well over

promise on the principle of the right to keep and bear arms.

McClure formed an unofficial political caucus called the Senate Steering Committee that was built entirely around issues. It had a partially floating membership, mostly of conservative Republicans and southern Democrats, who coalesced around specific legislation. In time of threat, the committee became a natural nucleus of power on the gun control issue. The issue that would bond McClure's efforts and NRA's grassroots lobbying was a petition by a Chicago-based anti-gun group, the Committee for Handgun Control, to force the Consumer Product Safety Commission (CPSC) into banning handgun ammunition from American private homes "as a hazardous substance."

When the CPSC was created in 1972, Congress denied it authority over any aspect of firearms or

300,000 individual letters in opposition, some of which contained petitions with additional thousands of names. It was spontaneous combustion at the grassroots."

But the battle had just begun. McClure and his staff met with Harlon Carter and ILA's Dick Corrigan, who asked McClure a simple question, "How can we help?" It was the first time anyone at NRA had offered McClure the Association's assistance. And the help would be needed. Senator McClure introduced an amendment to deny CPSC any foothold into firearms or ammunition under the Hazardous Substances Act. Corrigan and his staff began immediately garnering co-sponsors and supporters, which ultimately crossed all party and regional lines.

"We didn't talk about gun control," said Corrigan. "Instead, we began our forays by saying, 'We'd like to come in and talk about some consumer issues.' That got their attention, and then we would say, 'We are the largest group of consumers of certain products, and we believe it's important that we have our say on regulations, and we don't like what CPSC is being asked to do.'"

The immense amount of spontaneous mail had crushed the CPSC, and both houses of Congress were feeling the grassroots pressure as well. But more pressure was needed. Corrigan engineered NRA's first fine-tuned mailings, hitting specific states and congressional districts to make the right members feel the heat. One major problem loomed, however. The Senate Commerce Committee accepted legislation sponsored by Utah Democrat Frank E. "Ted" Moss to prohibit actions such as the proposed ban but to allow the CPSC to ban ammunition found to be "hazardous" and to require labeling of ammo in general as a "hazardous substance." This was utterly unacceptable to McClure and to NRA.

Harlon Carter sent mailgrams to all Life Members in Utah essentially explaining that the Moss amendment was the camel's nose under the tent. After Moss had received more than 12,000 constituent letters, Carter turned up the fire, with NRA holding grassroots meetings in Utah and with prominent supporters visiting Moss's state and Washington offices.

Norell remembered what happened next. "Because of NRA, Moss's anger began to dissolve

During the 1970s, American rifle shooters ruled the world's firing line in large measure because of the skills and dedication to hard work of champions. From left: John H. Writer, Margaret T. Murdock, Lanny R. Bassham, and Lones W. Wigger Jr.

into fear, and Senator McClure went to him with a perfect out. He invited Ted Moss to co-sponsor his legislation, shutting the CPSC out of the gun control business completely. No labeling, no oversight whatsoever. It became the McClure-Moss amendment."

Senator Moss worked hard for passage of the legislation, and NRA let its Utah members know that Moss was now totally on their side. The CPSC issue came up on the Senate floor on July 18, 1975, and after real debate with many Senators present and listening, the McClure-Moss amendment passed on a voice vote.

Ted Kennedy weighed in with his toehold amendment to ban "defective" ammunition and to require hazardous "labeling." Yet he didn't limit the power to the banning of "defective" ammunition. He demanded a vote, and the "nays" overwhelmed those supporting the Massachusetts Democrat. Then Kennedy demanded a roll call vote, and was defeated 75 to 11. A stunned and visibly angry Kennedy did not know what had hit him. He had confronted a new NRA lobby with a remarkably capable staff and a no-compromise, tough-as-nails leader.

THE CASE OF KENYON BALLEW

A TRAGIC FEDERAL ACTION BY GUN control police in Maryland would mark 1971 as a year of fundamental change and define the real dangers brought on by the 1968 Gun Control Act to peaceable gun owners.

On June 7, 1971, federal gun control agents from the IRS's, Alcohol, Tobacco, and Firearms Division (ATFD) and local police raided the apartment of NRA Life Member Kenyon Ballew— a 27-year-old Boy Scout leader and U.S. Air Force Military Police veteran. Ballew had committed no crime, but the raid left him totally disabled; he was paralyzed when a federal agent shot him in the head.

The raid began with bearded undercover agents crashing into the wrong apartment (armed with a search warrant that named only "occupant"), where they held small children at gunpoint and conducted an illegal search. After discovering their mistake, the agents went to Ballew's ground floor apartment. Ken Ballew and his wife heard nothing until the gang of federal agents and local plainclothes police knocked the door down with a battering ram and charged into the living room with guns drawn. Ballew grabbed a replica cap and ball revolver to defend his wife. The scruffy agents fired first, one bullet striking Ballew in the head. Ballew's gun discharged into the floor as he fell. Agents fired a total of eight shots in the apartment.

Everything about the handling of the Ballew case by federal authorities was flawed. The search warrant was based on third-hand information from a criminal informant claiming that Ballew had grenades. In fact, Ballew had dummy grenades, perfectly legal souvenirs of his military service. Immediately following the raid, agents smashed walls to dig out bullets they fired, thus tainting the scene. Adding needless insult to grievous injury, the government eventually apologized to residents of the first wrong apartment raid, but the Ballews never got anything,

even after internal federal investigation admitted a series of blunders by agents.

Ken Ballew would become a symbol for gun owners across the nation. Perhaps the outrage over the Ballew raid was best expressed by civil libertarian U.S. Representative John Dingell when he addressed Congress:

WHAT has come to pass? Bearded strangers in scruffy clothes smash down the door of a man's home. The man is shot in the head. His wife is thrown half naked outside as the man lies bleeding on the floor. The home is vandalized—walls smashed, furnishings ransacked, dozens of personal possessions carried away.

Where did this happen? Was it in Hitler's Germany? Or in Soviet Russia at the height of the Stalinist purges? No, it happened right here in suburban Maryland on the outskirts of the nation's capital. And it was not the Gestapo, or the NKVD . . . that perpetrated this act of terrorism. It was committed by agents of the Internal Revenue Service. . . . This kind of storm-trooper exercise may have been commendable in Nazi Germany, but it must be made unmistakably clear to the ATFD that it is intolerable here.

Congressman Dingell's outrage was communicated to NRA members and their friends and families as part of unprecedented coverage afforded the Ballew raid in month-by-month reports by Editor Ashley Halsey Jr. in *American Rifleman*.

The Ballew case was just the first in what would be hundreds of civil liberties abuse cases carried out in the name of gun control. The case also marked the beginning of serious efforts that would take years to complete—the legislative dismantling of dangerous and carelessly drafted provisions of the 1968 Gun Control Act.

After winning these fights, ILA took the unprecedented step of urging its members to thank their legislators. Legislators began to discover political benefits from supporting the rights of gun owners. More importantly, the CPSC victories enabled ILA to train and battle harden an effective Washington, D.C., lobbying corps and to develop a sophisticated grassroots capability for the fights ahead. The gun lobby was being forged.

Calm Amid the Storm

In many senses, for all the internal turmoil, the period saw dramatic new initiatives. Foremost among these was the emergence of a new magazine, with the premier issue of *American Hunter* appearing in October 1973. The magazine soon became self-supporting, operating in the black after only two years of publication. Initially it was offered on a subscription basis, and subsequently members could choose between receiving it or *American Rifleman* as part of their dues package. In time *American Hunter* would rival *American Rifleman* in terms of popularity, and it offered NRA members who were avid hunters a medium that appealed more directly to their interests.

Also popular with the hunting segment of NRA's membership was the *Hunting Annual.* Initially known as the *Denali Directory* (which published hunting regulations, seasons, listings of guides, and related information on a state-by-state basis, along with Canadian provinces and Mexico), the *Hunting Annual* expanded to incorporate feature articles on a wide range of hunting subjects. The organization also joined hands with the Boone & Crockett Club to produce the 1977 edition of *Records of North American Big Game.*

NRA took a number of significant steps in the field of public relations. A 1968 film, *The Story of the NRA*, was shown widely over the next several years. Successive NRA presidents, to a greater degree than ever before, appeared as guests on radio and television talk shows. The year 1972 saw the first National Hunting and Fishing Day, a tradition that has continued to the present, and from its outset NRA has been a key participant.

Pictured here in 1968, William W. McMillan made Olympic history by competing on every U.S. squad between 1952 and 1976 with the exception of 1956. His event was rapid-fire pistol, and at the Rome Olympics in 1960, he captured the gold medal.

By 1976, membership had reached an all-time high with 1,164,359 individuals on the roll. Still, the winds of change had begun to stir, and they would sweep through the 1977 convention with telling effect. The revolt in Cincinnati would be watershed in NRA's history, an event that would see a dramatically changed organization with entirely new leadership pursuing dramatically different agendas.

THE **AMERICAN RIFLEMAN**

JULY 1977 $1.00

OUTSTANDING
HANDGUNNER HEADS
NRA STAFF

IN THIS ISSUE:
ANNUAL MEETINGS
REPORT

Harlon B. Carter was awarded the "Outstanding American Handgunner" trophy two days before the Annual Meeting of Members in Cincinnati, where he was elected NRA Executive Vice President with a mandate to redirect the Association. "You, the membership, are entitled to have an NRA that is responsive to your wishes," he said to a tumultuous ovation.

CHAPTER SIXTEEN

REVOLUTION AND REFORM

1976–1977

You, the membership, are entitled to have an NRA that is responsive to your wishes. That is right, that is what you have demanded, and that's the way it's going to be. . . . You are the NRA, not I, not these gentlemen here. You are all we have.

—Harlon B. Carter, May 1977

THE CPSC VICTORY MADE MANY old hands in Congress understand that the real power of the gun lobby rested, not in a building in Washington, D.C., but in the hearts and minds of citizens across America who spoke with a single voice. This newfound respect for the grassroots strength of gun owners bought Harlon Carter and ILA a few months' time. Carter continued his search for dedicated people, recruiting Jim Norell from Senator McClure's staff as ILA's Director of Communications. Shortly thereafter he hired Mary E. Marcotte, who had run public information campaigns on health issues for the state of Maine, to fill out the communications effort.

It didn't take long for the new ILA staff to learn what Carter already knew all too well—that forces were at work to take control of the NRA Board of Directors and ultimately change what had evolved into the Association's core purpose—defense of the Second Amendment. These board members wanted NRA to shun its "gun lobby" image and become more active in environmental issues as a way to gain media approval.

The board created a Management Committee consisting of the NRA President, First Vice President, and Second Vice President and gave it unprecedented authority to act on virtually all matters in lieu of the full board or its Executive Committee. Merrill W. Wright, a retired industrialist and former President of the Massachusetts Rifle & Pistol Association, had recently been elected NRA's President. However, the leader of the movement to redirect the Association—by force of an iron personality—was First Vice President Irvine Reynolds, a Californian and President of Copley International. Reynolds and a cadre of board members under his control were deeply resentful of Carter and the Institute. Efforts to wrest control of ILA began immediately.

At its first meeting, the Management Committee moved to require that all ILA contracts be submitted to it for approval "prior to any formalizing agreements that might be made or considered if they run $1,000 per month or $5,000 per year or more." The action struck at the heart of ILA's ability to move quickly and independently. In preparing state and local mailings or organizing grassroots activities, ILA was involved in scores of contracts. Rapid response to legislative challenges was key to the Institute's success on the national and state levels, and its fiscal independence was what made rapid response possible. This directive ran counter to everything intended by the Dingell resolution

Journalist Neal Knox played a major role in drafting the bylaw changes enacted at the Members Meeting in Cincinnati.

Chairman of the Board of G. F. Wright Steel & Wire Company of Worcester, Massachusetts, Merrill W. Wright became NRA President in 1975. A police firearms training expert, Wright was the longtime Secretary of the New England Police Revolver League.

that had established ILA's total independence the year before. With the Management Committee order on contracts, a battle was joined.

What the People Really Think

While Harlon Carter dealt with the swirl of internal politics, ILA's staff prepared for battle. Part of that effort involved commissioning comprehensive polling of both the public at large and firearms owners in particular on every conceivable aspect of the gun control issue. Dick Corrigan linked up with a rela-

tively unknown California pollster, Dr. Richard Wirthlin, who ran Decision Making Information (DMI). Wirthlin and his partner, Dr. Gary Lawrence, spent long hours with the ILA staff working on questions and areas they wanted to probe.

The DMI poll was the most extensive measure of public knowledge on gun control and gun rights ever assembled. It revealed not only the thinking and beliefs of firearms owners and NRA members, but gave the ILA staff insight into the directions it needed to take to change the opinions of non-firearms owners. As an example, DMI asked the same simplistic questions on gun control used in newspaper polls conducted by Louis Harris and the Gallup organization. The percentages were identical. Wirthlin and ILA staffers had worked out another series of questions in which respondents would themselves begin to define terms like registration. When those questions were asked, percentages were reversed.

"It showed that Gallup's and Harris's lightweight and loaded questions produced a reaction to words the public only thought they understood," Mary Marcotte explained. "People whom Gallup said were for gun owner licensing actually overwhelmingly rejected the concept, as it would require them to get permission from police to own a firearm. That is the essence of licensing. After DMI, we knew the public would never buy into the concept once its terms were defined."

The DMI survey provided a remarkable roadmap for the future, and while ILA was arming itself with the kind of knowledge needed to educate the public, it was also boosting its power to organize and directly communicate at the grassroots. Dick Corrigan organized a Sportsmen's Policy Conference that brought together hundreds of activists from around the nation, representing diverse groups with common interests in firearms rights issues. For many, it was their first direct contact with NRA. The bonds forged during that meeting would endure and form the basis of a unified grassroots front.

Corrigan also staffed up, enlisting two very capable young women, Susan Reece and Kathryn Coe Royce, to be federal lobbyists. He also hired a prominent young African-American attorney, Peter S. Ridley, as a lobbyist. On Capitol Hill, these new faces were disarming. As a result of years of media hatred, people pictured "gun lobbyists" as the

thugs that had been portrayed in editorial cartoons. Instead, members of Congress were presented with articulate young people who quickly and forever broke the stigma. In addition, Corrigan made sure everyone knew NRA was politically ecumenical. The labels Republican and Democrat, liberal or conservative had no place in the individual lobbying equation. The only thing that mattered was how members of Congress individually stood on issues relating to firearms owners' rights.

Above: Advocating gun owner rights on Capitol Hill, early ILA federal lobbyists (from left) Susan Reece, Kathyrn Coe Royce, and Peter S. Ridley were disarming new faces who destroyed stereotypes of NRA cynically fostered on the editorial pages of anti-gun newspapers such as the *Washington Post*.

Left: Merle Preble, a former NRA board member and Director of Civilian Marksmanship, joined ILA after working with state and local activists in Kentucky to form a grassroots political organization called Unified Sportsmen. It would serve as a model for NRA-affiliated organizations across the nation.

While the staff was being organized and trained, Colonel Merle Preble was in the field helping state groups form highly motivated gun owner activist groups, first in the form of Unified Sportsmen of Virginia, then Unified Sportsmen of Florida. The Florida organization was headed by young Marion P. Hammer, who had been drawn into the battle with passage of the Gun Control Act of 1968.

On the communications front, Norell and Marcotte believed there were multiple audiences NRA needed to reach. The first was NRA's members, who needed fresh, up-to-date, and, above all, accurate information they could use to persuade others, including their elected representatives and local news media. ILA set up a new independent press operation and developed a biweekly newsletter, *Reports from Washington*, that was mailed to activists and outdoor writers nation-wide. Long-term plans for educational materials on major issues were also developed, and print advertising and a number of brochures, all written in plain-spoken words, specifically targeted the most current issues. The pay-off for all of this would be seen immediately in the difficult battles breaking out at the beginning of the new year.

Throughout the fall of 1975, as ILA organized its forces and developed the legislative and communications capabilities it would need, Michigan U.S. Representative John Conyers, who was pressing for legislation outlawing all private ownership of handguns, dithered away valuable House Judiciary Committee time with a drawn-out series of road-show hearings in select American cities. Conyers heard testimony, not on specific legislation, but on generic concepts of gun control.

Entire NRA Membership Mailed

Harlon Carter and his staff wasted no time. With no specific legislation moving in Congress but with many serious threats looming, Carter mailed a no-compromise letter to the entire NRA membership. He touched on the specifics

TO THE MEMBERS OF THE NATIONAL RIFLE ASSOCIATION

Writing a personal letter to 1,173,998 people is a difficult and expensive task. Bulk rate postage alone would cost $90,397.85. So I've decided to send my personal message to you through The American Rifleman. You can read it here just as well, and it's YOUR money I'm saving.

First, I want to say thank you for your support. Second, our dues must go up, just as everything else, and before they do, I want to be certain you have an opportunity to renew at the lower rates. And third, I want you to see what the NRA does, and how we go about our business. Look at the next few pages.

The NRA is a great organization. The future has never looked better. The NRA has reaffirmed its commitment to you. You are the National Rifle Association. We want to satisfy you. And we want to keep and further your rights and your participation in the American shooting sports tradition. Your dues and your support keep us doing just that.

All day-to-day operating expenses of the Institute for Legislative Action will be paid from your dues. This will concentrate contributions where you want them--fighting anti-gun legislation.

Competitive programs, hunter support, education, training and junior activities are all supported by your dues. The American Rifleman, the Hunter Information Service and the Firearms Information Service--you're vital to it all.

WITHOUT YOU, THERE IS NO NATIONAL RIFLE ASSOCIATION.

So that's why I'm writing. To thank you for being a member now, to show you how strongly I'm committed to working for you, and to say that I hope you'll be with us in the future.

Sincerely,

Harlon B. Carter
Executive Vice President

Above: ILA Executive Director Harlon Carter captivated the membership by appealing to them on a personal level. In this inspiring letter, Carter reminds members that "Without you, there is no National Rifle Association."

Right: Harlon Carter and *American Rifleman* Editor Ashley Halsey Jr. (left foreground taking notes) represented NRA at a January 28, 1976, White House meeting on firearms issues, where Secretary of the Treasury William E. Simon represented the administration. The first three speakers—former South Dakota Governor Joe Foss, former Air Force Chief of Staff General Curtis E. LeMay, and television personality Chuck Connors—expressed grassroots sentiments against gun control. Carter presented the findings of a DMI public opinion survey showing that 82 percent of Americans believed citizens have a private right to own guns and that only 11 percent felt new gun laws would reduce crime.

Above: NRA-ILA Executive Director Harlon B. Carter, flanked by ILA Director of Federal Affairs Richard L. Corrigan (left) and ILA General Counsel Michael J. Parker, tells the U.S. House Judiciary Subcommittee on Crime, "NRA is unalterably opposed to any further gun controls."

and theory of all of the major bills pending in both the House and Senate. Motivated by Carter's words, NRA members swamped Congress with letters, telegrams, and calls. Carter's letter also solidified his position with the NRA membership. "The news media is always writing about a 'gun lobby.' But that's really you and me—individual Americans—tens of millions of us," Carter wrote. "We can win this fight this year. . . . We can win it on a simple concept—*No compromise. No gun legislation.* That message must get to Congress from you—the voters."

Bicentennial Battles

For ILA, the 1976 legislative year opened on a variety of major fronts. The Institute was faced with more than 600 hostile bills and ordinances at the state and local levels, including a referendum effort in Massachusetts to ban handgun ownership statewide. Judiciary Committee Chairman Peter Rodino announced that when the new session of Congress opened, gun control would be a priority of his committee. He said a total ban on private possession of handguns "should be our ultimate goal" but counseled Congress to take a small bite. "I believe the political realities at present dictate a more modest approach."

That "modest approach" came in the form of John Conyers's bill, HR 11193, which took on a novel back-door concept: to curb lawful business and transport of firearms in federally licensed commerce. The measure would have given the Bureau of Alcohol, Tobacco, and Firearms (BATF) broad authority to eliminate 120,000 federally licensed dealers. It would have also created restrictions on common carriers designed to discourage the transport of firearms and ammunition, especially by smaller trucking firms. Billed by the media as a "weak handgun" bill, it was anything but. Because the media treated it as being "weak," Corrigan took the advice of Congressman John Dingell and decided to gamble that sometimes "worse is better." Worse soon came in the form of an amendment to the Conyers-Rodino legislation by Chicago Congressman Martin Russo. He sought to ban "Saturday Night Specials," and his absurdly broad definition covered 75 percent of all handguns, regardless of quality, size, or cost. After some very subtle work by ILA, the House Judiciary Committee accepted the Russo amendment.

Martin Russo of Illinois proposed legislation in 1976 that he claimed was a ban on so-called "Saturday Night Specials." To set the record straight, ILA created an ad pointing out that Russo legislation actually would have banned 75 percent of all handguns, regardless of size, quality, or cost.

Idaho Congressman Steve Symms held a press conference displaying a collection of very large pistols and revolvers, all of which Russo would ban as being "small, cheap and easily concealable." ILA designed a series of print ads capitalizing on the truth, showing life-sized photographs of what the public would have to admit were huge and expensive handguns. The life-sized photos covered two fold-out magazine pages. And a brochure called *The Myth of the Saturday Night Special* was produced, with thousands of copies distributed to activists, clubs, and the media. Most importantly, gun owners and NRA members were getting the same message—that virtually any handguns they might own would be banned, most now and the rest later. Russo's amendment would prove to be a bill killer. ILA's gamble had won.

Following NRA's Annual Meetings, the House Judiciary Committee considered a new version of HR 11193, minus the over-the-top Russo amendment. The bill was moved over the objections of staunch pro-gun congressmen such as Ohio Representative John Ashbrook. No hearing had been held on this new version, nor had there been any committee debate. The sidetracking of the nor-

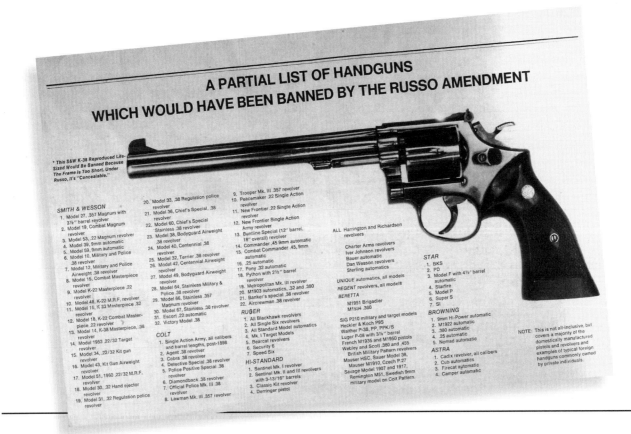

A PARTIAL LIST OF HANDGUNS WHICH WOULD HAVE BEEN BANNED BY THE RUSSO AMENDMENT

* This S&W K-38 Reproduced Life-Sized Would Be Banned Because The Frame Is Too Short. Under Russo, It's "Concealable."

SMITH & WESSON
1. Model 27, .357 Magnum with 3½" barrel revolver
2. Model 19, Combat Magnum revolver
3. Model 53, .22 Magnum revolver
4. Model 59, 9mm automatic
5. Model 59, 9mm automatic
6. Model 10, Military and Police .38 revolver
7. Model 12, Military and Police Airweight .38 revolver
8. Model 15, Combat Masterpiece revolver
9. Model K-22 Masterpiece .22 revolver
10. Model 48, K-22 M.R.F. revolver
11. Model 10, K 22 Masterpiece .32 revolver
12. Model 18, K-22 Combat Masterpiece .22 revolver
13. Model 14, K-38 Masterpiece, .38 revolver
14. Model 1953 .22/32 Target revolver
15. Model 34, .22/32 Kit gun revolver
16. Model 43, Kit Gun Airweight revolver
17. Model 51, 1950 .22/.32 M.R.F.
18. Model 30, .32 Hand ejector revolver
19. Model 31, .32 Regulation police revolver

20. Model 33, .38 Regulation police revolver
21. Model 36, Chief's Special, .38 revolver
22. Model 60, Chief's Special Stainless .38 revolver
23. Model 38, Bodyguard Airweight .38 revolver
24. Model 40, Centennial .38 revolver
25. Model 32, Terrier .38 revolver
26. Model 42, Centennial Airweight revolver
27. Model 49, Bodyguard Airweight revolver
28. Model 64, Stainless Military & Police .38 revolver
29. Model 66, Stainless .357 Magnum revolver
30. Model 67, Stainless .38 revolver
31. Escort .22 automatic
32. Victory Model .38

COLT
1. Single Action Army, all calibers and barrel lengths, post-1898
2. Agent .38 revolver
3. Cobra .38 revolver
4. Detective Special .38 revolver
5. Police Positive Special .38 revolver
6. Diamondback .38 revolver
7. Official Police Mk. III .38 revolver
8. Lawman Mk. III .357 revolver

9. Trooper Mk. III .357 revolver
10. Peacemaker .22 Single Action revolver
11. New Frontier .22 Single Action revolver
12. New Frontier Single Action Army revolver
13. Buntline Special (12" barrel, 18" overall) revolver
14. Commander .45 9mm automatic
15. Combat Commander .45, 9mm automatic
16. .25 automatic
17. Pony .32 automatic
18. Python with 2½" barrel revolver
19. Metropolitan Mk. III revolver
20. M1903 automatics, .32 and .380
21. Banker's special .38 revolver
22. Aircrewman .38 revolver

RUGER
1. All Blackhawk revolvers
2. All Single Six revolvers
3. All Standard Model automatics
4. Mk. I Target Models
5. Bearcat revolvers
6. Security 6
7. Speed Six

HI-STANDARD
1. Sentinel Mk. I revolver
2. Sentinel Mk. II and III revolvers with 3-13/16" barrels
3. Classic Kit revolver
4. Derringer pistol

ALL Harrington and Richardson revolvers

Charter Arms revolvers
Iver Johnson revolvers
Bauer automatic
Dan Wesson revolvers
Sterling automatics

UNIQUE automatics, all models
REGENT revolvers, all models

BERETTA
M1951 Brigadier
M1934 .380

SIG P210 military and target models
Heckler & Koch P9S
Walther P-38, PP, PPK/S
Luger P-08 with 3½" barrel
French M1935 and M1950 pistols
Webley and Scott .380 and .455
British Military Pattern revolvers
Mauser HSC, Sauer Model 38,
Mauser M1910, Czech P.27
Savage Model 1907 and 1917,
Remington M51, Swedish 9mm
military model on Colt Pattern.

STAR
1. BKS
2. PD
3. Model F with 4½" barrel automatic
4. Starfire
5. Model P
6. Super S
7. SI

BROWNING
1. 9mm Hi-Power automatic
2. M1922 automatic
3. .380 automatic
4. .25 automatic
5. Nomad automatic

ASTRA
1. Cadix revolver, all calibers
2. Cub automatics
3. Firecat automatic
4. Camper automatic

NOTE: This is not all-inclusive, but covers a majority of the domestically manufactured pistols and revolvers and examples of typical foreign handguns commonly owned by private individuals.

poration. If management meant a switch in product line, so be it.

The Fight in Massachusetts

Having locked down movement of federal anti-gun legislation, ILA turned its attention to Massachusetts's handgun ban referendum. While ILA staff focused on defeating the gun-ban ballot question, the state effort on behalf of firearms owners was headed by the Gun Owners Action League. Tanya K. Metaksa, a young Connecticut housewife and mother, would organize the grassroots action.

Left: The Second Amendment lost one of its greatest champions when 11-term Ohio Congressman John M. Ashbrook died unexpectedly in 1982 at age 53. Representative Ashbrook's efforts kept the House Judiciary Subcommittee on Crime hearings from becoming blatant propaganda vehicles for Representative John Conyers's radical anti-gun proposals.

mal legislative process was a powerful argument against moving the bill to the House floor. The reborn Judiciary Committee bill was sent to the Rules Committee, where action was stalled, and the legislation ultimately died. Killing HR 11193 was an extraordinary achievement that could only have been accomplished with a combination of grassroots organizing and political acumen and skill in Washington. ILA was up and running at full speed.

While the early political victories may have been heady stuff for Harlon Carter's young staff, all was far from rosy on ILA's first birthday. Despite an unbroken record of solid victories, Carter's ability to keep his young, independent lobbying organization from being dissolved was challenged anew when longtime NRA Treasurer Louis F. Lucas was replaced by Thomas Billings, an Irvine Reynolds colleague who knew virtually nothing about NRA's purpose, history, or membership. Billings had never belonged to the Association and was not a shooter; he was given a Life Membership to fulfill a requirement that officers be voting members. Given the title of Vice President, Finance, Billings appeared at NRA headquarters in July, determined to prove that the organization could be run like any other cor-

Below: Having worked with Harlon Carter for years at the Immigration and Naturalization Service, Hubert K. McGaffin was one of Carter's first ILA staff hirings. McGaffin served as the Institute's Fiscal Officer until 1986.

ILA commissioned a poll of Massachusetts voters, asking whether they agreed or disagreed with the statement, "No private individual should be allowed to own a handgun." More than 85 percent of voters answered that they disagreed. Moreover, 63 percent of registered voters believed they had an individual right to own a handgun. The Massachusetts referendum campaign fit Harlon Carter's adage that ILA was in "a fight for the minds of the people." When the smoke cleared on election night, the ban referendum was rejected by a two-to-one margin: 1,666,196 to 737,721.

"Streamlined" NRA Staff

That sweet victory, however, was dampened by two preceding events. First, Harlon Carter resigned as ILA's head, informing the NRA board that he had meant to remain in Washington only as long as it took to establish the Institute and to assure its strong future. ILA's reins were handed over to Carter's deputy, Robert J. Kukla, a Chicago attorney and former board member who had written the landmark gun rights book, *Gun Control.* A skilled debater, Kukla had made more than 300 major media appearances on NRA's behalf.

The second event took place on November 7, when 78 NRA employees were fired or forced into retirement—including all but two members of the acclaimed *American Rifleman* Technical Staff. "Why do we need a tech staff?" Tom Billings asked. Known inside headquarters as the "Weekend Massacre," the firings were carried out in very harsh terms, especially for men and women who had devoted long careers to NRA service. The toll was taken at all levels. Among those leaving were Secretary Frank Daniels and *Rifleman* Editor Ashley Halsey Jr.

As part of the makeover, Billings became "coordinator" of NRA's publications, and General Rich, who survived mainly as a figurehead, became Editor-in-Chief of *American Rifleman*. In any other corporation, this kind of arrangement might have been perfect for controlling all communications to stockholders. But NRA was, above all, an incomparable grassroots communication machine. And what ordinary members heard officially from headquarters was nothing compared to what they were hearing from each other.

In January, for example, the *Rifleman* published an article about the groundbreaking for a multimillion-dollar new headquarters building in Colorado Springs, Colorado. "We're making this move to give better service to our members while lowering operating costs," Rich said. The story also mentioned that the new headquarters was "within easy reach of NRA's new 37,000-acre National Outdoor Center," a real estate acquisition about which the membership had been told little.

The members, however, were staying informed through news delivered by sources such as *Gun Week*, the feisty tabloid published in Sidney, Ohio, and from *Handloader* and *Rifle* magazines, edited by Neal Knox, a long-time gadfly on the gun control legislative scene. What Billings referred to as "Streamlined NRA Staff," meaning the NRA firings and retirements, Knox referred to as "a cataclysmic house-cleaning." Knox also raised questions about the move to Colorado and about the plans for the Outdoor Center, which, he claimed, had nothing to do with NRA. In fact, Knox reported, the letters "NRA" were dropped from the center's name.

Although the Institute had been immune from the November staff cuts, a move was made in January to destroy its fiscal and personnel

independence, placing its fiscal operation totally under Tom Billings's control. This was done counter to NRA's bylaws, which established ILA's unique status.

The Oram Corporation Reports

In the summer of 1976, as part of the $30 million National Outdoor Center effort, the Oram International Corporation—which listed among its clients several organizations very actively opposed to NRA on gun rights or hunting—was given free office space at NRA headquarters, even while ILA was being charged rent. Oram produced a "fund raising feasibility" report on the Outdoor Center that said immediate past NRA President C. R. "Pink" Gutermuth was "convinced that a large number of NRA members like himself have little sympathy with present legislative policies but will be quite willing to support a major conservation program."

Furthermore, the report was rife with comments about the problems of overcoming NRA's "bad image" in order to garner support from major corporate or foundation donors. There was even the suggestion that in the year of America's bicentennial, the 105-year-old National Rifle Association should consider changing its name.

What if the Gun Lobby Moved Out of Washington?

In January 1977, the takeover attempt of ILA began in earnest with a series of Management Committee decisions, all designed to place the Institute under day-to-day control of Tom Billings. A two-page ILA advertisement headlined "What if the Gun Lobby Moved Out of Washington?" brought matters to a head. "The ad, on its face, was a fundraiser, but it said volumes about the precarious position of the Institute," said Jim Norell. "We told the membership, 'Not one thin dime from NRA general funds—not one penny from your membership dues—comes to the Institute.' Most members were outraged when they learned their dues didn't include the legislative fight."

The ad incorporated a photo of the U.S. Capitol with a trash can in the foreground containing a discarded newspaper with a banner headline declaring, "GUN BAN ENACTED—No opposition cited." In

so many words, the ad affirmed that what members had been hearing about NRA abandoning Washington was true. The ad also immeasurably reaffirmed Kukla's position by declaring, "The Institute for Legislative Action is built on a simple bedrock principle—we are unalterably opposed to any erosion of the individual's right to keep and bear arms. And we will uphold that principle anywhere, any time, and in any forum."

By the time the full membership of NRA was reading the ILA ad, they were beginning to hear about other aspects of the Billings team's plans for NRA's future. Specifically, they were learning about the Oram Corporation and its anti-gun and anti-hunting clients. And they learned about Oram wanting to change NRA's direction to environmentalism. A blistering article in the May issue of *Rifle* magazine quoted Billings as

After NRA's intent to move out of Washington became clear, ILA placed this advertisement in *American Rifleman* to remind NRA members of how much ILA had done to protect their gun rights. It also urged members to send financial contributions, reminding them that "not one penny from your membership dues . . . comes to the NRA Institute for Legislative Action."

saying that NRA's image as a "pro-gun lobby" was hurting the efforts to raise funds for the National Outdoor Center. It further quoted Billings as saying, "After Irv [Reynolds] becomes president we'll use the Nominating Committee process to get rid of those directors who won't go along with us and replace them with ones who will."

Whatever support Reynolds and Billings had on the Board of Directors began to evaporate after that news. Reynolds and Billings had planned to use a new, packed board majority to vote itself out of existence, replacing the 75-member governing body with a seven-member board. In what was almost a sermon, Knox laid out a long, well-documented case that NRA was about to be highjacked for uses that did not serve shooters and gun enthusiasts and that did not fight erosion of gun rights.

Federation for NRA

While members were getting riled over the condition and misdirection of their Association, forces were at work to direct that anger. Activists groups in every state—some of which had been helped into being by Merle Preble and Dick Corrigan, and others that had been old-line traditional NRA affiliates—began to do what they did best: grassroots lobbying. These groups and others formed a confederacy called the Federation for NRA, which coordinated virtually all of what was about to happen. At its head were several men: William Greif of New York, a union President and head of the Directors Guild; Francis Winters, President of the largest independent telephone company in Texas; and Red Latimer of Indiana.

The Federation also included a number of then-NRA board members—chiefly Kenneth Lee Chotiner, a California lawyer, and Edwin Topmiller, retired U.S. Border Patrol executive and longtime friend of Harlon Carter. The Federation organized the voting members of the Association to prepare to come to Cincinnati, Ohio, the site of the upcoming Annual Meetings, and return control of NRA back into the hands of the members.

The grassroots organizers knew what their purpose was because another group, composed of board members, staff on leave of absence, and prominent gun rights and corporate lawyers, had been at work studying New York's not-for-profit law. They realized that under the bylaws governing NRA, the voting members held extraordinary powers heretofore never exercised. This group began writing a series of bylaws and studying the order in which they would be offered. Among that group were two brilliant attorneys from New York, Dr. David I. Caplan and Sue W. Caplan, a husband and wife team largely responsible

This registration form urged members to attend the Annual Meetings in Cincinnati in May 1977. "One of the highlights," it declared, "will be the Firearms Legislation General Session." As it turned out, NRA's legislative efforts became the main focus of the Members Meeting after members revolted against NRA's leaders to elevate legislative matters to the top of NRA's agenda.

for bylaw changes that would redirect and restructure NRA. David Caplan was a physicist and patent attorney for Bell Laboratories, and Sue Caplan was a New York City criminal defense lawyer.

Showdown in Cincinnati

All efforts were focused on a single event, the Annual Members Meeting assembled the evening of May 21, 1977, in Cincinnati, Ohio. The opening gavel was struck at 7:30 P.M., and the meetings lasted a full eight hours, with more than 1,100 voting members present for virtually the whole session. Control of the floor had been organized largely though the efforts of Dr. Chick Chaconas, of Citizens Against Tydings fame, and Francis Winters, from the Greater Houston Sportsmen's coalition.

For the most part, participants in the meeting were polite yet forceful, even though matters easily could have gotten out of hand in the heat of battle. The orderly nature of the long meeting was due to the efforts of two men. Former NRA President Irvine C. Porter, a stately Alabamian who claimed to be "just an old country lawyer," agreed to take the chair. Demonstrating consummate legal skills, Porter remained on his feet, microphone or gavel in hand, for the full eight hours. Acting as parliamentarian, with equal skill and fairness, was board member and former U.S. Congressman Howard W. Pollock.

In all, 15 bylaws changes were introduced, debated, amended, and adopted. The Management Committee was abolished, along with the position held by Tom Billings. The move to Colorado Springs was halted, expenditures and activities for the Outdoor Center were ordered frozen, and a decision as to what to do with the Raton, New Mexico, property was postponed for study.

In essence those items were housecleaning measures. The members also removed the three officers who had served as the Management Committee. One among them, Dr. Alonzo H.

Garcelon of Maine, was a casualty of unintended consequences. A champion bench rest shooter, a legislative activist, and a founder of Sportsmen's Alliance of Maine, Garcelon had always been a true believer in NRA's cause. While the other Management Committee members would never again cross the NRA threshold, Garcelon would continue his service to the Association, eventually becoming NRA's President in 1985. Garcelon's ascendancy to that office was a tribute to his tireless efforts on behalf of America's gun owners. As NRA President, one of his first acts was to forcefully rebuke a slur on NRA members uttered by New York Governor Mario Cuomo in an April 18, 1985, radio address. When Cuomo attempted to dismiss his insult as being merely "inartful," Garcelon fired back: "Your statement could serve no other purpose except to stridently advance a simplistic, polarized, and extreme caricature, which induces conflict not resolution. Your past legislative record against the rights of gun owners gives credence to

Past President and Honorary Life Member Irvine C. Porter, a dedicated high power rifleman, was commended by NRA's board for exemplary service in presiding over eight hours of critical deliberations at the 1977 Members Meeting in Cincinnati.

The Cincinnati revolutionaries were careful to work with parliamentarians to ensure the legality of their actions. Here, Harlon Carter consults with lawyers, including David I. Caplan (center), regarding enactment of the organization's new bylaws.

the true intent of your recent verbal attack against our people."

The bylaw revision that changed the way the NRA board would be assembled was key. Members were given the means to nominate directors by petition and to place non-director NRA members on the Nominating Committee. Members also assumed the power to elect NRA's Executive Vice President at the Annual Members Meeting.

In the wee hours of the morning, the final chapter closed on what was to be known as pre-Cincinnati NRA when former NRA President Harold Glassen asked that Harlon Carter address the members. Carter strode to the podium and announced that he would be a candidate for Executive Vice President. Carter told the assembled throng that he would take the post only if "the job encompasses that of the Chief Executive of *all* the National Rifle Association."

After his election by acclamation, Carter announced to the roaring approval of the tired members, "Beginning in this place, at this hour, this period in NRA history is finished. There will be no more civil war in the National Rifle Association.

"You're America's greatest people, my friends. Don't ever forget that. You have afforded NRA this wonderful, historically important reaction of yours to the way the Association has been going, to the way you want it to be, and if I have anything to do with it—you are going to win, because you are the NRA!"

NRA Life Member Roy Rogers, the "King of the Cowboys," was an expert marksman, both on trap fields and in game fields. He appeared in NRA ads championing the Second Amendment and graciously lent his talents to the NRA film titled *Firearms Safety: First and Foremost. (Photo courtesy Rick Hacker)*

CHAPTER SEVENTEEN

A FOCUSED ORGANIZATION

1977–1980

The NRA is the faith, the confidence and the energy and dedication of its members. . . . We, those of us who have responsibilities to you, build upon your strength. We build upon your principles. And we build upon the priorities which you have agreed upon—our constitutional rights which you and I both have a lifelong dedication to nurture, to protect, and to extend.

—Harlon B. Carter, 1984

RENEWED VIGOR AND A DETERmined sense of purpose characterized NRA in the years immediately following the revolt in Cincinnati. The late 1970s saw Harlon B. Carter exert his forceful personality and clear vision on the day-to-day workings of the organization with the wholehearted support of his staff, the Board of Directors, and rank-and-file members.

The future Carter envisioned revolved around aggressive political action, a "no-compromise" stance on legislative threats against the Second Amendment, and a firm dedication to marshaling a membership force that would speak clearly to the civil rights mission of NRA.

As Edward Leddy noted in the conclusion to *Magnum Force Lobby*, in Cincinnati the organization had in effect been given "a mandate by its members to pursue the course of social activism on gun control." He acknowledged that while average NRA members were not inclined to "go to the barricades in the normal pattern of social movements," they were wholly committed to the protection of Second Amendment rights to the fullest extent. And Carter was unequivocally committed to meeting those membership demands—all amid the relentless anti-gun, anti-hunting assaults taken by the government under President Jimmy Carter.

Great emphasis was placed on the mission of the Institute for Legislative Action, and

Harlon Carter was ideal to lead the charge into the turbulent world of Washington politics.

Over a decade later, in a powerful, poignant tribute to Carter following his death in 1991, NRA Executive Vice President Wayne LaPierre delineated the characteristics that enabled Carter to exert such a remarkable influence on NRA. "Harlon was our champion and fiercest warrior, whose gift of intellect and conviction helped secure eternal safekeeping for the right to keep and bear arms . . . the very foundation of freedom. It was Harlon's leadership and vision that transformed a group of loyal Americans who love to shoot into the nation's largest and most effective defender of the Second Amendment."

In the 95th Congress, on the federal level alone, NRA would face 29 tough legislative and bureaucratic battles. Throughout each, Harlon Carter's overriding thought was that any loss would spell disaster for the fledgling lobby arm of the Association. To ILA staff, he made one command gospel: take the fight personally.

Harlon Carter had already predicted what the Jimmy Carter administration would mean for the

NRA's logo went through a number of transformations over the years.

Robert J. Kukla joined NRA's Board of Directors in 1966 and was a member of the Executive Committee. Before he became the ILA's Executive Director in 1977, he wrote a book, published in 1973, called *Gun Control,* which sought to "set the record straight" and expose the "less-than-truthful methods employed by gun control advocates."

nation's firearms owners with these prescient pre-election words: "The specter of questions raised about Jimmy Carter himself and about the people around him must loom foremost in the minds of millions of our citizens—40 million American men and women whose only 'transgression' is to own a firearm."

As incoming President, Jimmy Carter voiced his support of registering handguns and endorsed a waiting period for their purchase. And even before Carter took the oath of office, his closest political confidant had already issued a threat against the National Rifle Association, its mem-

bership, and all Americans who believe in the right to keep and bear arms. Hamilton Jordan, who later became Chief of Staff, promised that "Carter will really go on gun control and really be tough. We're going to get those bastards."

By the summer of 1977, the President approved a Justice Department draft bill that would have established a "de facto registration" and licensing system designed to give federal agents instant access to the names of every handgun owner in the nation "within one generation." Further, it would empower federal agents to put out of business the majority of the 160,000 federally licensed firearms dealers. Battle lines for the fight to come had clearly been drawn.

Under the direction of Robert J. Kukla, reelected in Cincinnati to the Board of Directors as ILA's Executive Director, the Institute staff girded for the fight. For serious family reasons, however, Kukla commuted from Washington to his home in Chicago. Harlon Carter soon concluded that the long absences from NRA headquarters portended gridlock in NRA's response to the looming legislative battle against the Carter administration's gun bill. By November, Carter sought Kukla's resignation, but negotiations soon reached an impasse.

No longer able to cast a blind eye to the crisis, NRA's Executive Committee convened in Sacramento, California, in January 1978 and ultimately removed Kukla from the ILA post by a 16-to-3 vote under the authority provided in NRA's bylaws. In a subsequent announcement to the membership, NRA President Lloyd Mustin noted that "Every committee member had a chance to state his views. None questioned Bob's personal knowledge of the gun control subject. Many seemed concerned over expected new gun control legislation and the readiness of ILA to win the fight."

Moving expeditiously, Carter named Neal Knox, Editor and Publisher of *Handloader* and *Rifle* magazines and founding Editor of *Gun Week,* as ILA's interim Executive Director "because of the emergency situation facing NRA and the nation's gun owners due to the expected administration's firearms bill and the need to quickly align ILA forces." Carter termed Knox "eminently qualified for this difficult assignment."

Carter White House Meets "Gun Lobby" Might

At ILA's helm, Knox at once commissioned a national survey designed to gauge American public opinion on crime and restrictive gun laws. The survey found a widely held conviction that gun ownership was a deterrent to crime. Of particular note, an overwhelming 89 percent of Americans believed they had the right to own firearms. In affirming those bedrock principles,

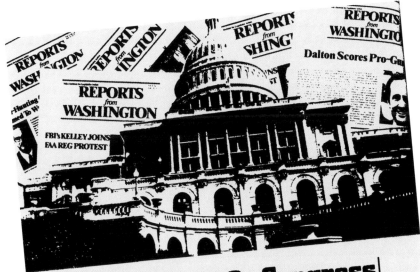

Your Check On Congress!

Without an informed, active NRA membership the private ownership of firearms in America would be past history!

You, THE GUN LOBBY, need and deserve the most accurate current, factual information on legislation affecting your right to keep and bear arms possible. You need the NRA Institute for Legislative Action's biweekly newspaper, "Reports from Washington."

In its new tabloid format, "Reports" provides in-depth bill analysis, investigative stories on the bureaucracy's "back door" gun control maneuvers, scholarly works on the Second Amendment, state legislative news, plus a host of articles of interest to hunters, collectors, competitive shooters, weekend plinkers and pro-Second Amendment activists in general.

The NRA Institute was founded on the bedrock principle of unalterable opposition to any erosion of the individual's right to keep and bear arms. The might behind that principle is you, the informed NRA member. Protect that right. Keep informed. Read the NRA Institute's "Reports from Washington."

Yes, I want to subscribe to "Reports from Washington." Enclosed is my check for:

_____ $6.00 for one year. _____ $11.00 for two years. _____ $16.00 for three years.

(Non-NRA member prices are $8.00, $15.00 and $23.00 respectively.)

Make checks payable to: NRA-ILA
Mail to: NRA Institute for Legislative Action, Dept. P
PO Box 2019, Washington, DC 20013

Please enclose the label from your *American Rifleman* showing your name and address.

Left: Among ILA's many undertakings was its biweekly publication, *Reports from Washington*, which provided members with in-depth analysis of any legislation affecting the right to keep and bear arms.

Below: John D. Aquilino Jr. edits ILA's *Reports from Washington* during the early days of the Institute. Formerly an investigative journalist, Aquilino was on the daily front line in dealing with hostile media, and he eventually formed NRA's Public Education Division.

POTENT ACTION BY THE NRA POLITICAL VICTORY FUND

IN 1976, WHEN IDAHO SENATOR JAMES A. McClure called for NRA to form a political force to change Congress, he both praised and issued a clear warning to the NRA Board of Directors. "NRA this past year has done a magnificent job," McClure said. "You have made it possible for your friends to be considerably more effective in the Senate and in the House. Yet something is missing. You are, in essence, fighting with one hand tied behind your back."

With the founding of the NRA Political Victory Fund (NRA-PVF), the Association entered the political arena to the fullest by reelecting friends and defeating foes. On the cutting edge in 1978, the NRA-PVF scored its biggest triumph of the primary season when eight-term Minnesota Congressman Donald Fraser was ousted in his bid for the Senate seat left vacant after the death of Senator Hubert Humphrey.

A massive, all-volunteer "Dump Fraser" campaign spearheaded by NRA-PVF and the Minnesota Gun Owners' Victory Fund resulted in one of the major political upsets of the year. One of the darlings of the firearms prohibition move-ment, Fraser was considered a certain winner in both the Democratic primary and general election. The *Washington Post* had even predicted that Fraser would win with 60 percent of the vote.

In an election postmortem, Governor Rudy Perpich, a Fraser supporter, termed NRA's efforts a major factor in Fraser's defeat and in electing Minneapolis businessman Robert Short. Acting on behalf of the NRA membership, the NRA-PVF brought about the long-promised change in electoral politics, symbolized by the Fraser primary election defeat. In 1978, it supported 256 candidates, including 90 non-incumbents, and saw 213 elected for a victory margin of 83 percent nationwide.

When Massachusetts Senator Ted Kennedy entered primary challenges to President Jimmy Carter's reelection bid, the NRA-PVF was ready to wield its new-found clout against gun owners' most ardent foe. Kennedy's dreams of unseating Carter were dashed in the Pennsylvania primary as gun owners cast ballots in droves under the NRA-PVF banner: "If Kennedy Wins, You Lose."

these findings became building blocks on which to launch ILA on both offensive and defensive fronts against the Carter administration's attacks.

Through ILA legislative alerts, massive grassroots opposition to the draft proposal carried the day, temporarily forcing the Carter administration to back down from a face-to-face fight with Congress.

Instead, the administration chose to make an "end run" around Congress and attempted to create a computerized system of national firearms registration by means of the bureaucratic rulemaking process—through regulations published by the Treasury Department's Bureau of Alcohol, Tobacco, and Firearms (BATF). Convinced the regulations were a "sure thing," the White House staunchly believed the plan could be enacted and funded without congressional approval and that the back-door maneuver was impervious to "gun lobby" pressure. In fact, Assistant Treasury Secretary Richard Davis was so confident that he admitted to firearms purchasers' names being omitted from the proposed regulations simply out of "political" considerations. He also asserted that BATF did indeed have the authority to include the names and would once the system was in place and operating. All past federal firearm purchase forms listing the purchaser's name, address, occupation, race, and other data, were to be included, and the system was to be funded from existing BATF surpluses.

That set the stage for the election of a true pro-gun, pro-hunting U.S. President, California Governor Ronald Reagan, a longtime NRA member and recipient of the coveted "Outstanding Public Service" award from the California Rifle and Pistol Association. For the first time in its 109-year history, the National Rifle Association formally endorsed a candidate for the presidency of the United States, and with Ronald Reagan's victory, the nation's firearms owners awoke to a whole new beginning.

The 1980 elections were marked by electoral upsets all across the nation, most dramatically in campaigns for the U.S. Senate that pitted anti-gun incumbents against upstart pro-gun challengers. Such a campaign was waged in Iowa, where Senator John Culver, a longtime friend of Ted Kennedy, was deemed unbeatable. On the Republican side, a relatively unknown Congressman, Representative Charles "Chuck" Grassley, took on his own party and beat its anointed candidate. The general election square-off between Culver and Grassley was remembered as a "suicide mission" by Kayne B. Robinson, an NRA board member and Executive Director of the Iowa Sportsmen's Federation.

"It wasn't a campaign; it was a crusade that turned into a very happy victory for Chuck Grassley in the caucuses and in the general election," said Robinson. "We organized all 99 counties and all 2,000 precincts and won—that was the beginning sign that we were onto something big. In the general election, though, Ted Kennedy appeared in ads for his old friend. He didn't wear very well in Iowa, and the issue of gun control became the biggest single factor in the election." NRA weighed in with statewide mailings that clearly defined the differences between the two candidates' positions on gun ownership, and Grassley's tracking polls spiked when those mailings hit. As Robinson put it, "Grassley's tough pro–Second Amendment stand was an enormous asset in a state where 1 million of its residents own firearms. Grassley went on to win every one of Iowa's 99 counties."

That upset victory was played out in other hotly contested Senate races: Bob Kasten over three-term Senator Gaylord Nelson in Wisconsin; Al D'Amato over Senator Jacob Javits and Representative Elizabeth Holtzman in New York; and Representative James Abdnor, who unseated Senator George McGovern in South Dakota. Those victories were mirrored in key House races.

With President Ronald Reagan, gun owners were empowered to take offensive action to roll back the onerous provisions of the 1968 Gun Control Act.

With grassroots mobilization and intense lobbying by ILA that covered every office on Capitol Hill, the BATF regulations went down smoking under the union of pro- and anti-gun congressional forces. The 314-to-80 House and 61-to-31 Senate votes cutting BATF's budget by $4.2 million—the amount intended to fund the BATF computer banks—proved an irrefutable poll of congressional sentiment. Likewise the 43-to-1 margin of public responses protesting the BATF power play was seen as proof positive that public opinion did not favor more federal firearms controls. That national referendum saw more than 337,000 protests filed, and only 7,800 letters of approval sent—an overwhelming poll, particularly with major segments of the media urging support of the regulations. BATF not only lost that round with the regulations lying dormant, but it also lost its leader. Rex Davis, BATF Director and longtime arch foe of NRA, announced his premature retirement at the height of the controversy.

By the fall of 1978, *Time* magazine had recognized the effectiveness of the post-Cincinnati NRA. "The pro-gun lobby, embodied in the National Rifle Association," the magazine stated, "stands as a pluperfect example of the single-issue factions. The NRA's traits and methods—passionate, uncompromising zeal combined with keen organization and ruthless skill at pressure tactics—are widely copied." That grudging praise offered quiet satisfaction to those in the forefront of the Second Amendment fight.

than 80 percent of all commercial explosive compounds, all military explosives, and all foreign-made explosives. Under the proposal, BATF would have been granted authority to tag smokeless and black powders, increasing costs by an additional 30 percent due to additional recordkeeping. It also would have the authority to knock all propellants off the market until safety and ballistics tests were conducted, a process that would have required several years. Grafted onto the "anti-terrorism" bill, BATF's tagging scheme met stiff opposition, and ILA battled the measure to a standstill where it remained until Congress adjourned.

No less controversial, ILA went to the mat in its opposition to President Carter's nomination of Illinois Representative Abner Mikva, an avowed gun prohibitionist, to the powerful U.S. Circuit Court of Appeals for the District of Columbia. In announcing its full-bore opposition to the nominee, ILA Executive Director Knox warned that

Above: Born in the Philadelphia Navy Yard, Vice Admiral Lloyd M. Mustin's naval roots trace back to his great, great grand-father, a naval squadron commander during the War of 1812. Admiral Mustin was elected NRA President in 1977, in the aftermath of the Cincinnati reforms.

Right: Washington, D.C., native, John B. Layton joined his hometown's police force as a foot patrolman in 1936. He would retire as Chief of Police. An expert marksman, Layton fired on the 1948 U.S. Olympic rapid-fire pistol team. He became NRA's President in 1979.

BATF's regulations setback in no way diminished that agency's flair for public relations. With the media's focus off firearms, BATF turned its rhetoric to explosives "tagging." Touted to the media as an attempt to control terrorist bombers, the scheme, upon close examination, was anything but "bomb control." It would have exempted more

Mikva "would hold a lifetime position of tremendous power to legislate by judicial fiat that which he has failed to accomplish in Congress. And he firmly believes in an advocacy court which he has referred to as an 'important non-legislative road to reform.'"

During contentious Senate Judiciary Committee hearings, Mikva was grilled on whether he would disqualify himself in cases involving gun ownership or NRA, which he had defamed as the "National Rip-off Association." Mikva refused to commit to any such recusal. As a member of the congressional "club," Mikva ultimately won Senate confirmation, but the fight would forever color any future promise of his nomination to the U.S. Supreme Court, an outcome not without a measure of victory for NRA.

McClure-Volkmer Reform Bill Introduced

Though less visible than his endorsement of Mikva, Jimmy Carter's federal gun police, which systematically carried out a brutal crusade against licensed firearms dealers and against the civil liberties of firearms owners, was without a doubt the Carter administration's worst bureaucratic assault. Going against the spirit and the letter of the federal firearms law passed in 1968, the BATF built a shameful record of trampling the rights of thousands of American citizens through a campaign of harassment, systematic abuse, and persecution of an entire class of citizens. That record became the focal point of major congressional inquiries and led to the introduction of the McClure-Volkmer Federal Firearms Reform Act.

In calling for congressional hearings at the start of the 96th Congress, Neal Knox stated that

ILA's General Counsel James J. Featherstone (left) and Communications Director James O. E. Norell discuss civil liberties abuse cases and pending reform legislation in 1980. Formerly a U.S. Justice Department attorney, Featherstone turned his considerable legal experience and talents to defending the Second Amendment. His unique understanding of government gave ILA's efforts to curb abuses of gun owners' rights a considerable boost.

"it is apparent to us that agents of the BATF are concentrating their efforts not against violent criminals but against citizens who have never before run afoul of the law. In the process of creating statistical felonies and statistical felons, the agency is destroying the lives and livelihoods of hundreds, perhaps thousands, of citizens."

Knox believed that only with the cloak of congressional protection would victims speak out without fear of BATF reprisal. Declaring war against the decade-old Gun Control Act marked another turning point in history for the National Rifle Association.

Empowered Membership

The marathon Cincinnati session had produced amendments to the NRA bylaws that were "designed to reduce the tremendous power of the President to perpetuate the board in his or her own image." One key change gave the board the

together we can spread the word!

YOU . . . give us the names and addresses of your friends who should become NRA members . . .

WE . . . will send each of them information about NRA benefits and services and a membership application . . .

TOGETHER . . . we will have a bigger, stronger NRA!

Send these people membership information:

NAME _____
ADDRESS_____
CITY _____
STATE _____ ZIP_____

NAME _____
ADDRESS_____
CITY _____
STATE _____ ZIP_____

If you have more names, please use an additional sheet of paper.

National Rifle Association
1600 Rhode Island Avenue, N.W.
Washington D.C. 20036

During the two years following Harlon Carter's election as Executive Vice President, NRA membership spiked by 60 percent, a sure sign America's gun owners felt that the organization was moving in the right direction.

power to elect the Nominating Committee and mandated that the board choose at least three of the committee's nine members from the membership at large. A second change provided a relatively simple way for any eligible member to be nominated as a board candidate, by submitting a petition signed by at least 250 voting members.

These changes underwent their first test in 1978, and the results of that board election attested to the vibrancy at work within NRA. The board's Nominating Committee submitted the names of 35 candidates for 27 vacancies, a striking departure from the oligarchic days when nomination was virtually tantamount to election since invariably the number of nominees matched the number of positions to be filled. With 15 candidates nominated by petition—three of whom also appeared on the Nominating Committee list—voting members had real choices, making subsequent boards more representative.

A new era dawned with a significant upsurge in membership numbers, as Harlon Carter turned his enormous energies to reinvigorating the Association. Avid firearms enthusiasts such as Slim Pickens, Roy Rogers, Robert Stack, Robert Fuller, John Russell, and Bert Jones voluntarily lent their celebrity status to a commercial advertising campaign promoting NRA membership. After exceeding the 1 million mark in the late 1960s, the membership rolls remained stagnant until 1978, when membership once more climbed above 1 million, and by the end of 1979 that figure stood at 1.6 million. In just two years, the NRA ranks saw a 60 percent increase.

Membership numbers in all categories—NRA Life, Endowment, Patron, and Benefactor—were at all-time highs. The Life Membership Fund had reached $16.7 million, and the organization's overall book assets increased $11.2 million in the two years following the Cincinnati revolution.

Membership growth spoke eloquently to the strong sense of mission exuded by Harlon Carter in his national tours, where he consolidated his power and influence over America's gun owners who had come to regard him as an icon, a legendary figure who pulled NRA from the abyss of failure.

Programs for Every Need

The influx of new members figured prominently in a number of significant initiatives beyond NRA's full-force move into legislative and political arenas.

To directly assist Carter, Joseph C. White was named Deputy Executive Vice President. He brought to the post an extensive firearms and successful management background. White's multifaceted background included stints as an instructor pilot in World War II and Chief Intelligence Officer for the Immigration and

Naturalization Service. To many NRA members, White was better known as a highly respected pistol shooter, with a number of national championships and honors to his credit.

Harlon Carter also seized the opportunity to install a new team to raise the stature, visibility, and effectiveness of NRA's shooting sports programs. To fulfill that vision, he appointed Gary L. Anderson, one of the greatest riflemen of all time, as Executive Director of General Operations. Anderson held two Olympic gold medals, seven world championships, and had set world records.

To Anderson, a former state legislator, the hand-in-glove duality of ILA and General Operations was a given. "The Institute for Legislative Action works to protect our right to exist as an organization and our right to participate in shooting activities while General Operations provides the programs and activities for people to participate in as they are exercising those rights," he said. "Both of these respon-

sibilities come together as one, just as a skeleton and flesh form a living body."

The Hunter Services Division was formed to provide a wealth of services to that diverse constituency. Staff of the Hunter Information Service, for example, handled members' inquiries on where to hunt, how to plan a hunt, what equipment to use, and other issues. The division also published a registry of guides, outfitters, and shooting preserves and even administrated a hunting awards program.

The Education and Training Division was also formed after splitting off training functions from the former Competitions and Training Division. Among its priorities was a mission to improve the lesson plans and curricula used in NRA Basic Firearm Education courses and to increase the number of instructors qualified to teach such courses. Additionally, a similar effort was accelerated to train and certify coaches who could help lead competitive shooting programs, especially for juniors. Nearly 1,000 certified coaches helped bring competitive youth shooting programs to groups such as the American Legion, the U.S. Jaycees, the National Guard, the Boy Scouts, and others. Another initiative, sponsored in coopera-

Even while NRA delved deeper into legislative action, it continued sponsoring a number of outstanding programs, such as this NRA Police Firearms Instructors Workshop.

WHAT IS NRA?

by Harlon B. Carter

WHAT IS THE NATIONAL RIFLE ASSOCIation? The answer is quick and easy. The National Rifle Association is its membership. The membership reflects its character and dedication. The membership is in command of whatever is done. Without **you,** there would be no political respect; there would be a decline and finally the end of the protection and the furtherance of our right to keep and bear arms. This is why it is overwhelmingly important for the membership of NRA to grow, both in numbers and knowledge of what is being done and what should be done.

NRA is growing rapidly. New members are joining by the thousands. The **net** increase has been 130,000 during the last six months. This translates into greater strength for NRA's objectives. This translates into a sound and vibrant fiscal situation. This translates into public respect and political persuasion, giving strength and direction as our membership points the way. Growth gives support to NRA's programs for participation. We should never forget that a vital ingredient in the nature of NRA and its success is that we are an organization of participants. No one joins the NRA to be a spectator. We are active. We are numbered among those who participate in society and its problems, and we participate in the outdoor shooting sports, which more than any other, are sports of personal involvement—of self-discipline, self-respect and self-qualification. These are things of the family and of friends. We have pride in our membership.

I have said it before, and it will bear repetition that we are a people who have revered our NRA membership somewhat in the manner in which we have revered our American citizenship. In the great public debates of the last fifteen years, our lot has been invariably cast with those who participate, with those who are involved in the future of our country to see whether we shall be a free people.

I have been chilled by public figures who have tried restricting our Fourth Amendment rights when they have said the Fourth Amendment right against unreasonable searches and seizures impairs enforcement of gun laws.

We are shocked when those who say they are opposed to any restraint upon the press

tion with Trinidad State Junior College's School of Gunsmithing, was a series of one-week courses teaching specific gunsmithing skills.

In what was deemed a long-overdue move, Competitions was made a division unto itself. In 1978, participation in the National Matches reached 5,581 participants, the highest level in a decade. Two years later, the NCAA held its first national rifle championship with help from NRA. Yet another new division, the Police Activities Division, was formed to interact with and support law enforcement officials at all levels of training and competition.

Shortly following creation of the new division, former Washington, D.C., Chief of Police John B. Layton, a member of the 1948 U.S. Olympic pistol team, was unanimously elected by the NRA board to become the Association's 45th President. Another veteran lawman, Keith Gaffaney of Anaheim, California, a retired member of the Los Angeles Police Department, was chosen First Vice President.

During the Board of Directors meeting on May 4, 1980, Harlon Carter announced the formation of the Police Activities Division and named G. W. "Eliot" Ness its director. Ness was charged with ensuring that NRA would bring increased support to law enforcement training and police competition programs. The division had two departments: Police Firearms Training with Jim Daugherty as Manager, and Police Competitions with Marie Rittue as Manager. The NRA conducted 18 local and regional police firearms instructors schools with 600 officers prior to an offense at the same time urge such prior restraint upon us.

We oppose that any people be punished, restricted or restrained by the might and weight of a great and centralized government merely because they have the means to commit a crime, although they have never committed one. A free people will not long survive free when they have been deprived of a right, not because they have abused it, but because they could do so.

We are foremost in the defense of the presumption of innocence, the presumption that a man is innocent of a crime until proved guilty in a proper court. On this precept, even if on no other, the right of the people to keep and bear arms is solid and unassailable.

Some of our opponents are, in fact and in deed, the new totalitarians, and we must have the courage to face it and say it. They have spoken in public of electronic surveillance on streets and sidewalks. They have advocated random searches without cause—roundups. They have spoken, and some of them affirmatively, of preventive detention. They have rejected identification cards of every category of people exposed to government restraints, save one, and this is us. They advocate I.D. cards and registration for us, for law-abiding and decent people who

have never committed a crime and concerning whom there is no evidence we shall ever do so. The right to privacy they claim for themselves, they reject for us.

Our NRA Members stand foremost in the struggle to protect and preserve all our God-given, constitutional and long-accepted rights. We stand foremost among those who see and recognize clearly the unfailing mix and combination of those rights with the right of the people to keep and bear arms.

This is great battle. Strong men will not shirk or flinch. Free men cannot do so. Ours is a great revolution, which began on this continent 200 years ago. The members of NRA have been involved in it for more than 100 years. Never will we give an inch. Never will we relax the forward motion to protect and to further our right to keep and bear arms. This right, more than any other, symbolizes the difference and the reality between free men and those who are not free.

Ours is not the light-hearted pursuit of a sport, though there's nothing wrong with that. Ours is the deep and serious voice of a people determined to be free.

Tens of millions of Americans support what we are doing and what we are saying.

We invite all good citizens to join us. We need millions to come forth and share with us.

successfully completing the course of instructions that first year. These 600 represented departments totaling more than 90,000 officers.

NRA field operations underwent an immediate and impressive expansion when Carter established the new Field Services Division and named retired Marine Major Edward J. Land Jr. its leader. "The winds of change at Cincinnati demanded new leadership pursuing dramatically different directions," Land remembered, "and the field team became a solid local presence for the membership." Newly hired field staff were exposed to intensive

training and were expected to focus their efforts in three primary areas: promoting NRA programs, working with ILA to keep abreast of state legislative and political issues, and fostering solid public relations.

Building for the future of the shooting sports, NRA helped underwrite educational shooting sports programs for youngsters through

Edward J. Land Jr. served as Director of the Field Services Division from 1978 until 1982, when he became Director of the Membership Division.

school programs, Boy Scouts, and 4-H clubs. H. T. "Tom" Davison had been Executive Director of the 4-H Foundation in 1975, in charge of training volunteers to work with youth. Though various companies helped sponsor 4-H's shooting program, it wasn't until the Texas 4-H partnered with NRA in 1977 that the program really began to take off. Within a few years, NRA was hosting a nationwide 4-H program, teaching youth everything from safety awareness and basic marksmanship to hunting skills and sportsmanship.

NRA became more active in international shooting as well when, during the 1978 Annual Meetings, a resolution was passed authorizing the establishment of an International Shooter Development Fund. This tax-deductible contri-

butions fund provided money to support the training and development of shooters bound for the Olympics and other international shooting competitions.

NRA's video series expanded with the release of *Olympic Shooting* in 1978 and an educational film on firearms safety called *Firearms Safety—First and Foremost*, starring Roy Rogers. In new publishing efforts, 1978 saw the advent of *American Hunter* magazine as an alternative to *American Rifleman*, NRA's flagship publication offered as a membership benefit. The move was tacit recognition that hunters were an integral and important part of the organization's membership ranks, and that tangible benefit would give hunters a sense of "belonging." The same was true for a much smaller but dedicated cadre of gun collector members, and the 1980 reintroduction of a quarterly newsletter was devoted to their interests.

Along with the magazine option for members, NRA made a significant move

NRA's youth programs give young people the opportunity to learn shooting safety, responsibility, and marksmanship.

Colonel Jim Crossman, pictured here in 1968, authored *Olympic Shooting* and *NRA Deer Hunters Guide,* both of which were published in 1978 by the NRA Book Service Department.

into the book publishing business. Beginning with the 1978 releases of Colonel Jim Crossman's *Olympic Shooting* and *NRA Deer Hunters Guide,* the NRA Book Service Department would fill a niche, offering a representative library covering all aspects of hunting and the shooting sports. Volumes offered detailed insight from experts on topics ranging from home firearm safety to the skills and proper techniques connected with rifle shooting, all written and photographed by teams of experts.

NRA's efforts connected with the publication of books were not confined to in-house works. The organization's leaders realized that one highly effective way of getting their message out on gun control and the Second Amendment was through solidly researched, lucidly argued books. In that context, NRA assisted in the 1979 publication of Dr. Don Kates' *Restricting Firearms: The Liberal Skeptics Speak Out.* The next year NRA would offer support in publishing David T. Hardy's *History on the Right to Keep and Bear Arms,* Dr. David I. Caplan's *The Role of the Second Amendment in the Constitutional System of Checks and Balances,* and Dr. James Whisker's *The Right to Hunt.*

A Vital Ingredient

Harlon Carter embraced gun owners' activism and recognized their unique role in the organization's success, as he noted in NRA's 1978 annual report: "We should never forget that a vital ingredient in the future of NRA and its success is that we are an organization of participants." In 1980, NRA formed a Volunteer Resources Department to coordinate the efforts of individuals willing to give their expertise. One of its first projects, appropriately, was a newsletter called *Camp Perry Satchel* for Camp Perry volunteers.

When Harlon Carter delivered his rousing inspirational speech in Cincinnati, accepting the position of Executive Vice President, he concluded by saying, "You, the membership, are entitled to have an NRA that is responsive to your wishes." By 1980, with record membership rolls, solid finances, program expansion, and a headquarters team exuding a clear sense of purpose, it was obvious that he and his staff had surpassed that express goal.

In November 1979, the NRA Police Training Department was reorganized into a separate division called the Police Activities Division and placed under the guidance of G. W. "Eliot" Ness. The firearm curriculum was standardized into a five-day firearm (handgun and shotgun) instructor development school. In 1981, NRA expanded the Police Activities Division to include police pistol combat competitions as well as training and certification for security officers. The division's title was then changed to the Law Enforcement Activities Division.

CHAPTER EIGHTEEN

LIVING THE GREAT ROLE

1981–1984

If the majority of the 85th Congress had envisioned the intrinsic flaws of the Gun Control Act of 1968; if the majority of Congress had looked upon that legislation with a sensitivity toward probable civil liberties abuses—the Gun Control Act would never have become law in its present form.

—Senator James A. McClure, 1981

AS A NEW DECADE DAWNED, with the White House and control of the United States Senate in pro-Second Amendment hands, prospects for passage of the McClure-Volkmer Federal Firearms Reform Act seemed within reach. Between 1977 and the 1984 Annual Meetings in Milwaukee, Wisconsin, NRA's membership almost tripled, from under 1 million to 2.9 million members, and was continuing to expand at a rate of some 3,000 new members each week.

With that revitalization, never content with the status quo, Harlon Carter vowed to take back lost ground.

Federal firearms law enforcement had been the subject of four congressional oversight hearings on civil rights violations suffered by American citizens. Upon introducing his bill, Idaho Senator James A. McClure minced no words when he told the U.S. Senate that the reform effort was nothing short of "an act of legislative decency."

Before 1980, passage of the reform bill faced impossible odds with Ted Kennedy chairing the all-powerful Senate Judiciary Committee. That all changed when pro-rights Senator Strom Thurmond of South Carolina assumed the Judiciary Committee chair upon Republican takeover of the Senate. And President Ronald Reagan, true to his word, affirmed his full support for the measure.

On the anti-rights side, Kennedy aligned with New Jersey's Representative Peter Rodino and reintroduced a gun bill that would place severe restrictions on the acquisition of handguns and more burdens on their legitimate possession. The ultimate thrust of the bill would give the federal government a virtual free rein on the total prohibition of private handgun ownership.

With Rodino controlling the House Judiciary Committee, Kennedy saw his bill as a checkmate against any serious momentum behind passage of the McClure-Volkmer Bill headed for Senate floor debate that fall.

Since the media had largely ignored oversight hearings on the McClure-Volkmer Bill, NRA produced a hard-hitting documentary entitled *It Can't Happen Here* that finally exposed to America untold stories of the lives and livelihoods that had been ruined under the color of the Gun Control Act and its abusive enforcement. Airing on

---

The Education and Training Division published a "Shooter's Diary," a training aid for the shooting disciplines conducted under the Junior Olympic Shooting Program.

more than 30 U.S. television stations, it quickly became the center of attention, especially in the nation's capitol. The Bureau of Alcohol, Tobacco, and Firearms reportedly feared that the potency of the documentary "may indeed put BATF out of business."

That hyperbole notwithstanding, by 1982 Senator McClure's reform effort had secured 58 cosponsors in the Senate. Spearheaded by Missouri Representative Harold Volkmer, the effort garnered 170 cosponsors in the House of Representatives. That momentum was further propelled when the Senate Judiciary Committee released a compelling,

extensive, formal report that cited "clear proof" based on historical and legal evidence that the Second Amendment indeed upheld the individual right to keep and bear arms. Entitled *The Right to Keep and Bear Arms,* it gave unqualified endorsement to the reform movement while citing its findings on Second Amendment history, an analysis on gun law enforcement, an anthology of legal decisions, and numerous articles by constitutional scholars.

While the anti-gun axis was forced into defending the indefensible on Capitol Hill, the National Coalition to Ban Handguns (NCBH) and Handgun Control, Inc. (HCI), shifted strategy, moving to what

INTERNAL DISSENT

AT THE 1981 MEMBERS MEETING IN Denver, Colorado, aftershocks rumbled through NRA that traced back to events at Cincinnati. Some NRA members saw danger in leaving the vote for Executive Vice President in the hands of Life Members attending the meeting rather than returning the decision to the Board of Directors, where it had traditionally rested. Moreover, even as they praised Harlon Carter personally, several protested a move to elect Carter to a five-year term instead of only a single year, noting that the change had potential for reducing leadership accountability.

After considerable debate, the proposal for a five-year term was defeated handily. Carter dramatically approached the podium and in no uncertain terms announced that he would hand in his resignation unless the membership reconsidered its action. After moments of embarrassed silence, a new vote was called. With no debate whatsoever, stunned voting members gave Carter the unprecedented five-year term he wanted with a rousing show of hands—leaving no doubt as to just how powerful he had become.

Just two years later, at the Annual Members Meeting in Phoenix, Arizona, Harlon Carter's authority was challenged anew by the Federation for NRA, a faction that had put forth bylaw amendments that would provide

for NRA officers to be independently elected. The change would make the four top-paid officers autonomous, answering directly to the membership, and no longer under the control of NRA's Executive Vice President.

In vehemently opposing the amendment, Carter wrote an "Open Letter" that appeared in NRA's magazines one month before voting members would decide the issue in Phoenix: "Prior to the Member's Meeting in Cincinnati in 1977, four of the top officers of NRA were separately and independently elected—each independent of the other, with no one at Headquarters in charge. Each cultivated and maintained the support of his own internal political clique. This fragmented leadership led to a lack of accountability to the membership, to inaction, and ineffectiveness." To drive the point home, Carter concluded that such fragmentation would doom the organization: "This is undeniably a scheme for NRA's decline and defeat—eventually the loss of your right to keep and bear arms."

No one doubted that NRA was at a crossroads and that the amendments were clearly a move to drive Carter from office. As with the Denver meeting, voting members once again stood shoulder-to-shoulder with Harlon Carter and overwhelmingly quashed the insurgents.

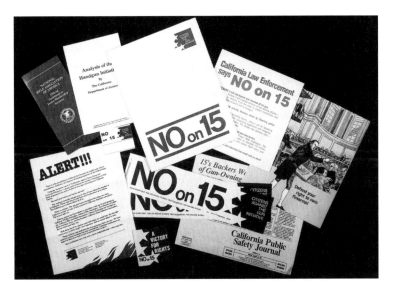

Above: The National Rifle Association joined with a coalition called Citizens against the Gun Initiative, which published a plethora of literature and promotional material to help defeat California's Proposition 15, a gun ban and registration scheme.

Below right: After 30 years in the Los Angeles Police Department, Keith M. Gaffaney became a lobbyist representing gun owners and sportsmen. Elected NRA President in 1981, his more than 35 years of service to the Association were recognized with his election as Honorary Life Member in 1985.

A ballot initiative titled Proposition 15 would put the test to Golden State gun owners in November 1982. Proposition 15 mandated a gun ban and registration scheme designed to choke off private handgun ownership in the state.

The California initiative drive, deemed unstoppable by the media, had the backing of influential politicians. These included San Francisco Mayor Dianne Feinstein, who had proposed a Morton Grove–type handgun ban in her city; Jerry Brown, who made the initiative a cornerstone of his campaign bid for a U.S. Senate seat; and Los Angeles Mayor Tom Bradley, who endorsed the gun ban in his campaign for Governor.

With that battleground set, Harlon Carter once again took stock of his armamentarium and found it wanting. Under the surface, fissures had developed between Carter and Neal Knox as ILA's head, not only because of their vastly different management styles but also due to their divergent opinions as to NRA's public affairs policies and operations.

In reflecting on that time, Colonel Wayne Anthony Ross, an activist board member and

they deemed more conducive turf: state and local action. That move promised to force NRA to battle on multiple fronts, thereby dividing its resources and diluting its strength.

Long a hotbed of anti-gun sentiment, Illinois was the ideal gun ban laboratory, and quite predictably it did not disappoint HCI operatives. The tiny Chicago suburb of Morton Grove passed the nation's first ban on the private ownership of handguns. And while the ordinance was aggressively challenged in court as unconstitutional under both the United States and Illinois Constitutions, the handgun ban was sustained in what its opponents called a "manifest error in interpretation." Ultimately, in upholding the ban, the Illinois State Supreme Court rested its argument on the "police power" clause contained in the state's constitution. That court victory emboldened the anti-rights coalition to set its sights on the next showdown, in California.

A PRESIDENTIAL FLINTLOCK

*Firearm photo courtesy
National Firearms Museum*

U.S. PRESIDENT AND NRA HONORARY Life Member Ronald Reagan is one of the greatest champions of the Second Amendment to sit in the Oval Office. In 1983, President Reagan told the NRA members gathered at the Annual Meetings in Phoenix, Arizona, and the world, "We will never disarm any American who seeks to protect his or her family from fear or harm."

This Pennsylvania-style flintlock rifle, made by Texan Christopher Scott Hirsh, was presented to Reagan in the Oval Office in December 1981. The 42"-barreled rifle is based on the work of John Rupp of Lehigh County and features a Siler lock, German-silver furniture, and handmade iron trigger and an engraved patchbox. Said Reagan of the rifle as he threw it up to his shoulder with well-practiced ease: "This is great. It's beautiful and it feels fine."

"We will never disarm any American who seeks to protect his or her family from fear and harm," President Ronald Reagan declared in addressing the 1983 Annual Members Meeting in Phoenix. Introduced by Executive Vice President Harlon B. Carter, President Reagan was the first President to address NRA's membership while in office.

prominent attorney from Alaska, commented that, "The situation had really come to a head. Harlon saw Neal as a 300,000 member guy in a 3 million member organization. He was a micromanager and couldn't delegate authority to the people that he oversaw. He had to edit every communication that ILA produced, and staff had to come to him for every decision. So things at ILA were slowing down substantially."

With such high stakes riding on the outcome of the California challenge, Carter made what he termed "a painful and reluctant" choice and

removed Knox as NRA's chief lobbyist. Carter then appointed J. Warren Cassidy, an NRA Director and insurance executive from Massachusetts, to ILA's top post. Cassidy had been a leader of the Gun Owners' Action League, which had crushed a gun ban ballot measure in Massachusetts in 1976.

Knowing they were favored by a two-to-one polling margin, Proposition 15 supporters boasted that referendum passage would "break the myth of the invincibility of the gun lobby," and "will sweep across the country." Charles Orasin of Handgun Control, Inc., boldly predicted that the "message will not be lost on the politicians in Washington." But once again gun ban advocates had severely underestimated NRA's grassroots muscle.

In launching a statewide multimedia campaign, Cassidy castigated the proposal as a "hoax" and predicted that "the more the issue is debated, the more people come to understand the complexities, the contradictions and the inherent failures of Prop. 15, the less likely they are to vote for it."

Support for the measure eroded as silver screen legend Charlton Heston volunteered his persuasive skills to narrate a 30-minute documentary that exposed the initiative's flaws. California's law enforcement community lined up in force; vocally opposed to the gun ban were 55 of 58 sheriffs, more than 100 police chiefs, and 33 law enforcement organizations.

United under a campaign committee called Citizens Against the Gun Initiative, 30,000 volunteers manned phone banks and canvassed neighborhoods in a massive organizational effort against Proposition 15. It was estimated that 250,000 citizens registered to vote solely based on their vehement opposition to the gun initiative.

In the end, voters rejected the measure by the landslide margin of 63–37 percent. Election analysts credited the debate to bringing an unprecedented 73 percent of eligible voters to the polls. And that turnout was key to the election of Attorney General George Deukmejian as Governor over Tom Bradley, and to the election of San Diego Mayor Pete Wilson over Jerry Brown in the U.S. Senate contest.

The result was, in Harlon Carter's words, "an undeniable testament to the strength of a united and active membership participating in the political process of our society." Even the *Los Angeles Times,* an avid champion for Proposition 15, reluctantly admitted that "by all reports, the opponents were better prepared, better organized and better at raising money than the sponsors."

Winning the Minds of Men

"To win the war for the hearts and minds of men," in Harlon Carter's words, NRA launched a major national advertising campaign in 1981 featuring distinguished Americans from all walks of life. Tagged "I'm the NRA," the campaign appeared in popular magazines and showcased

Over the years, "I'm the NRA" advertising has featured American icons such as General Joe Foss as well as a host of NRA members from many walks of life, bringing home to millions the simple fact that the Association is a slice of America.

former astronaut Wally Schirra, champion rifle competitor Noma McCullough, and motion picture star Roy Rogers, among others. The campaign reached more than 231 million Americans through widely read publications such as *Readers Digest, Time, Life, Esquire, Newsweek, Smithsonian,* and *Boy's Life.* "Thought Leader" advertisements by writers such as Simon & Schuster Editor-in-Chief Michael Korda, entitled "Guns Are Not the Problem," were aimed at targeted audiences and placed in publications such as the *Atlantic Monthly* and the *National Journal.*

To counter media distortion and misinformation, the newly configured NRA Public Education Division produced hard-hitting brochures for broad-side distribution, and complimentary subscriptions to ILA's *Reports from Washington* were provided to members of the Outdoor Writers Association, a group of journalists likely to understand and carry the NRA message to their readers. And high-profile celebrities like entertainers Barbara Mandrell and Hank Williams Jr. conveyed NRA messages to the American people.

Year of Champions

In competitive shooting events, Americans performed exceptionally well at the Summer Olympics in 1984, prompting air pistol silver medalist Ruby

INSTRUCTION AND TRAINING

"THE INSTRUCTORS ARE SOME OF the unsung heroes in the NRA," said Mark Ness, who authored a course book titled *Basics of Pistol Shooting* and later became Operations Research Analyst for the Office of the Secretary. "They never ask you, 'What's NRA doing for me?' They always tell you first how many new members they've signed up and how many people they've trained."

Students of NRA-trained instructors gain valuable experience, but not necessarily in expert marksmanship. "That's not the intent of our training program, although they will learn the rudiments of marksmanship," said Joe Roberts, whose duties as Communications Editor include publishing a newsletter for NRA instructors and coaches. "Students who graduate from an NRA training course, regardless of the discipline, will be safe gun handlers, responsible gun owners, and they'll know about the type of firearms they're dealing with."

Education and training are key to NRA's mission and have been since its founding in 1871. Thousands of NRA-certified instructors across America train hundreds of thousands of citizens each year on the safe and proper handling of firearms.

Fox to say, "The NRA has supported U.S. shooters all the way—with funds for training centers, coaches, equipment, and thousands of tournaments. They listened . . . and they do a fantastic job." Pat Spurgin, who was the gold medalist in women's air rifle competition, said, "The NRA has played a significant role in my shooting. Almost all competitive shooting goes through the NRA [and] . . . it's always been the behind-the-scenes factor in all the shooting I've done."

Later the same year, NRA's Gary Anderson and U.S. Olympic Committee Executive Director Don Miller broke ground for the new shooting sports building at the U.S. Olympic Training Center in Colorado Springs, Colorado.

While the events of the XXIII Olympiad received most of the attention, 1984 was also noteworthy in other competitive shooting fronts. It was the inaugural year of the NRA Action Shooting Championships. The National Matches at Camp Perry logged record participation, and the number of NRA-sanctioned tournaments was at an all-time high, with close to 11,000 separate events taking place during the year.

Traditional Services Handed New Charters

Beginning in 1981, the *NRA Gun Collecting Newsletter* was issued quarterly, and an agreement was reached with the American Society of Arms Collectors to reprint material from presen-

Above: Wayne LaPierre began his NRA career as one of the "young kids" in the Institute for Legislative Action. By the mid-1980s, he had become Director of ILA's Governmental Affairs Division.

Below right: Harlon B. Carter and NRA President Howard W. Pollock congratulate Olympic silver medalist Ruby Fox at an NRA reception held to honor medalists at the 1984 Games. Fox would join medal-winning teammates Matt Dryke, Ed Etzel, Wanda Jewell, and Pat Spurgin at the White House to receive personal congratulations from President Ronald Reagan.

Left: Rifleman Lones W. Wigger Jr., one of the most decorated athletes in American history, was a finalist for the Amateur Athletic Union's 1981 James E. Sullivan Award. Wigger passed along his shooting prowess to his daughter Deena, herself a national champion.

FEDERAL FIREARMS REFORM ACT

by Idaho U. S. Sen. James A. McClure

THE ABUSES SUFFERED BY GUN OWN-ers and dealers under the Gun Control Act of 1968 must be halted legislatively. It's time for a . . . FEDERAL FIREARMS REFORM.

When the Congress enacted the Gun Control Act of 1968, promises were made in the preamble of the legislation that the new law would not be used "to place any undue Federal restrictions or burdens on law-abiding citizens. . . ." That promise was never kept . . . because of the very nature of the Federal gun law itself.

GCA '68, aptly described as "legal flypaper that not even competent lawyers claim to understand," gives almost unlimited police power to the agencies enforcing it and provides only vague descriptions of what should be legal and what should be illegal.

It is a law under which any and all transgressions, even the slightest technical violation, are Federal felonies and under which Federal prosecutors are not required to prove criminal intent in order to establish guilt so that a totally unintentional violation can lead to criminal felony conviction. All this adds up to a lethal combination for the civil liberties of those citizens whose lives have been touched by GCA '68.

In any hard look at the GCA '68 or into the agencies which enforce it and prosecute violators, one fact keeps surfacing above all—most of the people charged with GCA '68 felonies are not criminals. Most are law-abiding citizens—gun dealers or gun collectors—who have become ensnared into technical violations of the law they clearly don't understand.

This brings up the record of the agency which enforces the law, the Bureau of Alcohol, Tobacco and Firearms, and the agency which prosecutes, the U.S. Department of Justice.

For its part, BATF has built much of its seizure and arrest record on statistical felonies involving mere technical violations. It means riskless raids upon otherwise law-abiding citizens,

tations made at its meetings. *American Marksman,* which was available on a subscription-only basis, covered competitive shooting, while *InSights* was being published for NRA's junior members, which were 50,000 strong by 1984. Annual sales of volumes offered by the NRA Book Service topped the 100,000 mark, and in 1983 the entire department was revamped with a target of seeing at least six new titles printed annually.

After the advent of the Hunter Clinic Program in 1982, well-attended clinics for turkey hunters led to dozens of similar outreach programs, covering many aspects of deer, waterfowl, and upland game hunting, as well as bow hunting.

Junior competitive shooting continued to receive strong emphasis, especially under the NRA Junior Olympic Shooting Program. This extensive system of camps reached all the way to national levels and brought together some of the nation's finest coaches, including several from the U.S. Shooting Team, with the country's best young shooters.

Representing the highest levels any shooter could achieve, NRA Director and Olympic gold medalist Lones W. Wigger was one of only 10 athletes from all amateur sports nominated for the Amateur Athletic Union's 1981 James E. Sullivan Award. Commenting on the nomination, Harlon Carter said, "It represents a recognition of the great contributions that shooters have made to amateur athletics as a whole." (Track star Carl Lewis was the eventual winner of the award.)

In 1982, the NRA Police Activities Division was renamed the Law Enforcement Activities

and it means impressive sounding lists of "crime guns seized." To the BATF, a "crime gun" is not a gun used to commit a crime, but any and all guns belonging to an individual or dealer who violates any provision of the gun law. For example, a dealer charged with a recordkeeping technical violation involving just one firearm may see all his guns seized.

The U.S. Department of Justice must also accept a large share of responsibility for civil liberties abuses committed under the provisions of the 1968 Act. Federal prosecutors have routinely pressed ahead with cases which, if considered in the light of criminal intent, should never have been before a court.

In reviewing the widespread excesses of the BATF, it has become apparent that there are very clear categories of abuse, and that they all are due to the vagueness of the law itself. For example, large portions of the statistical records built by BATF during the mid-1970s were centered around something called "straw-sales." "Strawman" usually involves two Federal agents, one posing as a non-resident of a state, the other posing as a resident. An attempt is made by the non-resident agent to purchase a gun. When the dealer informs him that under Federal law he cannot sell a gun to a non-resident, the other agent steps in, usually claiming to be a relative or friend of the non-

resident. He offers to buy the gun, showing proper identification and filling out the Federal form. When the transaction is closed, BATF believes the dealer has committed a felony.

Recently, one Federal judge wrote to me about his deep concerns over the efficacy of "strawman" sales. In his letter, U.S. District Court Judge Robert F. Chapman explained: "After trying three of these cases in various parts of the state, I became convinced that dealers . . . did not realize that the 'straw-sale' was illegal. I advised the U.S. Attorney's Office and the head of the BATF in South Carolina that no further cases would be tried until a letter was written and mailed to every gun dealer in South Carolina explaining the meaning of this language and that a 'straw-sale' was illegal." Judge Chapman went on to say that following his order, no further "straw-sales" operations were conducted in the state. But previous to his letter, 37 "straw" cases had been made by BATF.

Another vague aspect of the GCA '68 which has contributed to a record of BATF abuse is the question of what constitutes a firearms dealer. Again, BATF has built a statistical record of felony arrests where gun collectors or gun fanciers were charged with "engaging in the business" without having a required Federal Firearms License. What constitutes "engaging in the business?" Is it the

Division to better reflect the full array of its functions and responsibilities. A record number of NRA Law Enforcement Instructor schools were held, and by the end of the year, close to 2,000 law enforcement organizations were enrolled with NRA. The number of firearms instructors earning NRA certification likewise grew, with some 80,000 individuals on file nationwide. Almost 1.4 million individuals had been trained by NRA-certified instructors and coaches in 1983.

Political Victories

With the 1984 presidential election year, the Reagan-Bush team had solid NRA support and was in the forefront of a resounding national triumph for Second Amendment supporters. Of 237

candidates who garnered support from the NRA-PVF, 214 won. By then, Wayne R. LaPierre Jr. had been promoted from Director of ILA's State and Local Affairs Division to Governmental Affairs Director, wielding enormous influence over NRA's national political action. LaPierre's goal was to enter every race where Second Amendment rights were threatened. That year saw the introduction of "I'm the NRA and I Vote," campaign, and voter registration drives were the keystone for NRA-PVF victories. LaPierre took personal pride in the Texas U.S. Senate race victory in which Phil Gramm won with strong NRA-PVF backing.

LaPierre also scored victories on federal legislative fronts when ILA took back lost ground with passage in the U.S. Congress in 1982 of an amendment to exempt registration of .22 caliber sale of six guns per year, or one gun per year? That question cannot be answered.

The truth is there has been no definition except the off-hand opinions of individual agents in the field. And yet there have been many arrests and there have been convictions and forfeitures of property based on charges of dealing without a license. Because of the increasing awareness of BATF abuses, especially in the Congress, the agency finally—after almost 12 years—has proposed a Federal Regulation to define the term "engaging in the business." What about those past convictions? What about those arrests?

There is yet another standard practice in BATF's arsenal of abuse—the mass confiscation of whole gun collections and inventories and the "trashing" of those seized guns by BATF agents. Often firearms are seized where no formal charges are leveled. Collections seized in the past have found their way into BATF's own gun museum or have been intentionally damaged by agents.

Other standard abuses center around the question of whether or not a Federally licensed dealer can own and sell firearms from his own private collection. Recently a young Maryland firearms dealer—a former police officer and military veteran with an impeccable record of personal conduct—was convicted in Federal court of selling firearms from his private collection without registering the transactions in his Federal book. In finding the young dealer guilty, the Federal judge said he did so with "great reluctance" and called the violation "an isolated act of wrongdoing in an otherwise lawful and productive career." Just one week after the judge found the dealer guilty, the then acting Director of BATF informed U.S. Sen. S. L. Hayakawa that a dealer could indeed sell all private guns legally without running them through his books. So where was there a crime? Yet this young man's life is ruined.

And then there is perhaps the worst abusive practice of BATF—vindictive pursuit, where the government fails to win a criminal case and files a series of civil actions against the same defendant involving exactly the same allegations.

The case of Paul Hayes of Bosque Farm, N. Mex., is among the best of many examples of malicious pursuit. Hayes, a Federally licensed firearms dealer, and his wife, Billie, own a mercantile, gun shop and gas station. Hayes was charged in April 1978, with eight counts of "straw-sale" violations. (His entire gun store inventory of 170 guns was seized, and in the process of confiscating those firearms, federal agents removed the guns from protective boxes and wrappings and threw them in barrels.)

After a week-long trial, Hayes was acquitted of all charges. Subsequently, BATF informed

---

rimfire ammunition sales prohibited under the federal Gun Control Act. It was followed by passage of a federal law providing long-needed tax relief for custom gunsmiths. At the state level, ILA's Legal Affairs Division spearheaded the overturning of San Francisco's handgun ban ordinance. And in 1984, ILA celebrated passage of a trade bill amendment favorable to gun collectors that overturned a provision of the 1968 Gun Control Act. It allowed the import of foreign-made rifles, shotguns, and handguns listed as curios and relics.

A Popular Presence

On January 25, 1985, in a farewell address to the Board of Directors, Harlon B. Carter announced his decision to retire. He looked back fondly with an understated sense of pride on what he considered the high points of his tenure and reflected on 55 years as a member of NRA and the passage of 35 years since he was first elected to the Board of Directors.

His tenure as Executive Vice President had seen no passage of restrictive firearms legislation, even while there had been important roll-backs to the 1968 Gun Control Act. Membership had tripled. Contributions from members to the Institute for Legislative Action had risen to $4.5 million annually while the overall NRA budget had quadrupled as it passed the $50 million mark. Even as the budget soared, the organization's assets had doubled to reach some $70 million. And the organization exuded strength through unity.

Hayes that his Federal Firearms License renewal was denied. The reason: the same eight "straw-sale" charges on which Hayes had been found not guilty in the U.S. District Court. Hayes appealed and won the return of his license, but there was more to come. The government then filed an action in Federal court seeking forfeiture of all 170 guns seized from the Hayes shop. Again, the reason boiled down to the same eight "straw-man" counts. After years of fighting for their rights, the Hayes' property was returned in damaged condition. In all, this battle has cost the Hayes family their savings, their health and their livelihood. And where can there be any protection for people like Hayes or any of the other countless victims of BATF?

The answer is in changing the law. . .

The Federal Firearms Reform Act . . . would shield against entrapment of law-abiding citizens by requiring proof that a violation was committed willfully. It would narrowly define which citizens would be required to obtain a firearms license and would provide statutory recognition of collectors and their rights.

It would protect against malicious or vexatious charges by providing that:

- If criminal charges are brought, and the defendant is acquitted, the BATF and Justice Department cannot use those same charges to deny or refuse to renew a dealer's license. Nor can they use them to justify withholding or seizing firearms from the defendant.

- If firearms are confiscated from a collector and the government fails to bring criminal charges within 120 days, the firearms must be returned.

- If firearms are confiscated and the gun owner brings suit for their return, the court must award him a reasonable attorney's fee if he wins.

And the bill would provide protection against wholesale gun confiscations by prohibiting government seizures of guns not involved in specific violations.

The final impact would be to redirect federal agencies away from the "path of least resistance" over law-abiding and easily induced citizens and toward criminals who genuinely and knowingly violate the laws.

Reprinted with permission from *American Rifleman*, April 1980

Carter's departure came on his own terms and with his own sense of timing. It was the end of a stunning era, and he left NRA as it rode the crest of a wave of success. The essence of Carter's rich legacy, as noted in a board-approved tribute, was to leave a "National Rifle Association of unprecedented strength and influence."

Without question, Harlon B. Carter was beloved and respected by the rank and file membership, and his was a deep, heartfelt devotion to NRA. Carter expressed his "full confidence in the future" and reminded the board that neither its members nor the membership were "seeing me go. You are instead seeing me but one more time changing my relationship in the National Rifle Association, changing my position in it. I am not leaving." Implicit in that message was the reminder that he had been elected to the Executive Council for life and intended to stay closely attuned to the pulse of NRA.

In tribute to Harlon Carter's unparalleled career, the Board of Directors unanimously elected him to Honorary Life Member status, the Association's highest honor.

The NRA Youth Hunter Education Challenge (YHEC) allows young hunters to build on skills learned in hunter safety classes. Shotgun shooting is one of eight events in the YHEC program.

CHAPTER NINETEEN

STAYING POWER

1985–1990

*Trashing NRA is all that counts these days. The anti-gunners espouse
a personalized "hate" campaign to discredit the only organization standing between them and their destruction of our Constitution.*

—J. Warren Cassidy, 1988

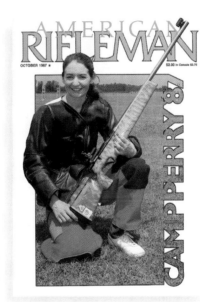

THE ANNOUNCED RETIRE-
ment of Harlon Carter as
Executive Vice President
created a vacancy to be auto-
matically assumed, under NRA
bylaws, by the Executive Director of General Operations,
Gary L. Anderson. However,
Anderson declined the position, for as Carter put it, "He
has no desire to get entangled
in the fickle tides of NRA internal politics."

It fell to the NRA Board of Directors to select
Carter's successor. After an extensive national
search, G. Ray Arnett was chosen. Arnett had been
U.S. Interior Department Assistant Secretary for
Fish and Wildlife and Parks under President
Ronald Reagan. Highly influential in the hunting
community, Arnett welcomed the opportunity as
"an honor and a challenge I accept with both
pride and a sense of respect." An ardent out-
doorsman and past NRA Director, Arnett was
elected by the board for an interim period until
the selection could be ratified at the Annual
Members Meeting in Seattle, Washington,
that April.

Ratification would not be gained easily, however. A dissident faction seized on Carter's departure as a singular opportunity to run an opposi-

tion candidate to challenge Arnett:
namely former ILA Executive
Director Neal Knox.

Before the largest attendance
of voting members in history,
NRA President and former Alaska
Congressman Howard W. Pollock
and others on the board labored
arduously to keep the meeting
orderly while members voted on
numerous bylaw amendments and,
ultimately, the election for Executive
Vice President.

Always genial and a consum-
mate gentleman, Howard Pollock was uniquely qualified to meet the challenge. Pollock learned patience
the hard way. As a World War II Navy pilot, he was
severely injured in a firefight while throwing what
turned out to be a defective hand grenade. He lost
an arm and punctured both lungs and remained
hospitalized for two years. After retiring from the
service as a Lieutenant Commander, Pollock moved
to Alaska, where he served as Civilian Officer for
Headquarters Army. He entered the political world

While NRA kept busy on the legislative front, it continued devoting
ample coverage to shooting events, including the National Matches
at Camp Perry, through *American Rifleman, Tournament News,
American Marksman,* and *Shooting Sports USA.*

first as a state legislator while simultaneously earning a law degree and later was elected to Congress, gaining fame as one of the few courageous leaders to fight passage of the 1968 Gun Control Act.

At the Members Meeting, Pollock brought his skills as a masterful parliamentarian to the floor, moderating what otherwise could have become a bitter and contentious session.

It was clear that Arnett was Carter's logical and anointed successor. Arnett's name was placed in nomination by renowned NRA Director Alice Bull, who dubbed him "a dedicated champion of our rights" and "a tough and capable and no-nonsense type of administrator."

Weighing heavily in the final vote was a ringing endorsement for Arnett by Congressman John Dingell, a man of historic achievement in the pro–Second Amendment movement. In the end, Arnett gained the membership's seal of approval by a margin of better than two-to-one, and in his address following the divisive election campaign, he called for unity. Significantly, a bylaw amend-

Above: G. Ray Arnett succeeded Harlon Carter as Executive Vice President. Though Carter and other prominent leaders endorsed Arnett, his tenure was short, and he was replaced in 1986 by J. Warren Cassidy.

Left: Once chosen "One of the Ten Outstanding Young Men in the United States," Howard W. Pollock served as Alaska's Congressman from 1967 to 1971, during which time he actively fought against passage of the Gun Control Act of 1968. He became NRA President in 1983.

ment was approved that enabled members to vote by mail ballot, expanding the franchise to all eligible voting members, not just those who could attend the Annual Members Meeting.

Arnett's five-year term began auspiciously enough, but the infighting that flowed from Seattle did not end. Inside NRA headquarters, the situation was not much different. Warring camps emerged while Arnett "assessed" the "who" and the "what" of NRA operations with a clinical eye and a bureaucratic hand. Though Arnett was personally liked, his penchant for organizational

NRA's First Lady: Alice H. Bull

WHEN HEART FAILURE CLAIMED THE life of Alice H. Bull on November 26, 1998, at age 88, a remarkable chapter of NRA history concluded. That chapter was about a trailblazer who left behind a legacy of commitment to the shooting sports, to the Second Amendment, and to the National Rifle Association.

In 1949, Alice Bull became the first woman elected to the NRA Board of Directors. A year later, she became the first woman to serve as President of a state rifle and pistol association in her home state of Washington. As an NRA Director, from 1949 to 1988, she chaired many committees and was elevated to the Executive Council in 1988. Her lifetime of service to NRA was recognized in 1981 with her unanimous election as an Honorary Life Member, the Association's highest honor. It has been bestowed on only 15 other individuals, and, again, Alice Bull was the first woman to be so honored. In 1996, for her outstanding career as a shooter, lifetime dedication to protecting the Second Amendment, and contributions to NRA, Bull received the Sybil Ludington Women's Freedom Award at the NRA Annual Meetings in Dallas.

Alice Bull's competitive shooting career began in 1929 at the University of Washington, where she was a member of the women's rifle team. She went on to win numerous state, regional, and national titles, including four National Women's High Power Rifle Championships. She was the first woman to make the President's 100, placing 33rd out of the 1,400 shooters competing in the match in 1936. The President's 100 were honored with a parade through Camp Perry. "She often said that was her greatest pre-war distinction," said her son, former NRA Director Leland L. Bull Jr. "She was the only woman in that parade until the mid-1960s."

In 1961, Bull became the first woman to earn the Distinguished Rifleman Badge, the Department of Defense's highest honor given for marksmanship excellence with a military rifle. Thirty years later, during the High Power Rifle Awards Ceremony at Camp Perry, the Alice Bull Trophy was unveiled. Presented to the civilian shooter with the highest combined aggregate score from the President's Match and the National Trophy Individual Match, it stands more than seven feet tall and has a triangular base that supports the three service rifles used by Bull during her shooting career—a Model 1903 Springfield, an M1 Garand, and an M1A. Atop the elaborate base stands a bronze statue of Bull in circa 1936 shooting gear holding the Springfield that earned her place in the President's 100.

Over the years, Bull gave tirelessly of her time and expertise to promote shooting. She organized the Greater Seattle Shooters Council, a federation of 66 rifle and pistol clubs, in order to teach marksmanship skills to civilians who were going to war in Korea. She later became the first woman to be appointed to the National Board for the Promotion of Rifle Practice.

Future generations of shooters will remember Alice Bull for her remarkable achievements. Anyone fortunate enough to have known her remembers not only a trailblazing champion but a gracious woman devoted to the service of others.

Honorary Life Member Alice H. Bull, the first woman elected to the NRA Board of Directors, was honored with the Sybil Luddington Women's Freedom Award for 1996 at the NRA Annual Meetings in Dallas for her lifetime of service to NRA and the shooting sports.

During his tenure as Executive Director of the Institute for Legislative Action, J. Warren Cassidy lobbied fiercely to achieve passage of the McClure-Volkmer Bill.

charts and order was an unseemly replacement for the zeal and passion for the cause that marked the post-Cincinnati mindset of the membership and staff. Moreover, Arnett failed to work closely with the Board of Directors, even in matters that demanded board oversight.

In a move reminiscent of the "Weekend Massacre" that presaged the Cincinnati revolt, Arnett unilaterally eliminated the Public Education Division, dismissed its staff, and outsourced its public relations functions to a contract agency, all in a move "to reduce operating costs immediately." Combined with ongoing staff turmoil and low morale over Arnett's creation of powerful executive posts filled with operatives that were seen as "barriers" to action, the firings fueled the board to take action.

In a specially called meeting on May 17, 1986, a resolution adopted by the Executive Committee of the Board of Directors set Arnett's termination in motion. That same resolution authorized and directed ILA's Executive Director, J. Warren Cassidy, to perform the duties of Executive Vice President until a permanent replacement could be elected in accordance with the bylaws. In a final stroke, the committee prevailed upon Harlon Carter to assist in the transition.

In speaking for the NRA Board of Directors, President James E. Reinke subsequently alluded to a "year of turmoil" and the need to take "forceful action to correct some severe management problems." He further told NRA's membership that "the callous expulsion of employees from their offices—in large number and with little notice—went far beyond any acceptable action of management in our Association. An Executive Vice President who presided over such an action was not to be kept in office, as the membership dictated in Cincinnati."

Although Arnett's tenure was brief, the period witnessed noteworthy achievements as NRA membership reached the 3 million milestone.

Edward J. Land Jr. had been promoted to Director of the Membership Division, and he approached membership drives with new ideas that paid dividends. Among them were three-year, five-year, and Life Member promotions, which produced more than 150,000 multiyear members in a single year, and recruiting efforts such as the "American Rifleman" radio series that helped swell membership ranks.

Landmark Legislative Victory

Significant as membership growth was to the organization, it yielded center stage to a historic legislative achievement: passage of the McClure-Volkmer Firearms Owners Protection Act. After seven years of painstaking work, the reform act passed in the U.S. Congress, and President Reagan signed it into law on May 19, 1986.

Although the bill had been introduced in 1979 by Senator McClure and Representative Volkmer, it was stonewalled in Congress until the Reagan years. Ultimately, the bill's passage came in no small measure because House Judiciary

U.S. Senator James McClure (left), a Republican from Idaho, and U.S. Representative Harold Volkmer, a Democrat representing Missouri, were coauthors of the McClure-Volkmer Firearms Owners Protection Act, which President Reagan signed into law in 1986. The law undid many of the burdensome and poorly crafted provisions of the Gun Control Act of 1968.

Committee Chairman Peter Rodino declared the measure "dead on arrival." In 1985, with the tireless support of Senators Orrin Hatch, Ted Stevens, and Robert Dole, Senator McClure achieved an overwhelming 79-15 Senate passage of the long-awaited act. Utah's Senator Hatch called it a "victory for freedom, fairness, and common sense," adding that it "should be the beginning and not the end."

Not only did the bill pass the Senate for the first time, it did so free of any of the restrictive amendments that the anti-gun lobby had promised. But the salvo handed down by Judiciary Chairman Rodino assured a very different, hand-to-hand combat in the U.S. House.

THE HARLON B. CARTER–GEORGE S. KNIGHT FREEDOM FUND

IN DECEMBER 1989, THE HARLON B. Carter—George S. Knight Freedom Fund was established due to a generous cash contribution of $100,000 by NRA Board of Directors member George Knight.

The Freedom Fund is awarded to those persons whose exemplary activities have been vital and instrumental in defense of the right to keep and bear arms. The fund is awarded annually to three individuals—one at the federal level, one at the state level, and one at the local level.

The corpus of the fund can be used if there exists an emergency situation regarding the protection of the Second Amendment of the United States Constitution.

In addition, Freedom Fund awards may also be given to a deserving high school student, grammar school student, or author, who researches and writes a paper concerning the best method to inform citizenry about the Second Amendment to the U.S. Constitution.

Award Recipients

1992: Professor Robert J. Cottrol
      Dr. Suzanna Gratia
      General H. Norman Schwartzkopf
1993: Dr. Linda Miller
      Deputy Chief Joseph Constance
      Mr. Phillip B. Journey
1994: Dr. Ed Suter
      Mr. Landis Aden
      Mrs. Mary Warner
1995: Dr. Paul Craig Roberts
      Virginia State Senator Virgil H. Goode Jr.
1996: Mr. James Bovard
      Mr. Robert Damron
      Mr. Ken Blanchard
1997: Sheriff Peter J. "Jay" Printz
      Mr. Mark Harris
1998: Mrs. Alice H. Bull (posthumously)
1999: Professor Raymond T. Diamond
      Mr. Kenneth Christopher Foss
         (posthumously)
      Ms. Victoria "Vickie" Buckly
         (posthumously)
      Sergeant Kenneth R. Edwards

Executive Council member George S. Knight served as founder and chairman of the NRA Firearms Civil Rights Defense Fund and established the Harlon B. Carter–George S. Knight Freedom Fund to bestow annual monetary awards on defenders of the Second Amendment: activists, scholars, and other deserving individuals.

Representative Larry Craig, a pro-gun stalwart who represented Idaho's First District, helped launch the offensive against Rodino. In a rare defiance of House leadership, supporters of the measure forcefully set in motion a parliamentary strategy to gain the upper hand by pushing a discharge petition to circumvent the House Judiciary Committee and bring the bill directly to the floor for a vote.

Leaving their mark on history were 218 courageous House members who signed the discharge petition, thereby resurrecting the bill from Rodino's intended graveyard. That action would mark only the eighth time since 1960 that a discharge petition had been successfully activated in Congress—a major legislative accomplishment in itself.

"Being able to get that bill passed was an important test—not only for NRA but also for gun control and the country's leadership," said Congressman Craig, who was elected to the U.S. Senate in 1990.

"We were taking back a lot of very bad policy that had grown out of a very emotional time in America with the assassination of President Kennedy and the rush to judgment that followed. And we were able to restore the balance following the politics of the Watergate era that had swept so many anti-gun congressmen into power."

NRA made signing the discharge petition the equivalent of a vote "for or against" firearms owners. It sent members an undiluted, unqualified, and unmistakable message: "What your Congressman does

on the discharge petition will tell you whether or not he's concerned about your firearms and hunting freedoms. It will tell you whether or not your Congressman is willing to act on behalf of your rights in Washington, D.C. Don't let your Congressman 'take a walk' on your gun and hunting freedoms—THIS IS THE LITMUS TEST."

After two days of heated debate that saw New Jersey Representatives Rodino and William Hughes offer amendment after amendment intended to gut the reforms, on April 10, 1986, the Firearms Owners Protection Act was finally approved by a 292-130 floor vote, a better than two-to-one margin. While the bill did not pass unscathed, it remained largely intact and was a first step in taking back lost rights.

Widely acclaimed for orchestrating the act's passage were two key NRA figures who would become influential national leaders in the organization's future: Wayne R. LaPierre, Director of the Governmental Affairs Division, and James Jay Baker, the division's Deputy Director. Both were

Above: Upon the death of Alonzo H. Garcelon in late 1985, James E. Reinke, retired Vice President of Government Affairs for Eastern Airlines, assumed NRA's presidency. Reinke's dedication to the Second Amendment led to his election as an Honorary Life Member in 2000.

Left: Maine dentist Alonzo H. Garcelon, a shooter, hunter, and conservationist, was elected NRA President in 1985. Soon after taking office, Dr. Garcelon dramatically confronted New York's anti-gun Governor Mario Cuomo and forced him to apologize for slurring NRA members.

rising stars not only in NRA's galaxy but also inside Washington's political corridors of power.

"The McClure-Volkmer Law was undoubtedly ILA's finest moment," said James O. E. Norell, ILA's first Communications Director. "It fixed some things that had no business being in any sort of criminal law. McClure-Volkmer happened because of the way the law had been abused by federal officials. It couldn't have been done otherwise—and the truth won out."

Media-Made Myths

That same year saw an end to the bullet ban frenzy that had begun in 1982 over so-called "armor-piercing" ammunition capable of penetrating bullet-resistant vests worn by many law enforcement officers. The media-made issue first gained notoriety through a controversial exposé on "Cop Killer" bullets that NBC—over law enforcement protests—televised nationally. In reality, the ammunition had never been distributed to the general public and was available only to the military and law enforcement agencies.

Despite these facts, the media tempest intensified, and the ever opportunistic Handgun Control, Inc., issued calls for its prohibition. Federally, New York Representative Mario Biaggi introduced legislation that officials from the Treasury Department, Secret Service, and Justice Department all resoundingly criticized as "unworkable." Associate Attorney General Rudolph Giuliani testified that legislation such as Biaggi sought would have the effect of "rendering illegal virtually all available ammunition."

Grabbing headlines, Biaggi persisted in his bullet ban crusade, even though government ballistics and legal professionals had themselves been unable to come up with a practical,

SERVING WITH DISTINCTION

BEHIND THE MAELSTROM ACCORDED gun control issues in the late 1980s, steady, stellar work was being accomplished in a wide range of areas.

Throughout the years in which a "rift" with the nation's police was allegedly growing, NRA's Clubs and Associations Department reported no decline in membership among affiliated law enforcement agencies or law enforcement clubs. Additionally, NRA's Law Enforcement Activities Division continued to conduct police firearms training schools at a record pace, consistently certifying more instructors than any other agency in the country.

A publication intended specifically for the law enforcement community, titled *The Badge*, made its debut in 1989 with distribution to 150,000 officers, and thousands of requests for copies poured into NRA. A separate Law Enforcement Relations Division was also formed, giving due recognition to preserving the long-standing linkage between NRA and the nation's law officers. Other highlights of NRA's relationship with law enforcement include the following:

- NRA helped pass the landmark Law Enforcement Officers Death Benefit Bill,

which was signed into law by President Ronald Reagan.

- Annually, NRA selects a Law Enforcement Officer of the Year and honors him or her with a cash award and recognition at its Annual Meetings.

- Thousands of law enforcement officers and security personnel hone their shooting skills in NRA-sanctioned police tournaments, including the National Police Shooting Championships, held annually since 1962.

- NRA kept the cost of its law enforcement training schools to roughly half what private, commercial groups charged.

- NRA instituted a $25,000 insurance program for families of NRA-member officers killed in the line of duty.

- NRA's Jeanne E. Bray Memorial Scholarship Fund provided scholarships to the children of NRA-member law enforcement officers who are killed in the line of duty.

enforceable definition that would not penalize millions of law-abiding gun owners. The International Association of Chiefs of Police also weighed in, calling for further study on the issue "to avoid potentially damaging legislative overreactions."

Caught in the crossfire, NRA's opposition to the Biaggi Bill was singled out as if it stood alone. So shrill was the media assault on NRA that its precisely crafted legislative definition—working with Reagan administration officials and police groups— never saw the light of day and received no mention outside its own publications.

That all changed in 1984 with the introduction of a bipartisan measure, sponsored by Senator Strom Thurmond of South Carolina and Texas Representative Jack Brooks, that provided what its sponsors hailed as an "eminently fair balance" between the legitimate interests of the nation's gun owners and the need to protect America's police officers.

Endorsed by NRA and every major law enforcement organization, the Thurmond-Brooks legislation swiftly moved through the U.S. Senate only to meet a roadblock in the House. The House Subcommittee on Crime was chaired by anti-gun Representative William Hughes, who denounced the Reagan administration for introducing the bill without consulting him and moved to approve a more restrictive measure. The legislative wrangling would persist until August 1986, when a bipartisan federal bill that clearly and narrowly defined "armor-piercing" ammunition was passed, finally putting the media-inflamed issue to rest.

After stoking the national brouhaha, Representative Biaggi was forced to admit, "Significantly, our final legislative product was not some watered-down version of what we set out to do. In the end, there was no compromise on the part of police safety."

No less controversial, the media, after the introduction of the Austrian-made Glock 17, fabricated the notion of an "all plastic gun" capable of evading airport security detection systems. Amid heightened national concern over terrorism, in 1986 columnist Jack Anderson had Libyan leader Muammar Kaddafi's hit men, in imminent danger to America, toting all-plastic guns.

Mario Biaggi was among the first to seize the issue, assailing the Glock 17 as a unique security

A forceful advocate for the rights of America's firearms owners, NRA-ILA Executive Director James Jay Baker testified on Capitol Hill on numerous occasions, drawing on his experiences as an attorney and prosecutor.

threat when in fact the Glock was readily detectable; the "all-plastic gun" contained 19 ounces of steel. In response to a Biaggi inquiry, Astrophysics Research Corporation stated, "Fully assembled, the Glock 17 looks exactly like any other automatic pistol when viewed on the television monitor of our Linescan airport X-ray security machine." Notably, Astrophysics Research was the world's largest manufacturer of X-ray security equipment, and its units were used at more than 90 percent of U.S. airports. Without letting those readily available facts get in the way, the anti-gun lobby leapt into action.

Ohio Senator Howard Metzenbaum introduced a bill to "prohibit the manufacture, importation, sale or possession of firearms not detectable by metal detection and X-ray systems commonly used at airports in the United States." The bill would empower three separate federal agencies—BATF, the Federal Aviation Administration, and the Food and Drug Administration—to ban firearms simply by changing standards of detectability. The openended phrase "readily detectable" could be expanded to eliminate the private ownership of commonly owned pistols and revolvers.

In opposing the gun ban bill, NRA was castigated as an impediment to airport security. In fact, the organization exposed the truth by calling for improved training of screening personnel and systems. At hearings on Capitol Hill, ILA's James Jay Baker forcefully made the case that security procedures, not firearms, were at issue, as the security work was contracted out to private firms on a low-bid basis rather than to the most qualified. He noted that the government's own tests proved that any pistol or revolver currently made could pass undetected through security systems that were improperly manned and operated.

That unvarnished truth, those early warnings about life-threatening voids in airport security, fell on deaf ears. Such practical solutions to what should have been readily apparent did not square with the avowed goal of ban-the-gun politicians.

Ultimately, the issue over non-existent "plastic guns" was resolved under a Reagan administration initiative that achieved bipartisan support in Congress. That legislation required all firearms in existence to contain enough metal to be detectable by equipment found in airports. It did not ban one existing firearm and did not allow any discretion in its enforcement by government agencies. In a clear victory for the nation's firearms owners, only non-metal firearms—yet to be developed—were targeted, leaving the rights of American citizens intact.

Action Moved to the States

At the same time, unprecedented numbers of pro-gun, pro-hunting bills were being introduced in state legislatures. They focused principally on

During the height of the "plastic gun" uproar, *American Rifleman* Technical Editor Pete Dickey (right) interviewed Gaston Glock, inventor of the Glock pistol. Dickey's May 1986 *Rifleman* feature article, one of the more than 150 he wrote as Technical Editor, exploded the "plastic gun" myth.

state firearms preemption, the right to carry firearms for self-protection, and range protection laws, among other initiatives. Florida became a key battleground state, where flagship initiatives were passed through the perseverance and masterful strategy devised by Marion P. Hammer, head of Unified Sportsmen of Florida (USF), who worked with ILA and every major law enforcement organization in the state. The media-fanned myth of NRA's "rift with police" was shattered under the statewide coalition forged to make "right to carry" and preemption laws a reality.

"We demonstrated, once again, the ability of NRA and USF to work together with law enforcement—our natural allies—to achieve a common goal," Hammer said. "I believe the alleged 'rift' between NRA and law enforcement is primarily a figment and has been manufactured and contrived by the media, hostile to gun ownership and indeed the Second Amendment." These achievements in Florida cast Hammer into the national spotlight as an NRA board member.

Advertising Wars

Immediately following his elevation to Executive Vice President, J. Warren Cassidy appointed Wayne R. LaPierre to head the Institute for Legislative Action, and James Jay Baker was selected to direct its Governmental Affairs Division.

Cassidy proved all too prophetic when he warned, even while savoring passage of the McClure-Volkmer Act, of the "backlash that is sure to come from the anti-gun organizations and the media." Driving a wedge between law enforcement and NRA had long been a strategic goal of the anti-gun lobby. It stretched back to the California Proposition 15 debate in which law enforcement support was critical to the massive pro-gun victory.

In what Cassidy characterized as the "Advertising War," Handgun Control, Inc., turned up the media heat. HCI distributed to newspapers around the country ready-made editorials, embellished with headlines like "NRA undermines police safety" or "NRA and cop-killer legislation." In case readers missed the point with the HCI-planted editorials, advertising space was purchased and carried similar messages featuring Sarah Brady, wife of former White House Press Secretary James Brady who had been felled from an assassin's bullet intended for President Ronald Reagan in 1981.

In the media spotlight, Sarah Brady blatantly used her husband's tragedy to tout a national waiting period and gun registration scheme, a proposal defeated during debate over the McClure-Volkmer Act and rejected by a majority of states. Though portrayed as a suburban housewife, Brady had become a hired HCI lobbyist.

Leaving no attack unchallenged, NRA countered with its own campaign in a bold nationwide ad series that carried the message, "DEFEND YOUR RIGHT TO DEFEND YOURSELF." NRA

Medal of Honor winner, Marine Corps fighter ace, two-term Governor of South Dakota, first Commissioner of the American Football League, and host of two weekly television series, Brigadier General Joe Foss became NRA President in 1988. He was elected an Honorary Life Member in 2000.

critics predictably howled at the campaign, but, as LaPierre noted, mainstream America had a different reaction. "The ads were frank, yet they had a gut-level appeal to millions of Americans who face the reality of crime every day—a vast, frightened, and angered America that's not ready to hand over its individual freedoms," he said.

In an open display of hostility to the organization, two broadcast outlets in the Washington, D.C., area flatly refused to air a series of NRA-produced commercials on the "gun control" issue. With no explanation, the CBS television affiliate rejected paid advertising that featured NRA's President-elect, Brigadier General Joe Foss. The NBC television affiliate also barred the ads, saying it did not air "controversial advertising." NRA's messages were designed to set the record straight on ammunition bans, "plastic guns," the nation's law enforcement community, and America's unique constitutional rights.

NRA saw the rejections as a clear denial of its right to free speech as guaranteed under the First Amendment. To General Foss, the rejection amounted to nothing short of a personal affront.

Retired Detroit PD Inspector and six-time National Pistol Champion Harry Reeves (left) and Medal of Honor winner Joe Foss, who became NRA President in 1988, admire targets shot by Elizabeth A. Callahan of the Washington, D.C., PD, at the National Police Shooting Championships.

A TRIBUTE TO NRA PRESIDENT JOE FOSS

JOE FOSS WAS ONE OF AMERICA'S GREATest heroes of World War II. As a Marine fighter pilot in the "Cactus Air Force" on Guadalcanal, Foss earned the Medal of Honor for his leadership and bravery and for downing 26 Japanese aircraft. Foss later became the Governor of South Dakota, a Brigadier General in the South Dakota Air National Guard, and Commissioner of the American Football League. He also hosted "The American Sportsman" television series. Foss, who served as NRA President from 1988 to 1989, was a dedicated champion of the right to keep and bear arms, a shooter, and a hunter.

In 1989, Colt honored Foss's military and civilian accomplishments with an engraved commemorative M1911A1 "Joe Foss Limited Edition" pistol.

Photo courtesy the National Firearms Museum

Fierce Second Amendment supporter U.S. Senator Phil Gramm of Texas (second from right) joined Charlton Heston, NRA President James E. Reinke, and ILA Executive Director Wayne R. LaPierre at the first Charlton Heston Celebrity Shoot in 1987.

Foss had gained national fame as a World War II fighter ace responsible for downing 26 enemy planes and had received the nation's highest military decoration, the Medal of Honor.

In an ad designed as a direct response to HCI's vicious attack on NRA as an "extremist" organization, General Foss had this to say: "I read where some say the NRA is 'extremist.' Well, let me ask you. Is it extremist to spend tens of millions of dollars promoting gun safety and wildlife management? Or to sponsor Olympic shooting teams? Is it extremist to support laws that protect and benefit crime-fighting legislation? Is it extremist to believe in every American's right to choose whether to own a firearm? And his right to defend his home and family? That's not extremist. Nor are the millions of NRA members. They're like you and me. Extremely American."

If any question ever existed, the rejection of NRA's ads by the big-city media elite further imprinted the belief that firearms owners could depend only upon themselves to convey the truth where it counted: in Congress, state legislatures, city councils, local clubs, and indeed, in their own neighborhoods.

Making Safety Matter

Concerted youth education efforts featured a primer on the Second Amendment for elementary school children, an outreach to educators willing to delve into constitutional issues in the classroom, publication of a *Guidebook for Gun Safety and Shooting Education in Schools,* and myriad other educational activities. As the bicentennial of the Bill of Rights drew near, NRA also undertook sponsorship of a national essay contest for students in grades 1–12 on the topic of "The Second Amendment to the Constitution: Its Meaning, Past, Present and Future."

The Eddie Eagle GunSafe® Program, introduced into school systems to teach firearms safety messages to young children, garnered national attention and accolades. There had been previous safety messages aimed at young children, but Eddie Eagle captured the moment as the character captivated kids. Its basic concept was to teach children, when they saw or found a firearm, to **"Stop! Don't touch. Leave the area. Tell an adult!"** Created by NRA Director Marion P. Hammer in response to a rash of accidents in Florida, NRA worked with child psychologists and elementary education specialists to produce student workbooks and an animated video that teachers and police departments could use, free of charge, while teaching gun accident prevention.

NRA actively sought feedback for Eddie Eagle from the teachers and law enforcement officers who taught the program. One teacher from Jamaica, New York, wrote: "Very good. I am appreciative you have provided this valuable service to our youngsters." Another, from Pasadena, Texas, commented, "I have been looking for this type of material for two years. I only found it through a friend who has guns. This is an important topic."

The program became so popular that, in 1989, 850,000 youngsters put their crayons to the Eddie Eagle coloring book. Another positive response came in a write-up in *Association Management* magazine, which praised NRA for being among the national associations educating the public about safety issues.

Programs for Women

The *Personal Protection Program Handbook* was inaugurated, providing instruction in handgun use for self-defense, with women as its key intended audience. Jeanne Bray, a five-time winner of the National Women's Police Combat Pistol Championship and a member of NRA's Board of Directors, was a pioneer in this field.

With the creation of the Office of Women's Issues and Information in 1990, NRA signaled its intent to take its many programs directly to women and "to network with women's organizations to expand the scope of NRA activities." The Office of Women's Issues found itself in the spotlight almost immediately, appearing at the 1990 annual meeting of the League of Women Voters to argue against "Gun Control Concurrence," which proposed banning lawful access to many firearms and limiting access to others.

Junior Programs

The ranks of junior members reached a historic high, topping the 50,000 mark in 1985. That same year, *InSights* magazine was expanded in format and changed from a bimonthly to a monthly publication. A youth advisory board for the publication was established to provide reader feedback on the type of coverage youthful readers wanted. In 1988, the publication launched a wildlife art contest. In testament to its impact, one of the early winners, Ohio's Adam Grimm, went on to become the youngest artist to win the federal duck stamp competition.

By this juncture, NRA was also offering a wide range of shooting sports opportunities for youth. Among these was a newly established program called the NRA North American Hunter Education

Championships. Later known as the International Youth Hunter Education Challenge, the program was designed as a contest to advance specific hunting skills such as orienteering, wildlife identification, and rifle, shotgun, and archery marksmanship. Thousands of volunteer parents and hunter education instructors conduct this program at state and local levels, graduating safer, more responsible, and more skillful American hunters. Other activities included the NRA Junior Olympic Shooting Championship, continued close coordination with 4-H club shooting programs, and work with the Boy Scouts of America to develop requirements for expanded merit badge opportunities in the shooting sports.

Out in the Field and on the Range

In keeping with its fundamental goal of providing gun safety and marksmanship training to civilians, NRA taught a record number of students in 1984. A total of 908,460 men and women went through NRA courses in basic pistol, rifle, shotgun, home firearms responsibility, and voluntary practical firearms. The training was accomplished by 21,000 NRA-certified firearms instructors.

Recognizing the need to perform more efficiently in the oversight of close to 12,000 sanctioned tournaments annually, the Competitions Division was reorganized in 1986.

Colonel M. S. "Gil" Gilchrist, a West Point graduate and 26-year Army veteran, began working at NRA as Assistant Manager of Youth Programs and later became Director of the Competitions Division,

One thing never changes concerning the NRA Annual Meeting and Exhibits; shooting air pistols and air rifles at the hall's air gun range is a favorite with many youngsters, who are provided with the proper safety gear and expert instruction.

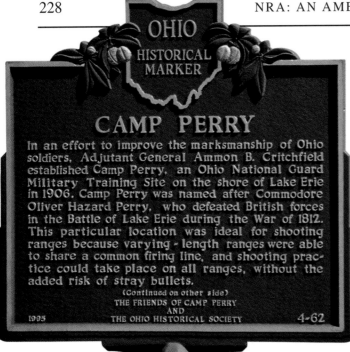

OHIO HISTORICAL MARKER

CAMP PERRY

In an effort to improve the marksmanship of Ohio soldiers, Adjutant General Ammon B. Critchfield established Camp Perry, an Ohio National Guard Military Training Site on the shore of Lake Erie in 1906. Camp Perry was named after Commodore Oliver Hazard Perry, who defeated British forces in the Battle of Lake Erie during the War of 1812. This particular location was ideal for shooting ranges because varying - length ranges were able to share a common firing line, and shooting practice could take place on all ranges, without the added risk of stray bullets.

(Continued on other side)
THE FRIENDS OF CAMP PERRY
AND
THE OHIO HISTORICAL SOCIETY

1995   4-62

managing 52 core programs all revolving around tournaments. He remembered his first look at the junior competition at the 1985 National Matches. "Before I retired from the Army, my last assignment was Director of Civilian Marksmanship, and the maturity level I saw among the youth on the firing line at Camp Perry astounded me. It was like a rite of passage into a lifetime sport," Gilchrist said. The division promotes amateur shooting activities at local, state, regional, national, and international levels. Conducting 27 national championships a year, Gilchrist termed Camp Perry "the grandaddy of them all." It drew more than 4,000 competitors each year.

American Marksman was revived to announce upcoming events in competitive shooting, previously covered through *Tournament News* and *American Rifleman.* NRA also began publishing *Shooting Sports USA* and continued, through the International Shooter Development Fund, to help the national shooting team. In 1987, the U.S. Shooting Team Division was formed to help with training on the NRA Range at the U.S. Olympic Training Center in Colorado Springs.

The following year, the Field Services Division became an independent division reporting directly to the Executive Vice President. As part of this change, the Range Development Department was renamed Range Assistance and came under the Field Services umbrella. In an effort to recruit new members, the

Hunter Services Division made its first venture into metropolitan hunting shows in 1988. In 1990, NRA joined the United Conservation Alliance as a major player, hearkening back to its traditional interest in issues important to hunters.

Year after year, tens of thousands of copies of *The Hunter's Guide* were distributed, with 1989 being a truly banner year for the publication: more than 250,000 copies were sold or distributed in conjunction with membership promotions and educational programs. The ongoing book publication program saw the appearance of new titles, including several in the *NRA Hunter Skills Series* (on turkey, deer, waterfowl, and western big game hunting), along with the revision of older, popular favorites. A new approach to members involved a series of hunting videotapes, which members could purchase. Other membership benefits included launching a credit card program and a Sportsman's Premium Package, which offered bargain coupons to shooting sports suppliers.

Doug Koenig of Alburtis, Pennsylvania, is a three-time winner of the Bianchi Cup, which became formally known as the NRA National Action Shooting Championships in 1985.

By 1986, the NRA Whittington Center featured eight functioning ranges with more under construction. It offered a wide range of opportunities for NRA members, including training and competition, game management, and hunting.

Inset: NRA held Range Development Conferences around the country in 1987, and those who attended received the 250-page *NRA Range Manual* covering all aspects of range design, construction, and maintenance.

The NRA Whittington Center in Raton, New Mexico, which had its official dedication and ground-breaking ceremonies on June 26, 1978, provided an ideal meeting place for special events. Adventure camps utilized not only the center's housing units and dining facilities but offered exposure to various aspects of the outdoor experience, including hunting and recreational and competitive shooting. With its 33,000 acres and ranges for everything from trap and skeet to high power rifle, the center was designed for all shooting interests.

On these and many other fronts, "in spite of all the lies and negative headlines that characterized the treatment of NRA by our opposition over the past year," said NRA President Richard D. Riley, NRA programs continued to grow and flourish as the organization prepared to begin a new decade.

NRA's roots in competitive marksmanship run deep and have spread in many directions since the Association's founding in 1871.

CHAPTER TWENTY

ANOTHER THRESHOLD

1990–1995

The right to keep and bear arms is not a privilege given to us by the Constitution. It is a birthright, confirmed for us by the Constitution. . . . Freedom is only ours to enjoy, to protect, and to pass intact to those who follow. And to do that, we've got to be brave. We've got to be visionary. We've got to be strong. We've got to be inflexible. We've got to be uncompromising. In other words, we've got to be leaders.

—Wayne R. LaPierre, 1994

AS AMERICA MOVED INTO THE final decade of the 20th century, the nation's media elite, in an intensity that echoed the late 1960s, hammered the National Rifle Association for its refusal to concede ground on the Second Amendment.

Media slurs such as "Public Enemy Number Two" (behind the Mafia) and "The Evil Empire" were hurled at the organization and its members in an effort to demonize, isolate, and demoralize the nation's firearms owners and break their will to fight gun bans, ammunition bans, gun rationing, and a national gun registration scheme—all of which were pending before the U.S. Congress.

It was a time when *NBC News* President Michael Gartner boldly proclaimed in *USA Today,* "There is no reason for anyone in this country, anyone except a police officer or a military person, to buy, to own, to have, to use, a handgun. . . . The only way to control handgun use in this country is to prohibit the guns. And the only way to do that is to change the Constitution."

NRA member Charlton Heston went to the heart of the matter in his address to the membership at the 1989 Annual Meeting in St. Louis, Missouri. Having grown up in rural northern Michigan during the Depression, Heston spoke of the pride he felt when he was old enough to put venison on the table and of his later years in Chicago, Illinois, as a member of his high school rifle team. In those simpler times, Heston remembered, Americans didn't really need NRA. But "NOW WE DO," he thundered, as the drumbeat to enact national gun ban legislation grew louder and more strident.

The seven-time President of the Screen Actors Guild and acclaimed civil rights champion emphasized the importance of firearms rights to a free society. "It matters a lot, not just for us," he said. "It matters for the millions of Americans who've never owned a firearm, don't want to own one, and never will. . . . Every American, every single citizen, has a stake in the future of democracy. That's what's at issue here."

Heston's address came when "gun control" lobbyists and the nation's monolithic media had the upper hand, demanding a ban on semi-automatic firearms in reaction to the cold-blooded murders of five children in a Stockton, California, schoolyard.

Heston spoke on the theme of "Eternal Vigilance" with the stirring eloquence NRA members would come to treasure during his years as NRA's

---

With Wayne LaPierre at NRA's helm, the organization devoted more resources to programs that appealed to hunters. These programs included NRA SuperClinics, the first of which kicked off in 1991 at the Valley Forge Convention Center in Pennsylvania.

Right: In celebration of the Second Amendment's 200th birthday in 1991, NRA created an eye-catching poster featuring relevant quotes from the nation's Founding Fathers.

Below: Attorney and NRA Second Vice President Sandra S. Froman, a grassroots activist and staunch supporter of the Second Amendment, was instrumental in conducting a Second Amendment Symposium commemorating the bicentennial of the Bill of Rights and has been actively involved in NRA's Refuse to Be a Victim® program.

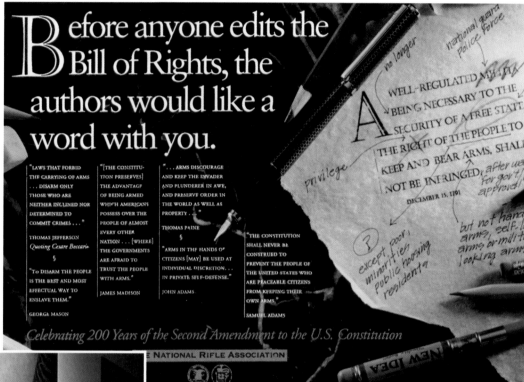

President. His remarks were a clarion call to action— an augury for the challenges the 1990s would hold in store.

In the face of media-driven hysteria over the ownership of semi-automatic firearms, Heston was quick to tell fellow NRA members, "Beside my bed, dictated by common sense and protected by the Second Amendment of the Bill of Rights, I keep a service .45 I brought back from World War II. . . . I do not plan to surrender it." His words were plain reference to provisions in proposals awaiting congressional action.

Although that year would mark the bicentennial anniversary of the Bill of Rights, the flood of anti-gun regulations and gun ban legislation, from the Bush administration down to state and local levels, found the organization battered simultaneously on multiple fronts. Even Sarah Brady's signature piece, a national waiting period for gun purchases, would take a back seat to the outcry against semi-automatic firearms, portrayed in the media as "machine guns" that were "preferred by criminals and drive-by shooters." Hearkening back to the 1968 Gun Control Act debates, anti-gun forces resurrected the "sporting purposes" test, as if sport was the only legitimate reason to own firearms.

The Educational Fund to End Handgun Violence would manipulate emotions to achieve its endgame, saying, "The weapon's menacing looks, coupled with the public's confusion over fully automatic machine guns versus semi-automatic assault weapons—anything that looks like a machine gun is assumed to be a machine gun— can only increase the chance of public support for restrictions on these weapons."

In defending gun ownership for all lawful purposes, Dr. Edward Ezell of the Smithsonian

Institution made clear before the Senate Sub-committee on the Constitution on May 5, 1989, that proposed bans on semi-automatic firearms were "ill-conceived."

Dr. Ezell produced data showing that "despite the current mythology, few, including drug dealers, seem to have much use for the cumbersome rifles for criminal acts." He cautioned the committee that action should not be taken out of a "personal dislike for firearms." Said Dr. Ezell, "It is not enough to have dislike for personal ownership of specific classes of firearms. It is not enough to believe that people should not own guns. Justification for additional federal legislation only can be found if there is, in Justice Oliver Wendell Holmes' words, 'a clear and present danger.'"

Facts were inevitably shoved aside in the media clamor surrounding the issue. NRA Executive Vice President J. Warren Cassidy noted that *Time* mag-

azine "even told readers who criticized its biased reporting that the issue was too important for attempts at fair and objective reporting."

Before Congress, NRA repeatedly pointed to the heinous Stockton murders as the grisly symbol of a failed criminal justice system. The perpetrator's numerous felony arrests had been plea-bargained down to misdemeanors: seven times arrested and seven times freed, despite a final probation report that noted he posed a danger to himself and others.

Concluding that the killer should have been roaming a jail yard, not a schoolyard, ILA's Federal Affairs Director James Jay Baker repeatedly warned, "The predators in our society are free to rape and murder, not because our laws are too weak, but because nobody is strong enough to enforce them."

Before the Senate Judiciary Committee's Subcommittee on the Constitution, Baker testified that "the attack on semi-automatic firearms is no less an attack on an entire class of firearms that has been owned by millions of law-abiding Americans throughout this century. In a sense, the NRA's historic position on gun control, at times characterized as paranoid by our opponents,

---

Despite what anti-gun politicians claim, the semi-automatics they would ban aren't on the streets in the hands of criminals, but in collectors' gun cabinets, in game fields, and on the firing line of ranges such as Camp Perry.

NATIONAL RIFLE ASSOCIATION'S CRIME-FIGHTING PROPOSAL

delivered by James Jay Baker, NRA-ILA Federal Affairs Director, February 10, 1989

TODAY WE ARE HEARING THE SAME tired proposals that sportsmen and gun owners have been hearing since the early 1900s. In the face of violent crime currently linked to massive drug smuggling and its financial profits, elected representatives in Congress and state legislatures call for making felons out of law-abiding citizens who insist on their right to own firearms. At the same time, the criminal justice system is apparently unable or unwilling to prosecute and jail the real felons. The NRA asks Congress to explore and consider every possible means of restricting criminals and improving the criminal justice system before legislating any restrictions that will only impact the law-abiding citizen and that may well aid the criminal.

Law-abiding Americans believe that criminals who violate existing laws should suffer the penalties. But the fact is, violators are not suffering those penalties. Criminal justice failures were widely reported earlier this week. *USA Today* called it "Getting Off Easy." That's an accurate phrase when the average drug trafficker received a sentence of only six years—and then actually served less than two years. The *Wall Street Journal* reported that fewer than half the people convicted of felonies nationwide went to prison. And that doesn't begin to address the real issue, since an indeterminable number of people charged with penalties plea bargain down to obtain only a misdemeanor conviction.

Therefore, we propose a series of crime-fighting initiatives. We pledge to Congress that we will *support* these initiatives with the same vigor with which we *oppose* restrictive firearms laws. These proposals can be supported by sportsmen, law enforcement, and any gun control advocates who really care about fighting crime.

1st: We propose the assignment of at least one assistant U.S. attorney in each district to prosecute felon-in-possession-of-a-firearms cases under 18 U.S.C. 922(g). Increased funding for U.S. attorneys was a feature of the omnibus Anti-Drug Abuse Act, and we support that funding.

2nd: We propose a five-year freeze on plea bargain agreements when individuals are charged with violent- or drug-trafficking crimes. The Purdy crime [the Stockton murders] alone demonstrates the result of a plea-bargain policy that has become all too common in the face of overcrowded court dockets and prison systems.

has been vindicated. Advocates of gun control have finally admitted that they are not interested in protecting the rights of law-abiding gun owners—they are merely interested in eliminating any type of firearm whenever presented with an emotionally charged opportunity to do so. What was once an attack on handguns is this year an attack on rifles and shotguns."

NRA had already suffered a serious setback in 1989 when the Bush administration capitulated on the issue and imposed an import freeze on 42 foreign-made semi-automatic firearms.

In voicing the organization's reaction, ILA's Executive Director Wayne LaPierre was incredulous: "Does the Bush administration seriously believe that drug dealers smuggling cocaine by the planeload won't find room for black market guns?" He termed it "sad" that an American President would "break a campaign pledge in the face of short-term political hysteria." For America's gun owners, that act

3rd: We call for increased enforcement of the provisions of the Firearms Owners Protection Act, Public Law 99-308. As you know, the law made it a federal felony, to be punished with mandatory penalties, to use a firearm while committing a drug-trafficking offense. Last year, Congress increased those penalties in the omnibus "Anti-Drug Abuse Act." Any reluctance by the government to prosecute federal gun-law violators who have been arrested and charged with local offenses, but who are also violating federal laws against possession by felons, particularly of Title II weapons such as sawed-off shotguns or unregistered machine guns, must be addressed.

If the Justice Department finds that firearms were acquired from out-of-state in an investigation of gun-running rings, the federal government should step in. This would assist local government in a number of ways. First, it would make real the largely rhetorical federal assistance described in the "State Firearms Control Assistance Act, which was the first title of the 1968 Gun Control Act." Second, it would mean tougher jail sentences than may occur with local prosecution. And third, it would help with the problem of expensive and overcrowded state prisons by diverting the most serious of drug-trafficking offenders to the federal system.

4th: We support those measures aimed at increasing the nation's prison space. Initially, the federal government should look to those military bases scheduled for closure. With minimal expense, these bases could be converted to prisons for use by the federal government or by the states in which they are located. As a second step, the NRA is prepared to support reasonable funding mechanisms earmarked solely for the construction of Level III prison facilities to house the most violent criminal offenders.

5th: We support the establishment of a special, expedited death penalty for those who kill police officers in the course of committing a felony or who kill police officers' family members in retribution for the performance of their duties.

6th: We look forward to working with members of Congress and the Administration to ensure that the mandate of the McCollum substitute to the so-called Brady Amendment is carried out: That the Attorney General report to Congress this fall with a program that will allow for the accurate and instantaneous screening of firearms purchasers at the point of purchase.

We are confident that broad support for these proposals can be garnered from most of the groups represented in this room today. We are also confident that reasonable individuals will agree that these proposals hold far greater promise for reducing the nation's appalling level of violent crime than does any ill-conceived and misdirected gun control proposal.

was a wake-up call—one that would live to haunt President Bush in the 1992 national elections.

Though "assault weapons" bans were defeated in 22 states, bans were enacted in California and in cities such as Cleveland, Dayton, and Boston that would be challenged in court for years to come.

More highly publicized shootings by killers in Jacksonville, Florida, and Louisville, Kentucky—again stark examples of justice system failures—were exploited by Handgun Control, Inc., to breathe

new life into its national waiting period proposal that had been derailed in Congress.

For its "no compromise" stand on gun ban bills, NRA was widely chided in the media as doomed to political failure. Even the *Wall Street Journal* picked up the theme with the headline, "Mighty Gun Lobby Loses Its Invincibility by Taking Hard Line."

Never "sunshine soldiers," NRA members were resolute in freedom's fight, though some openly feared that Warren Cassidy had not been hard-line enough.

On the outside, Neal Knox wrote critically about NRA operations and pointed to sharp friction between Cassidy and ILA's leadership team of LaPierre and Baker. There were other growing indications of dissatisfaction with Cassidy's leadership. Harlon Carter was quoted in the February 1991 issue of *Guns & Ammo* as having said to fellow NRA members, "The matter of leadership and direction is in your hands. If you don't like the way the NRA is going—then get after it."

In short order, those fears would resonate within the ranks of NRA's Board of Directors, a body already torn by internal dissent and alarmed by management missteps.

Though gravely ill, Carter returned to Washington from his Arizona home. Flanked by NRA President Richard D. Riley, an enterprising and influential state lawmaker from New Hampshire, Carter set about the business of restoring the organization's diminished clout.

Above: Maryann and Harlon Carter worked as a team during the formative days of NRA-ILA, and she served on many NRA committees. Mrs. Carter received a framed copy of *American Rifleman*'s obituary of the former NRA President, Executive Vice President, and Executive Director of NRA-ILA from his fellow Honorary Life Member James E. Reinke.

Left: Richard D. Riley started a gunsmithing business at age 23 and turned it into one of New England's largest shooting supply centers. A former New Hampshire State Senator, competitive shooter, hunter, and lobbyist, Riley was elected NRA President in 1990.

Carter felt the organization had become increasingly vulnerable and unfocused and that it was in danger of losing its credibility with mainstream America. The facts were plain: a referendum campaign to overturn a handgun ban in Maryland had been defeated, membership numbers had plummeted, deficit spending had jumped, a $10 million computer system had proved a bust, and key staff were at best alienated and at worst discredited by Cassidy. This was especially true for ILA's LaPierre and Baker, when ILA faced its most critical juncture in fighting simultaneously the Brady Bill and federal gun ban legislation.

Cassidy's removal had long been debated in back-room meetings of board leaders who, for external political reasons, had opted instead to curtail his authority as a means of regaining organizational control. But that temporary fix failed to stop the hemorrhaging of both financial and personnel issues. It was time for decisive action. Ultimately, Cassidy's time as Executive Vice President would end in 1991.

Jostling for the vacated post fell to a number of candidates from the Board of Directors, staff, and outside contenders, all to be judged by a Screening Committee prior to the organization's Annual Meetings that year in San Antonio, Texas. There, Harlon Carter once again took center stage, exhorting the membership to keep NRA unified, growing, and strong.

With major backing from pro–Second Amendment stalwarts on Capitol Hill, Wayne LaPierre was elected Executive Vice President by the board. After 13 years in NRA service, he brought to the table an undisputed, highly visible record of achievements. He had substantially increased ILA's effectiveness, resources, and national clout, especially in taking the debate to the American people through media campaigns and prime-time interviews on nationally televised broadcasts.

Following passage of the McClure-Volkmer Firearms Owners Protection Act—NRA's crowning achievement—LaPierre had been honored as *ABC News'* "Person of the Week." The honor was a tribute to LaPierre's success as a national spokesman, taking NRA's message across America and into the halls of Congress.

In his first "Standing Guard" column, which appeared in NRA's magazines, the new Executive Vice President pledged "every ounce of energy, talent, and experience at my disposal to maintain a powerful NRA presence nationwide to ensure the preservation and protection of our Second Amendment rights."

Outlining his vision for rebuilding the organization, LaPierre noted, "Critics in the media have

---

The Exhibit Hall has been the focal point of NRA Annual Meetings for many years. It is a place where NRA members can visit manufacturers' booths to view and discuss the latest models of firearms and related accessories and visit fascinating collector exhibits from across the country.

SYBIL LUDINGTON WOMEN'S FREEDOM AWARD

THE SYBIL LUDINGTON WOMEN'S Freedom Award was established in 1995 so that the National Rifle Association of America could express its profound appreciation and gratitude to the many women who have selflessly advanced the purposes and objectives of the Association. Recipients are presented with a bronze sculpture by Jane Tucker entitled "Freedom."

Sybil Ludington was a Revolutionary War heroine. On April 26, 1777, a wounded messenger barely reached the home of New York militia officer Henry Ludington with desperate news of a British attack on nearby Danbury, Connecticut. With no time to spare, Colonel Ludington enlisted the help of his 16-year-old daughter, Sybil. While her father organized the local militia, Sybil rode through the night on horseback to alert the troops in the surrounding countryside. By risking her life, Sybil made a profound difference in America's successful pursuit to become a free and independent nation. It is in this spirit of freedom that the National Rifle Association of America bestows its prestigious Sybil Ludington Women's Freedom Award to modern-day heroines.

Candidates for this award shall exemplify more than two of the following criteria:

- Be current National Rifle Association members in good standing
- Have demonstrated outstanding performance in competitive shooting, outstanding dedication to hunting ethics and conservation, or outstanding promotion of recreational shooting activities
- Have made outstanding educational contributions to advancing the purposes and goals of the National Rifle Association, including appearances for the purpose of public education and/or significant writings
- Have demonstrated meritorious performance under perilous conditions through the lawful use of a firearm in defense of self and/or others
- Have demonstrated dedication to the protection of the Second Amendment through extensive legislative and/or legal contributions
- Have demonstrated outstanding volunteerism through personal involvement with and promotion of NRA programs and issues with significant recognized impact.

Award Recipients

1995: Marion P. Hammer
1996: Alice Bull
1997: Representative Suzanna Gratia Hupp
1998: Tanya K. Metaksa
1999: Marianne Jensen Driver
2000: Sue King
2001: Susan Howard

referred to me as 'hard liner,' probably not realizing that I accept their words as a compliment. What they refer to as hard line is in fact my bottom line. I do not intend to waver from my belief that the rights of law-abiding American citizens must be protected, no matter the cost. This belief is set in stone, and it will serve as the foundation of every policy that originates from this office."

LaPierre called for conveying NRA's "message and programs to the American people with renewed energy and vision," and he reminded members that they had a "weapon our opponents are lacking. This weapon is the truth." Joining LaPierre in that rebuilding effort was James Jay Baker, whom LaPierre appointed ILA Executive Director. Baker subsequently

Above: Joe Foss officially welcomes outgoing NRA President Richard D. Riley to the informal association of former presidents by pinning on the "Old Goat" insignia. President Robert K. Corbin stands by to offer his congratulations.

Right: NRA launched CrimeStrike with a direct message to politicians: The way to save lives is by enforcing existing gun laws against violent armed criminals, not by imposing further restrictions on constitutional rights. The message in CrimeStrike ads was not lost on criminals either.

named Mary Marcotte Corrigan as Deputy Executive Director.

Influential voices within the gun owning community, including some who had become disenchanted with NRA, welcomed LaPierre and the tenor of his message. Representative of those voices was that of John Wooters, one of the country's best-known outdoor writers, an NRA Life Member, and a Director from 1979 to 1985, when he gave up his seat on the board. He did so because "the NRA power structure at the time didn't want to hear from the hunters among the membership." During the latter part of the 1980s until LaPierre's assumption of the executive vice presidency, Wooters, like countless other hunting members, asked the question, "What has NRA done for me lately?"

The answer, he concluded, was precious little, but he saw welcome changes almost immediately under LaPierre and Baker. "LaPierre and his staff have accomplished near miracles in six months,"

he wrote. "They're fashioning a genuinely new NRA, one that's dedicated to protecting hunters' rights as well as those of non-hunting gun owners." He found the changes to be "very, very encouraging," with "the negative trends of the last few years seeming to have been reversed." Wooters predicted, as did many others, that "the best is yet to come."

Positive Initiatives

Changes came at a fast and furious pace, especially in rebuilding NRA's membership, which LaPierre hailed as "our lifeblood and power plant." A special Membership Task Force was assembled, comprising experts in marketing, communications, and data processing, to tailor direct-mail messages to NRA members' special interests and to rally new

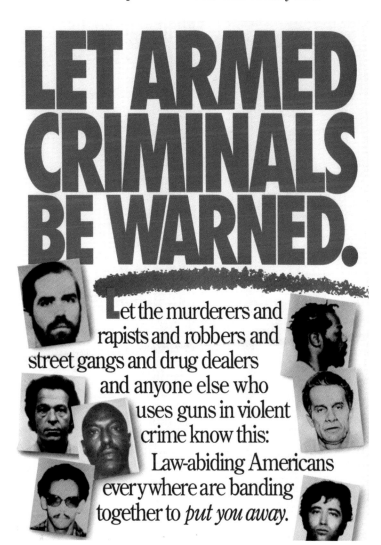

LET ARMED CRIMINALS BE WARNED.

Let the murderers and rapists and robbers and street gangs and drug dealers and anyone else who uses guns in violent crime know this: Law-abiding Americans everywhere are banding together to *put you away*.

members to the Second Amendment cause. With the advice and proven talent of Bradley S. O'Leary, President of PM Consulting Corporation, the team worked hand-in-hand with NRA staff to reverse a five-year spiral in membership recruitment and retention. The effort was a marked success. In the first nine months of 1992, a half million members were brought into NRA's ranks, and total membership surpassed the 3 million mark.

The first of NRA's SuperClinics for hunters was held at Valley Forge, Pennsylvania, in 1991, with four more scheduled for 1992. The SuperClinics paved the way for the NRA Whitetail Tour and SuperClinics, traveling seminars featuring nationally known authorities and the best hunting knowledge, equipment, and expertise available. These were expanded into the Great American Hunters Tour, the most ambitious effort yet undertaken in hunter outreach. In further outreach to hunters, LaPierre moved to have Hunter Services report directly to him.

NRA Targets Violent Criminals

Pinpointing violent armed criminals as the greatest threat to Second Amendment freedom, NRA launched CrimeStrike designed to put teeth back into the nation's collapsed criminal justice system. In declaring war against violent criminals, its message to lawmakers was direct: Enforcing penalty provisions of existing gun laws rather than imposing further restrictions on constitutional rights would save lives through dramatic reductions in violent crime. That issue would be a recurrent theme, begin-

Above: Some of the biggest whitetail deer ever taken are on display in NRA's Great American Whitetail Collection, established in 1993.

Below: Wayne LaPierre commanded press attention in June 1992, when he publicly battled media giant Time Warner—long known for its assaults on Second Amendment rights—over its marketing of rapper Ice-T's viciously anti-police album, "Body Count."

ning with the 1992 elections, for the remainder of the 1990s decade.

"NRA is one of the largest police organizations in America," observed Kayne B. Robinson, board member and former Assistant Chief of Police of Des Moines, Iowa. "If you surveyed hundreds of thousands of police officers all over the country, you'll see the real predominant view is that law-abiding citizens owning firearms are not the problem. Armed violent criminals are, and harsh gun laws only affect the law-obedient," he said.

CrimeStrike's "Three Strikes and You're Out" campaign caught fire across the nation. NRA worked closely with the Washington State Council of Police Officers to collect signatures for a referendum effort to gain passage of such an act in that state. After that success, many other states followed suit. CrimeStrike also supported bond issues to build more prisons in Texas and Mississippi, lobbied to triple state prison construction funds in federal legislation, and presented expert testimony on the value of keeping violent criminals imprisoned.

Even as CrimeStrike found a receptive audience nationwide, a detailed survey concluded that three of four American women would, at some time in their lives, be victimized by a criminal attack. With increased awareness of the need for personal protection, NRA Gun Safety and Refuse To Be A Victim® seminars grew immensely in popularity, providing hundreds of thousands of women with personal protection strategies and the facts they needed to make an informed decision on whether or not they wanted to own a firearm and to learn how to use one.

A traveling Sporting Clays team under the new Recreational Shooting, Training and Ranges Division introduced shotgunners across the country to the "hottest new shooting around" while the Charlton Heston Celebrity Shoot provided enjoyable competition for event participants in addition to raising funds.

Hosted by the Missouri Department of Conservation, the first National Shooting Range Symposium, which initiated ideas to help the growth and preservation of shooting ranges nationwide, was held in August 1990 in St. Louis, Missouri.

In 1991, for the third straight year, the Youth Hunter Education Challenge (YHEC) took place at the 33,000-acre NRA Whittington Center. A record 241 excited finalists competed in the year's national event. Young hunter education graduates from around the country and Canada could demonstrate their skills and knowledge in eight events—rifle, shotgun, archery, muzzle-loading, wildlife identification, orienteering, hunter safety trail, and hunter responsibility—all designed to teach how safety and responsibility are vital to America's hunting heritage.

Another hunting initiative was a series of Western Big Game Schools, conducted in game-rich states such as Wyoming, Montana, and New Mexico. These schools were staffed by some of the nation's top outdoor writers, including Jim Zumbo and Wayne Van Zwoll, plus professional guides and outfitters, industry representatives, and other hunting experts. Topics included everything from gun and gear selection to pre-hunt scouting, field dressing, and game care.

Assisting in a major outreach program for women called Becoming an Outdoors Woman, NRA staff instructed 100 women in rifle and shotgun

A CrimeStrike brochure discussed NRA's solution to violent crime in America—turning our "catch-and-release" system into an honest criminal justice system that protects citizens, young and old, from crime by sending violent criminals to prison and keeping them there longer.

shooting at a seminar hosted by the University of Wisconsin at Stevens Point. NRA would provide sponsorship and other forms of support to this program for years to come.

On the hunting front, NRA accelerated action to counter an organized campaign of "hunter harassment." Animal rights groups had been encouraging confrontation between the anti-hunter and the hunter in the field. Verbal abuse, physical contact, blocking access to public hunting areas, and destroying personal property were among the tactics employed by anti-hunters. NRA alerted

Right: NRA Political Victory Fund ads let sportsmen in Congressman Mike Synar's district know that he was the only member of the Oklahoma delegation casting anti-hunting votes. Synar was later defeated for re-election in a political upset that drew national attention.

Below: With its many firearms training programs, NRA is dedicated to ensuring that the next generation of Americans will learn the safe, proper, and responsible use of firearms, but it is up to individual gun owners to make sure that shooting sessions are both safe and enjoyable for their youngsters.

IF SYNAR WINS, HUNTERS LOSE.

Last month Mike Synar voted to ban hunting and scientific wildlife conservation in an important wildlife refuge. He was the only Oklahoma representative to vote that way.

Only Synar voted to eliminate what the Assistant Secretary for Fish and Wildlife and Parks called "the only means of controlling excess deer populations" – a move that could've caused "widespread die-offs among the deer population, either by disease or starvation."

Once again Mike Synar put his personal anti-hunter views above the views of Oklahoma. He voted against every other Oklahoma congressman. He voted against hunters. And he voted against you.

ON AUGUST 25TH, VOTE AGAINST MIKE SYNAR. AND MAKE SURE HE LOSES INSTEAD OF YOU.

Paid for by NRA-PVF and not authorized by any candidate or candidate's committee.

members on how to handle such encounters peacefully and responsibly, and ILA campaigned for the passage of laws prohibiting harassment of law-abiding hunters.

During this time period, the Whittington Center became the site of a truly rare opportunity for juniors—the 12-day Whittington Adventure Camps for youths ages 13–17. The camps exposed participants to probably the most comprehensive and diverse shooting experience to be found anywhere. Expert instructors taught gun safety and marksmanship lessons in pistol, rifle, shotgun, muzzleloading, and silhouette shooting. Hunter education instructors led a three-day, two-night simulated big game hunt in Whittington's remote backcountry.

Enlisted by Wayne LaPierre, television person-alities volunteered their time to appear in an innov-ative campaign to deliver the Eddie Eagle GunSafe® message into homes throughout America in com-mercials that aired during prime-time program-ming. Through this new creative approach, celebri-ties such as Susan Howard (*Dallas*), Khrystyn Haje (*Head of the Class*), and Michael Talbot (*Miami Vice*) carried the life-saving Eddie Eagle message to the airwaves, encouraging young children, if they found a firearm, to act responsibly and prevent tragic acci-dents. And an animated Eddie Eagle video, starring Jason Priestly of television's *90210* fame was pro-duced to bring the message of gun safety home.

Six years after the Eddie Eagle Program was initiated, its creator, then-NRA Second Vice President Marion P. Hammer, was awarded one of the National Safety Council's highest honors: first-place national citation for outstanding Community Service. The Eddie Eagle Program also received the American Legion's National Education Award.

To further aid in the defense of constitutional freedoms and underwrite NRA's safety and training programs, the Second Amendment Task Force and Golden Eagles special programs were chartered, inviting members to make an annual financial com-mitment to NRA's frontline fight.

Investing in the Future

A paramount example of Wayne LaPierre's vision came with the 1994 relocation of NRA headquarters from Washington, D.C., to a new facility in Fairfax, Virginia. High taxes, disdain for the organization

Right: NRA President Thomas L. Washington cuts the ribbon at the formal opening of the new NRA Range, May 4, 1995. Treasurer Wilson "Woody" Phillips (left) and Secretary Edward J. Land Jr. are among the onlookers.

Below: In 1994, NRA moved its headquarters from Washington, D.C., to a new complex in Fairfax, Virginia, and realized an immediate cost savings of almost $1 million a year.

IMPLEMENTED BY THE FIELD SERVICES Division in 1992 to benefit the NRA Foundation, the Friends of NRA program was designed to generate support for NRA's educational programs on national and local levels—programs such as youth safety, education, training, and range development.

Working with NRA field representatives, members and volunteers organize fundraising banquets in their communities, complete with auctions, raffles, and door prizes. The events provide a social forum for friends, neighbors, and business people to share their enthusiasm for hunting, the shooting sports, and gun safety education and training. Larry Potterfield, President of Midway Arms, Inc., who had initiated the NRA Round-up Program in 1992 to benefit NRA's legislative efforts, was instrumental in developing and launching the Friends program and held the very first banquet.

"Friends of NRA put a face on NRA locally," said Steve Miller, Managing Director of the Field Operations Division. "The program has really taken off. In 1993, we held 191 banquets, and we netted a little more than $800,000. By way of comparison, in 2001 we held 700 banquets and netted $8.7 million." Because of the Foundation's charitable status, donations are tax-deductible.

Allan D. Cors, President of the NRA Foundation in 2002, expected Friends of NRA to net nearly $10 million that year, which "will fund local and national educational programs that get more people involved in the shooting sports," he said.

Half of the profit raised by each Friends of NRA banquet must be spent in the state in which it was sponsored. The other half supports qualifying national-level programs such as the Eddie Eagle GunSafe® Program, women's programs, disabled shooting, constitutional education, range development, and law enforcement. State Fund Committees made up of volunteers review grant applications from local organizations and make funding recommendations to the NRA Foundation on how the monies might best be used in their areas. Through the end of 2001, the NRA Foundation had awarded over $40 million in grants to NRA and 3,500 other organizations across America, making it the country's leading charitable organization in support of NRA and the shooting sports.

Gun enthusiasts all over the nation attend Friends of NRA fundraising banquets for food, fellowship, and fun. Participants can win valuable prizes, and the event's proceeds go toward vital NRA programs.

In 1992, Brenda and Larry Potterfield began the Round-up Program. Their Midway USA customers could "round up" purchases to the next highest dollar with the change being donated to the NRA-ILA Endowment for the Protection of the Second Amendment. The donations pushed past the $2 million mark at the end of 1999, and the Potterfields, shown with son Russ and daughter Sara, received the Distinguished Service Award from NRA President Charlton Heston, Executive Vice President Wayne R. LaPierre, and ILA Executive Director James Jay Baker.

on the part of D.C. officials, outmoded communications systems, cramped operating quarters for staff, an inadequate instructional and testing range facility, among many other factors, contributed to the move. Though not one D.C. official encouraged NRA to stay, Virginia state and county officials assiduously courted the organization.

The move meant an immediate savings of more than $1 million a year. Further, the organization could tailor its 300,000-square-foot space for its special needs—including the construction of a state-of-the-art range and world-class National Firearms Museum—streamline the infrastructure, take advantage of new technology, and consolidate its entire staff under one roof. "The purchase proved to be a tremendous bargain," said Wilson "Woody" Phillips, who was elected Treasurer in 1992. "Investing in the

future meant creating the whole environment, keeping membership informed, creating programs, streamlining the infrastructure, and taking advantage of technology. NRA did all this and more."

Strong in the Face of Adversity

Though anti-gunners in Congress would be sent home empty-handed in legislative battles waged in the late 1980s and in the dawn of the 1990s, that would all change with the campaign and election of Arkansas Governor William Jefferson Clinton as U.S. President in 1992.

Congressional support had grown for an NRA-supported instant criminal records check for handgun purchases. The legislation was introduced by West Virginia Representative Harley O. Staggers as an alternative to the seven-day waiting period bill. The U.S. Justice Department under the Bush administration had also weighed in, testifying that the Brady Bill was "useless" in controlling crime and that any check that could be done in seven days could be done in seven minutes under the "instant check."

Before the Staggers Bill could grow legs, however, New York Representative Charles Schumer ridiculed it, calling it "a ruse . . . a sham . . . a fake." But the "instant check" system had become a reality; it was already in place and operating effectively in Virginia, Florida, and Delaware.

ENSURING THE FUTURE: THE NRA FOUNDATION

ANOTHER MOVE THAT WOULD PROVE TO be a milestone in NRA's history was the establishment of the NRA Foundation, a 501(c)(3) charitable affiliate of NRA. Established in 1990, the NRA Foundation offers charitable donors a channel to support NRA's many safety and educational programs through tax-deductible contributions.

John R. Woods Sr. from St. Louis, Missouri, served as the Foundation's first elected President and led its early operations. Woods and his family continue to lead the way as philanthropists to the Foundation and gave it some of its first contributions. Championing the development of the NRA Foundation Endowment, Woods said, "Investment in the NRA Foundation Endowment is seed money that will fuel exponential growth in the years ahead. From the modest beginning, we will achieve our ultimate purpose of guaranteeing that our treasured American firearms heritage will be financially secured generation after generation." Sandra S. Froman of Tucson, Arizona, and Allan D. Cors of McLean, Virginia, succeeded Woods as President.

Members and NRA supporters can contribute tax-deductible gifts including bequests, life insurance, securities, real estate, and a variety of charitable trusts, to support NRA programs. Through the NRA Foundation's endowments, contributions are invested, and a portion of the interest earned is used to fund NRA's educational programs. The remaining interest is reinvested to grow and to ensure a funding source for the future. Endowment monies can only be used for their designated purposes. Over time many endowments have been established, including those for disabled shooting services, firearms and marksmanship training, law enforcement training, the National Firearms Museum, hunting and wildlife conservation, women's programs, range facilities and programs, and youth education.

To recognize significant donors for their philanthropy, the Foundation offers opportunities for donors to permanently name an endowment. Many significant names in NRA history and the firearms and related manufacturing industry have named Foundation endowments, including the following:

Countering the Media's Brady Bill Bias

To counter the media's one-sided coverage of the Brady Bill, ILA commissioned Lawrence Research of Santa Ana, California, to conduct a national poll gauging public opinion on the dueling concepts. It found an overwhelming 92 percent support for Representative Staggers's alternative bill, which required an immediate background check, the upgrading of criminal records, and the establishment of an appeals process to rectify wrongful denials.

"Had the facts of this debate been exposed at the beginning, perhaps the waiting period myths that were shattered by the Lawrence Research survey would not have become so pervasive," said ILA chief lobbyist James Jay Baker.

Brady supporters celebrated victory on May 8, 1991, when the Brady Bill was passed in the U.S. House of Representatives by a vote of 239 to 186. From there the debate shifted to the Senate, where a complicated patchwork amendment to an omnibus crime bill was approved on a vote of 67 to 32 that would place gun owners under a national five-day waiting period. The proposal mandated the development of a national instant check system within five years and specified complicated milestones before the waiting period would "sunset."

As it happened, the crime bill never moved out of the U.S. Senate that year. The Brady Bill

Beretta Endowment
Blue Book Publications Acquisition Endowment
David P. Bookman Endowment
William S. Brophy Endowment
Brownell Family Endowment
Eldon L. & Hope T. Buckner
Alice H. Bull Endowment
Harlon B. & Maryann Carter Endowment
Allan D. Cors Endowment
Charles Elder Endowment
F. R. "Rudy" Etchen Endowment
F. E. "Bud" & Willa Jean Eyman Endowment
Reinhart Fajen Endowment
First Shot Endowment
Joe & Donna Foss Endowment
Sandra S. Froman Endowment
Hal and Jean Glassen Endowment
Melvin Gordon Endowment
Charlton Heston Endowments
Hodgdon Family Endowment
Hornady Family Endowment
Eric Johanson Endowment
Keystone Endowment
Theodore J. LeVake Endowment
Lockton Companies/AGIA Endowment
Merrill D. & Lillian Z. Martin Endowment
Joel & Lydia Morrow Endowment
Microsoft Gun Club Endowment
Bruce Nelson Endowment
Edward J. Neumann Endowments

New Mexico Gun Collectors Association Endowment
John W. O'Donnell Endowment
Ohio Gun Collectors Association Endowment
Harry & Florence Reeves Endowment
Laura Revitz Endowment
William L. & Collette N. Roberts Endowment
Theodore Roosevelt Endowment
Robert F. & Ruth H. Rubendunst Endowment
William B. Ruger Endowment
Stehsel Family Endowment
St. Louis Big Game Hunters Endowment
Thomas L. Washington Endowment
R. L. Wilson Educational Endowment
James R. & Dorothy M. Wood Endowment
John and Jeanne Wooters Endowment

By the end of 2001, the NRA Foundation's endowments would total almost $14 million. Commenting on the success of the endowment effort, Executive Director of General Operations Craig D. Sandler said, "One need only look at the consistently rising endowment dollars, raised by the NRA Foundation through its many innovative programs and strategies, to realize that the goal of endowing all eligible programs within General Operations will become a reality. Through endowment we have the opportunity to change the course of history."

was signed into law on November 30, 1993, by Bill Clinton. The span of the waiting period had changed, as had the bill's provisions and sponsors, but one fact did not change: the bill was a "first step."

An emboldened Ohio Representative Edward Feighan confirmed that the bill would only be a "first step," to be followed by restrictions on the ownership of semi-automatic firearms. Missouri Representative William Clay chimed in, saying the Brady Bill was "a minimum step. We need much stricter gun control, and eventually we should bar the ownership of handguns except in a few cases." Scrambling on board the bandwagon, Representative Schumer announced plans to introduce legis-

lation to rescind many of the reforms adopted in the McClure-Volkmer Firearms Owners Protection Act.

Anti-gun collaborators in the national media saw initial passage of the Brady Bill the same way. Here's how the *Baltimore Sun* put it: "The Brady Bill is only the beginning. . . . The only acceptable solution . . . is the kind of laws that apply in virtually every European country—laws that generally ban handguns altogether and place the most stringent limitations on rifles and shotguns used for hunting and target shooting."

With Bill Clinton in the White House, holding the line against the nation's first gun ban would become a virtual impossibility in 1993.

Clinton Embraces Anti-Gun Lobby

On the campaign trail, Clinton, who had unabashedly sought NRA's support in his gubernatorial races, had already distorted truth and reality when he promised to "take a serious look at whether we need these automatic and semi-automatic weapons that are becoming instruments of mass destruction in our cities." With that distortion and his public embrace of Sarah Brady and her organization's endorsement, Clinton was well on his way to becoming Handgun Control, Inc.'s poster boy. As President, Clinton would unleash Janet Reno's U.S. Justice Department and the political muscle of the FBI to bolster the gun ban movement.

In reaction to Clinton's power play, NRA produced a television commercial exposing the failures of the criminal justice system and offering proven solutions to violent crime. Three Washington, D.C., network affiliates refused to air it, all but admitting they disagreed with the message and its messenger. The CBS network affiliate wrote, "It is our right and privilege, for reasons unto ourselves, to reject the ads."

In calling that blackout "atrocious," NRA President Robert K. Corbin, a former Arizona Attorney General, issued grave concerns about the First Amendment's future: "The real issue isn't about firearms ownership, gun control, violent crime, NRA or even the Second Amendment. The

Below: Rather than selling firearms that the military no longer needs and add dollars to the U.S. Treasury, the Clinton administration wasted tax dollars to reduce these small parts of American history into scrap metal. NRA succeeded in convincing Congress to impose a moratorium on the destruction.

Inset: For eight years, Bill Clinton served as the anti-gun "poster boy" for Sarah Brady's Handgun Control, Inc. After the 1994 elections, Clinton begrudgingly admitted his gun control agenda "cost 20 members their seats in Congress. The NRA is the reason the Republicans control the House."

If you still need convincing reasons to guard your guns, here's a couple.

Bill Clinton, President of the United States.

Sarah Brady, Leader of Handgun Control, Inc.

Bill Clinton accepts HCI endorsement at an October 17, 1992, political rally in Romulus, Michigan.

Director under Neal Knox. And with the Knox slate of Directors in clear control of the board in the 1990s, Metaksa was promised a free hand in executing legislative strategies.

Another leadership change was in the making as three board members launched campaigns to replace Warren L. Cheek, who had announced his retirement after serving for 17 years as NRA Secretary. Emerging victorious in that three-way contest, Edward J. Land Jr. was elected NRA Secretary by the board at its Annual Meetings in Minneapolis. With extensive prior experience as Field Services Director and Director of the

Left: Former three-term Arizona State Attorney General Robert K. Corbin drafted and helped enact passage of the first hunter harassment bill in the nation. Today, all 50 states have similar laws protecting the right of hunters to pursue their sport. Corbin became NRA President in 1992.

Below: ILA Executive Director James Jay Baker, in addition to being one of the most respected lobbyists on Capitol Hill, is an accomplished hunter who cohosted the *American Hunter* television series with actor Jameson Parker of television's *Simon and Simon* fame.

issue is the free traffic of ideas—and the consequences of suppressing this dialogue—in a democratic society. When the media deny the American people the means to decide for themselves and instead decide for them, then 'freedom of the press' means nothing more than freedom from dissent."

In the fall of 1993, NRA lost the gun/magazine ban vote by a 51-49 vote in the U.S. Senate when California Senator Dianne Feinstein's amendment was attached to an omnibus crime bill.

A grueling fight was promised in the U.S. House, but it was a fight that would not see ILA's Jim Baker at the helm. At year's end, he had made clear a decision to step down and return to the private sector, though LaPierre would retain his services as consultant on legislative and political matters.

Tanya K. Metaksa, an NRA board member and 30-year veteran in legislative action, was appointed ILA Executive Director at the 1994 winter board meeting. In the late 1970s, she had served as ILA State and Local Affairs Director and Deputy

Membership Division, Land was eminently qualified to assume the formal duties of that office. Distinguished in both rifle and pistol as a Marine Corps marksman, he was equally at home with the membership while skilled on the intricacies of board process, policy, and procedure. With its 76 Directors and 38 committees that had oversight over all Association programs, Land observed, "You have a situation where you don't merely have a Board of Directors, you have the complexities of a legislature."

The 10th Cavalry was formed on September 21, 1866, at Fort Leavenworth, Kansas, and along with the 9th Cavalry, 24th and 25th Infantry, made up the first all-black regiments in the Regular U.S. Army. The men were known as "Buffalo Soldiers," and their courage on battlefields around the world earned 20 Congressional Medals of Honor. On July 28, 1992, a Buffalo Soldier Monument—championed by General Colin Powell and constructed with NRA support—was dedicated at Ft. Leavenworth. Wayne LaPierre joined General Powell at the dedication, along with future NRA directors Charlton Heston and filmmaker John Milius.

Off-Year Election Victories

On the electoral battlefront, NRA scored victories in the 1993 off-year gubernatorial elections in Virginia and New Jersey, where violent crime was a huge issue. Voters in Washington overwhelmingly passed that state's "Three Strikes and You're Out" grassroots initiative. In the blink of a political eye, that battle cry would become a centerpiece of Bill Clinton's State of the Union address just a few months later, though he had by no means jettisoned his gun ban agenda.

While momentum was on NRA's side in shifting the debate from guns to criminals and from bans to punishment, the federal gun ban push in Congress was another matter entirely. On May 5, 1994, by a razor-thin vote of 216 to 214, the U.S. House passed a far-reaching amendment pushed by Representative Charles Schumer that banned the importation, manufacture, and sale of scores of then-legal semi-automatic firearms and sent its version of the crime bill to a joint House-Senate Conference Committee.

Attached to the Clinton administration's so-called crime bill, the omnibus bill hit unexpected

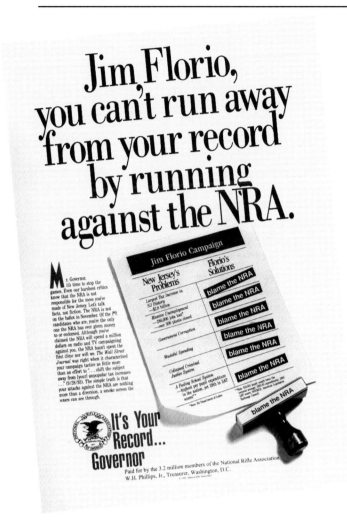

ning their Brady waiting period and recent bans on semi-automatic firearms and ammunition magazines, the anti-gun lobby is telling politicians that gun owners are no longer a threat. They claim you don't care enough about your rights to vote, so politicians shouldn't care about the Second Amendment. And if you don't prove them wrong November 8, if you do nothing, rest assured that's all you'll have left."

Left: When New Jersey Governor Jim Florio's unpopular tax increases got him in hot water with voters and threatened his re-election, his response was to attack NRA. NRA's response labeled Florio's attempted diversion "a smokescreen the voter can see through." Voters did.

Below: A prominent wildlife conservationist and skilled lobbyist, Thomas L. Washington served for many years as Executive Director of the Michigan United Conservation Clubs. Elected NRA President in 1994, he played a central role in NRA's acquisition of its state-of-the-art headquarters in Fairfax, Virginia.

roadblocks to its final passage as NRA-led firearms owners exerted intense pressure on their representatives to defeat the Conference Committee report. Though slowed down by procedural votes that reportedly left Clinton "sputtering with anger," the crime bill finally passed the House on August 21 and was signed into law on September 13, 1994.

Though Bill Clinton bullied a national gun ban on some semi-automatic firearms and a waiting period into law, his hold on Congress would be short-lived. As Wayne LaPierre foretold it, "You're going to see a revolution," as firearms owners vowed revenge at the ballot box on November 8, 1994.

NRA President Thomas L. Washington, an effective lobbyist who served as Executive Director of the Michigan United Conservation Clubs, termed the elections a clear turning point for Second Amendment freedom. In exhorting members to vote in record numbers, Washington warned, "After win-

Above: "We're building a new NRA with grassroots muscle, and we're starting with programs that will make everyone a part of the team," said Executive Vice President Wayne R. LaPierre, who presided over the largest membership expansion in NRA history.

Then-Texas Governor George W. Bush welcomes (from left) ILA State & Local Affairs Director Randy Kozuch, Senator Jerry Patterson, ILA Executive Director Tanya Metaksa, and Representative Ray Allen at a signing ceremony in Austin for Texas's Right-to-Carry Bill. Patterson and Allen sponsored the critical reform.

NRA leaders took to the airwaves as they criss-crossed America in support of NRA members' unprecedented efforts to elect pro–Second Amendment candidates at state and federal levels. Wayne LaPierre had already set the stage through a national tour promoting the Second Amendment through release of his compelling new book, *Guns, Crime, and Freedom,* which covered every point of contention in the debate. The book broke media barriers and reached the *New York Times* best-seller list.

NRA members were energized and on the march like never before. As an unpaid volunteer, Charlton Heston campaigned tirelessly for House and Senate candidates in more than a dozen states and appeared in hard-hitting television commercials to extend NRA's reach into the homes of the nation's firearms owners.

"Our duty is to our members, so we didn't get involved in races because the outcomes were certain," said ILA Executive Director Tanya K. Metaksa. "We fought some tough, uphill battles knowing that when people refuse to get involved because chances of winning are slim, that is not democracy in action, but democracy in decline. Our strength is local grassroots members—people of substance, talking about issues that matter. NRA

members were dedicated toward doing what they believed in their hearts to be in the best interests of law-abiding gun owners."

A Sea of Change in Congress

The result was a sea of change in Congress that witnessed the ousting of Washington Representative Tom Foley, the first U.S. Speaker of the House to be unseated in 138 years. Of 435 candidates elected to the House, 225 were A-rated by NRA, giving the organization the Clinton-proof Congress it had set out to assemble.

In the wake of NRA's massive election success across America, stunned anti-gun politicians and the media spoke out: "As candidates who backed gun control legislation fell one by one across the nation Tuesday night, the National Rifle Association re-emerged as a high-caliber force that politicians cross at their own peril," reported *The Hill,* a Washington, D.C., political publication. And the *Washington Post* reported, "After suffering big defeats in Congress this year on handgun control and a ban on certain assault weapons, the National Rifle Association made good on its promise not to get mad but to get even." President Clinton said it all when he blamed NRA for changing the face of Congress.

Ignited by the 1994 elections, ILA launched proactive campaigns on multiple fronts, including an aggressive effort to educate Americans about their Second Amendment rights. As part of that education plan, from April 2–5, 1995, ILA hosted the *Second Amendment: Right Under Fire?* conference in Washington, D.C. "We invited scholars, journalists, criminologists, doctors, lawyers, and civil rights activists on all sides of the issue to participate," said William F. Parkerson III, Director of ILA's Research and Information Division. "After spirited debate, at day's end, it was clear that honest historical and scholarly research proves con-

"You're going to see a revolution" was Wayne LaPierre's prediction for the 1994 elections, and he couldn't have been more accurate. Bill Clinton's anti-gun policies cost his party control of both houses of Congress, and Clinton begrudgingly gave credit where credit was due.

clusively that men such as Jefferson, Madison, and Mason revered the right to bear arms, and that they acted to secure that right for future generations. Those who attack the individual right interpretation of the Second Amendment today can not do so without first attempting to rewrite the history of this country."

With political clout that NRA members and the nation's firearms owners had not seen in years, NRA launched an aggressive campaign designed to educate Americans about the inalienable right to self-protection, to pass state preemption and range-protection laws, and to give honest Americans a fighting chance against violent criminals through criminal justice reform and the passage of right-to-carry legislation. That task would be formidable and daunting for the remainder of the 1990s.

History was made in a big way at the 1998 National Matches at Camp Perry. Nancy Tompkins-Gallagher (left) became the first woman to claim the High Power Rifle Championship, and Marine Sergeant Julia Watson became the first woman to win the National Trophy Individual Rifle Match. The NRA Long Range Championship was captured by Michelle Gallagher, 17, who took the title from her mom.

CHAPTER TWENTY-ONE
COMING OUT ON TOP
1996–2001

There's a cultural war being waged in America today, where the nation's influential elites are fighting to purge society, and obliterate from our culture, any trace of the right to keep and bear arms. You've heard of "ethnic cleansing"? This is "cultural cleansing"—and it's your First Freedom that's being washed down the drain.

—Wayne R. LaPierre, 1997

IN THE 1960s, AMERICAN gun owners were stunned and angered by the deluge of demands for harsh gun laws that surfaced amid enormous social turmoil. For a hundred years up until that time, NRA had predominantly been a shooting, hunting, and gun safety organization. But that had all changed. NRA members were forced to organize, lobby, and fight. And they were determined to win after suffering defeat with passage of the 1968 Gun Control Act.

In the mid-1980s, gun owners won back some lost freedoms with passage of the Firearms Owners Protection Act. Then, under the political anvil of President Bill Clinton, "holding the line" became NRA watchwords into the millennium.

Even as NRA members celebrated the organization's 125th Anniversary in 1996, the most anti-gun President in American history redoubled his efforts in declaring war against the nation's firearms owners, using every bureaucratic lever within his far-reaching grasp. The Bureau of Alcohol, Tobacco and Firearms systematically pushed thousands of federally licensed firearms dealers out of business. The Centers for Disease Control called gun violence a "disease" and prescribed gun control laws as a "cure." Through trade regulations, the White House banned imports of common, conventional firearms. Clinton even moved to establish a United Nations Task Force on global gun prohibition.

Under the strong will of Tanya K. Metaksa, the NRA Institute for Legislative Action more than held the line. ILA set down a marker when the U.S. House of Representatives voted to repeal the 1994 Clinton gun and magazine ban that spring. It was a bipartisan victory, but it was short-lived. The U.S. Senate failed to respond in kind. True relief meant there had to be a change in both the White House and in the Senate. And that meant NRA needed victory in the 1996 elections.

In the presidential election, Wayne LaPierre urged Clinton's defeat, calling on NRA members to remember, "Freedom is the most essential element in our nation's charter and character. . . . [U]nlike with other issues, with freedom there is no give-and-take. Freedom is fragile—and once lost, nearly impossible to regain, as European nations can well attest."

In the end, however, Clinton's 1996 reelection victory turned solely on employment and economic issues. Only the most optimistic could have foreseen ultimate triumph at decade's end for freedom's fight.

In 1996, more than 29,000 members gathered in Dallas, Texas, to celebrate NRA's 125 years of service to America.

After the 1996 elections, NRA struggled to regain its footing on multiple fronts. Following a dues increase, membership had declined predictably, and far too many gun owners believed that a Clinton-proof Congress—with pro–Second Amendment majorities in both the House and Senate—would halt Clinton's avowed goal of "eradicating the gun culture" in America.

Within NRA, internal wars waged by "armchair generals" who were new to NRA's Board of Directors threatened to tear the organization apart. All were recruited by First Vice President Neal Knox in his quest to pack the board with a voting block that would take his lead on any given issue. But for strategic missteps, the dissidents nearly succeeded in that power grab.

Marion P. Hammer Assumes Presidency

Wading into these turbulent waters, First Vice President Marion P. Hammer assumed the reins as NRA President earlier than expected after her predecessor, Thomas L. Washington, died while in office.

On assuming the presidency in late 1995, Hammer praised Tom Washington's legacy of accomplishments as a dedicated conservationist, originator of the Youth Hunter Education Challenge, and prime mover in acquiring NRA's new state-of-the-art headquarters.

Above: Launched in 1996, the Youth Education Summit (YES) gives qualifying high school students an expense-paid trip to the Washington, D.C., area, where NRA hosts a wide slate of activities for them. The youngsters attend Constitutional seminars, meet congressmen and other notables such as Oliver North, and tour the nation's capitol.

Left: Archery is one of the eight events conducted in NRA's Youth Hunter Education Challenge (YHEC) Program, which has involved more than 1 million youngsters since 1985.

With due respect to the fallen leader, Marion Hammer declined to give interviews immediately, though the media clamor was relentless. "My refusal started a better relationship, because we forced the media to have some respect and take a second look at both our principles and our programs," she said.

As head of Unified Sportsmen of Florida, Hammer was a tough, skillful, no-compromise lobbyist and was no stranger to "give and take" by the state's press corps. She was nevertheless stunned by the national media blitz on her election as NRA's first woman President.

"The exposure was intense," Hammer observed. "The media was very exercised because a woman was President of what they viewed as a man's organization, and they didn't quite know what to make of it. Profiles were written in a wide spectrum of the press. NRA's public affairs staff estimated that in the first four months of my presidency, the media coverage was valued at millions upon millions of dollars worth of paid advertising. Among the best articles was an interview that appeared in *George* magazine conducted by John F. Kennedy, Jr., himself."

Magazines such as *Harper's Bazaar, Ladies Home Journal,* and *Biography* also profiled her, as did national news broadcasts. The vast media coverage resulted in millions of Americans taking a fresh look at the organization.

Hammer saw the media flurry as "an opportunity to showcase the real NRA, who we really are— their friends and neighbors. It gave me an opportunity to cast a spotlight on our educational programs, the NRA Foundation, our constitutional rights, and the community services that are at our core."

Hammer had been a driving force in the creation of the award-winning Eddie Eagle GunSafe® Program, and her efforts as head of Unified Sportsmen of Florida led to passage of the nation's model "shall issue" Right-to-Carry reform law in 1987, which restored the right to self-protection in Florida and served as a blueprint for many other states.

As NRA President, Hammer turned her attention to building endowment funding for youth programs through the NRA Foundation and spearheaded the long-delayed construction of the National Firearms Museum. Its completion would stand as a tribute to her perseverance in tearing down obstacles put in its way for nearly a decade.

Internal War Wages Again

Hammer's toughest challenge would come in unifying NRA's Board of Directors as the dissident Knox faction tried repeatedly to wrestle management control from Wayne LaPierre and finally attempted a coup to oust him as top officer. The internal fight spilled into the streets and became a national spectacle, nearly self-destructing the organization.

An article in *American Spectator* on the organization's Annual Meeting in Seattle editorialized: "A bloody internal battle that threatens to destroy the powerful lobby will play out. . . . At stake is whether the NRA, the most feared special-interest lobby in America, remains an

Just one month after she assumed the presidency, Marion P. Hammer was interviewed at NRA headquarters by John F. Kennedy Jr. His article, "Granny Get Your Gun," appeared in the April/May 1996 issue of *George* magazine.

important force in American politics or consigns itself to the margins."

The commentary noted that "friends of the NRA on Capitol Hill such as Rep. Bob Barr, the Georgia Republican who serves on the House Judiciary Committee, worry that the political fallout from the current controversy, which is more ferocious and much more public than any prior battle, could be permanent. And if the NRA collapses, they fear, it will be time for gun-owners to bury their guns. 'Any time you have a vacuum at the top,' says Barr, 'the other side—the gun control movement and President Clinton—will try to step in and seize the moment.'"

LaPierre's popularity with the membership and their respect for his tough-fisted approach to legislative issues proved fatal to the Knox faction's takeover scheme. The membership validated its overwhelming support for LaPierre by giving him a resounding vote of confidence at the Annual Meetings.

That year proved a turning point.

CHARLTON HESTON ON AMERICA'S FIRST FREEDOM

ON SEPTEMBER 11, 1997, NRA FIRST Vice President Charlton Heston brought the battle for Second Amendment rights home to the American media—on their own turf. Appearing before a standing-room-only crowd at Washington, D.C.'s prestigious National Press Club, he challenged the journalists in attendance with a provocative speech on why the right to keep and bear arms is America's first freedom, the first among equals.

Today I want to talk to you about guns: why we have them, why the Bill of Rights guarantees that we can have them, and why my right to have a gun is more important than your right to rail against it in the press.

The original amendments we refer to as the Bill of Rights contain 10 of what the constitutional framers termed "unalienable rights." These rights are ranked in random order and are linked by their essential equality. The Bill of Rights came to us with blinders on. It doesn't recognize color or class or wealth. It protects not just the rights of actors or editors or reporters, but extends even to those we love to hate. That's why the most heinous criminals have rights until they are convicted of a crime.

I say that the Second Amendment is, in order of importance, the first amendment. It is America's first freedom, the one right that protects all the others. Among freedom of speech, of the press, of religion, of assembly, of redress of grievances, it is the first among equals. It alone offers the absolute capacity to live without fear. The right to keep and

bear arms is the one right that allows "rights" to exist at all.

Either you believe that, or you don't, and you must decide.

Because there is no such thing as a free nation where police and military are allowed the force of arms but individual citizens are not. That's a "big brother knows best" theater of the absurd that has never boded well for the peasant class, the working class, or even for reporters.

As a veteran of World War II, as a freedom marcher who stood with Dr. Martin Luther King long before it was fashionable, and as a grandfather who wants the coming century to be free and full of promise for my grandchildren, I am troubled.

The right to keep and bear arms is threatened by political theatrics, piecemeal lawmaking, talk-show psychology, extreme bad taste in the entertainment industry, an ever-widening educational chasm in our schools, and a conniving media—that all add up to cultural warfare against the idea that guns ever had, or should now have, an honorable and proud place in our society.

But all of our rights must be delivered into the 21st century as pure and complete as they came to us at the beginning of this century. Traditionally the passing of that torch is from a gnarled old hand down to an eager young one. So now, at 72, I offer my gnarled old hand.

We have raised a generation of young people who think that the Bill of Rights comes with their cable TV. Leave them to their channel surfing

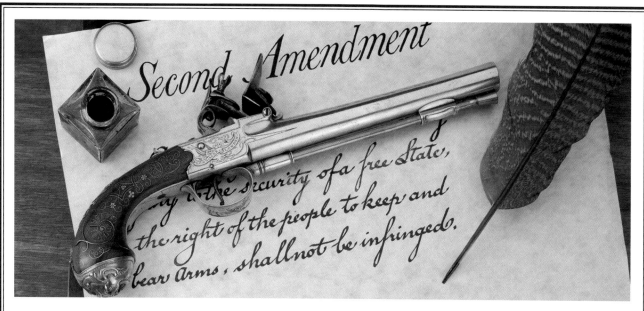

and they'll remain oblivious to history and heritage that truly matter.

Think about it: What else must young Americans think when the White House proclaims, as it did, that "a firearm in the hands of youth is a crime or an accident waiting to happen?" No—it is time they learned that firearm ownership is constitutional, not criminal. In fact, few pursuits can teach a young person more about responsibility, safety, conservation, their history, and their heritage, all at once.

It is time they found out that the politically correct doctrine of today has misled them. And that when they reach legal age, if they do not break our laws, they have a right to choose to own a gun—a handgun, a long gun, a small gun, a large gun, a black gun, a purple gun, a pretty gun, an ugly gun—and to use that gun to defend themselves and their loved ones or to engage in any lawful purpose they desire without apology or explanation to anyone, ever.

This is their first freedom. If you say it's outdated, then you haven't read your own headlines. If you say guns create only carnage, I would answer that you know better. Declining morals, disintegrating families, vacillating political leadership, an eroding criminal justice system, and social morals that blur right and wrong are more to blame—certainly more than any legally owned firearm.

I want to rescue the Second Amendment from an opportunistic President, and from a press that apparently can't comprehend that attacks on the Second Amendment set the stage for assaults on the First.

I want to save the Second Amendment from all these nitpicking little wars of attrition—fights over alleged "Saturday Night Specials," "plastic" guns, "cop-killer" bullets, and so many other made-for-prime-time non-issues invented by some press agent over at gun control headquarters—that you guys buy time and again.

I simply cannot stand by and watch a right guaranteed by the Constitution of the United States come under attack from those who either can't understand it, don't like the sound of it, or find themselves too philosophically squeamish to see why it remains the first among equals: Because it is the right we turn to when all else fails.

That's why the Second Amendment is America's first freedom.

Please, go forth and tell the truth. There can be no free speech, no freedom of the press, no freedom to protest, no freedom to worship your god, no freedom to speak your mind, no freedom from fear, no freedom for your children and for theirs, for anybody, anywhere, without the Second Amendment freedom to fight for it.

Charlton Heston—the Academy Award®–winning legend, hunter, activist, and World War II veteran—was elected at large at the Annual Members Meeting in Seattle to join NRA's Board of Directors. Along with that win, Heston announced his intention to confront Neal Knox directly by campaigning to unseat him as NRA's First Vice President.

Heston stepped into the arena and in a tight contest overthrew Knox. That election also elevated Kayne B. Robinson, former Assistant Chief of Police of Des Moines, Iowa, to the post of Second Vice President. Although the infighting on the board would not end until the organization's 1998 Annual Meetings in Philadelphia, Pennsylvania, the tide had been turned at last.

In unity with President Marion Hammer, NRA's new team of leaders moved quickly to put the internal strife aside and set in motion an ambitious grassroots campaign with the ultimate goal of electing a pro–Second Amendment U.S. President at the dawn of the 21st century.

Rallying gun owners to the cause, Charlton Heston was assured national media attention when he raised the campaign's standard with passion and conviction. "I believe the Second Amendment is America's first freedom," he said, "the one right that protects all others. Among freedom of speech, of the

Above: NRA First Vice President Kayne B. Robinson retired with the rank of Assistant Chief after a 32-year career with the Des Moines, Iowa, police department. He commanded the patrol division before becoming Chief of Detectives and also served as a police firearms instructor, among other postings with that department.

Left: President Charlton Heston, joined by Executive Vice President Wayne LaPierre and NRA-ILA Executive Director James Jay Baker, played lead roles at 16 get-out-the-vote rallies in key states—such as the home states of both Al Gore and Bill Clinton—leading up to election day 2000. More than 50,000 NRA members, families, and friends attended those events.

press, of religion, of assembly, of redress of grievances, it is the first among equals. The right to keep and bear arms is the one right that allows 'rights' to exist at all. I believe the doorway to all freedoms is framed with muskets. So now we move. Understand up front that there is no room in the middle. You must either stand aside or step forward with us in this partnership to save the Second Amendment. Will you walk with me? Together we can change the tide of human events."

THE HARLON B. CARTER LEGISLATIVE ACHIEVEMENT AWARD

My service to NRA, . . . my loyalty to NRA and my love for NRA are undiminished and will endure undiminished for as long as I live.

—Harlon B. Carter

HARLON B. CARTER, LIFELONG DEfender of the Second Amendment, joined NRA as a junior member at age 16, was elected to the NRA Board of Directors in 1951, served as NRA President from 1965 to 1967, created the NRA Institute for Legislative Action in 1975, and served as NRA Executive Vice President from 1977 to 1985. Through his vision and leadership, the Association substantially increased in membership, services, and programs, and the NRA Institute for Legislative Action began an unparalleled record of success on national and state legislative battlegrounds.

The Harlon B. Carter Legislative Achievement Award was established in 1992 by the NRA Institute for Legislative Action to honor leadership and outstanding achievements on behalf of America's firearms owners in defending individual rights guaranteed by the Second Amendment to the U.S. Constitution.

The following individuals have been honored with the Harlon B. Carter Legislative Achievement Award:

1992	Marion P. Hammer
1993	The Honorable Harold L. Volkmer
1994	Charlton Heston
1995	The Honorable John Dingell
1995	James E. Reinke
1996	The Honorable Harold L. Volkmer
1996	Senator James McClure
1997	Senator Mitch McConnell
1999	Alice H. Bull
2000	The Honorable John Dingell
2001	Attorney General Bill Pryor

NRA-ILA Executive Director James Jay Baker (left) presents Congressman John Dingell (D-Michigan) with the 2000 Harlon B. Carter Legislative Achievement Award in recognition of his outstanding service on behalf of the Second Amendment and America's firearms owners.

With those words, a three-year nationwide campaign commenced—a drive that would contribute greatly to the election of Texas Governor George W. Bush as U.S. President and end the Clinton-Gore administration's reign of terror against gun ownership.

Staying Free

Immediately after passage of the 1994 Clinton gun ban, the *Washington Post* editorialized that "No one should have any illusions about what was accomplished. Assault weapons play a part in only a small percentage of crime. The provision is mainly symbolic; its virtue will be if it turns out to be, as hoped, a stepping stone to broader gun control."

Seeking refuge from his scandal-plagued presidency, Bill Clinton stepped up his war on gun owners. Using high-profile, national tragedies as smokescreens, Clinton moved to expand the import ban on semi-automatic firearms, impose an unauthorized federal tax on all firearms sales, mandate trigger locks on handguns, and retain detailed records on firearms owners in a national computer database.

Countering these proposals as undue, unconstitutional, and unenforceable, NRA launched a nationwide campaign of its own, promoting Project Exile, a highly successful crime-fighting program in Richmond, Virginia.

Endorsed and financially supported by NRA, Project Exile put into practice what NRA had preached for decades: Crack down on and jail armed violent felons in violation of federal law.

Laws covering possession of firearms by felons and drug dealers had been made even more stringent under provisions of the NRA-endorsed Firearms Owners Protection Act, opposed in 1986 by Handgun Control, Inc. On paper, the provisions were tough; in practice, they were virtually ignored or plea-bargained into oblivion.

Project Exile put the law into action. Armed felons were taken off the streets and brought to trial in federal rather than state courts. They were subjected to the stiffer penalties proscribed under federal gun control statutes and sent to federal prison if convicted. Once among the top urban areas for homicide, Richmond's violent crime declined dramatically, with homicide down 55 percent after Project Exile took effect.

The U.S. Attorney for the Eastern District of Virginia, whose office initiated Project Exile, told the *Newport News Daily Press* on January 23, 1998, that "officials were shocked . . . at the extent of [Project Exile] suspects' criminal records. Several had between four and eight convictions for offenses as serious as robbery, abduction and murder."

Indeed, more federal prosecutions occurred under Project Exile in Richmond than were made nationwide under the entire enforcement history of the Clinton-backed Brady "waiting period" law since its inception in 1993.

NRA cast the national spotlight on Project Exile and the lawlessness of the Clinton administration in enforcing existing federal gun laws. That message was pressed aggressively, leading to a showdown between Congress and the Clinton-Gore administration.

No restrictive gun laws backed by Clinton saw the light of day, and the administration was forced to swallow funding to enact Exile programs in other cities under the budget bill signed into law on October 22, 1998.

New Directions

Just prior to the 1998 congressional elections, Tanya K. Metaksa announced that she was stepping down from the day-to-day operations of the Institute for Legislative Action. Returning to the post of ILA Executive Director was James Jay Baker, a formidable force who drew a wellspring of support from Capitol Hill, NRA members, and the firearms industry.

Patrick G. O'Malley was appointed ILA's Deputy Executive Director. Both he and Baker returned to the organization after representing the Sporting Arms and Ammunition Manufacturers Institute, which was then fighting a rash of liability lawsuits backed by headline-hungry big-city mayors around the country. What the anti-gun lobby could not achieve through legislation or back-door regulations, it sought to enact through such litigation, blaming gun manufacturers for violent crime.

"There is no end to the issues that the other side thinks up," said Baker. "And whether the

BRADY ACT CHALLENGE IN THE U.S. SUPREME COURT

IN 1997, THE U.S. SUPREME COURT STRUCK down sections of the Brady Act that commandeered the service of local law enforcement to administer a federally enacted program, declaring them unconstitutional on Tenth Amendment grounds. "The federal government may not compel the states to enact or administer a federal regulatory program," wrote Justice Antonin Scalia for the five-to-four majority.

In the landmark case of *Printz and Mack v. United States*—brought by Sheriff Peter J. Printz of Ravalli County, Montana, and Sheriff Richard Mack of Graham County, Arizona—the

U.S. Supreme Court had defined the boundary between federal authority and state sovereignty. Oral arguments were presented by noted constitutional scholar Dr. Stephen P. Halbrook, who represented Sheriff Printz, with assistance from former ILA Legislative Counsel Richard Gardiner.

The case was funded in part through NRA's Civil Rights Defense Fund. Founded in 1978 under the vision of George S. Knight, a long-time member of NRA's Board of Directors and a prominent Virginia attorney, the fund has supported more than 1,000 legal cases involving the civil rights of firearms owners.

issue of the day is 'Saturday Night Special' bans or 'cop-killer' bullets or semi-auto gun bans or gun show bans, every issue boils down to this: Do you trust law-abiding citizens with firearms, and do you attempt to control misuse of firearms by controlling law-abiding citizens or by prosecuting those who abuse the right? You can strip all the technicalities aside. They all devolve to this basic question: Do you control criminal behavior with firearms by controlling those people who misuse firearms, or do you add new restrictions on law-abiding people?"

Putting the firearms industry out of business had become the latest hobbyhorse for the White House. Anti-gun mayors and well-heeled trial lawyers joined in, filing lawsuits aimed at bank-

Florida Governor Jeb Bush congratulates former NRA President Marion P. Hammer for her efforts in helping to get a bill to his desk to protect the American firearms industry from reckless lawsuits. With Governor Bush's signature on May 1, 2001, Florida became the 26th state to adopt legislation since Georgia enacted the first such measure in February 1999.

rupting the industry. The White House further added lawful gun shows to its hit list, branding them "illegal arms bazaars for criminals."

On both fronts, ILA promised a bare-knuckled fight. It offered legal support to firearms manufacturers who stood steadfast in rejecting outside "settlements" to the lawsuits. The strategy paid off. One after another, municipal lawsuits were dismissed in court. And ILA's State and Local Affairs Division worked with legislators to enact state laws barring cities from frivolously suing the industry. By April 2002, 28 states had passed laws that banned cities from pursuing litigation, and the U.S. Supreme Court had declined to hear the issue.

Trying to make gun shows extinct ultimately fared no better and collapsed under the weight of a joint House-Senate Conference Committee, where the bill died. But the entire issue of "gun control" would be fought right up to the 2000 elections, a battle made all the more difficult in the wake of a horrible massacre at a school in the Denver suburb of Littleton, Colorado, in 1999.

In declaring war on American firearms owners in the aftermath of the Columbine High School tragedy, President Clinton charged that the mass murders stemmed from "the culture of hunting and sport shooting in America." In a ghoulish April 27 press conference mapping out his administration's assault against gun owners' rights, Clinton predicted his efforts would result in the death of pro–Second Amendment beliefs, saying, "When there are no constituents for this movement, the movement will evaporate."

That theme would be played out repeatedly in the national media. Said ILA's Jim Baker, "What you didn't find 10 to 20 years ago was the 24-hour news cycle, which foments a lot of the controversy and a lot of the issues today simply to fill programming time." Though the Clinton-Gore machine shamelessly tried to use the tragedy to enact new firearms restrictions, most Americans saw no connection between gun control and the twisted teenagers in Columbine who had carried out a year-long plan to slaughter dozens of their classmates. Telephone calls, mail, e-mail, and faxes into Capitol Hill offices ran anywhere from 100–1 to 500–1 against the White House gun control package.

NRA TOPS *FORTUNE* LIST OF INFLUENTIAL LOBBIES

NRA HAS ASCENDED TO THE TOP OF *Fortune* magazine's "Power 25," a listing of the most influential lobbying groups in America. The 2001 "Power 25," compiled by *Fortune*'s Washington Bureau Chief Jeffrey H. Birnbaum, is based on responses to a survey sent to more than 2,900 individuals, including every member of Congress, Hill staffers, senior White House aides, professional lobbyists, and top-ranking officers of lobbying organizations and companies.

In 1997, NRA ranked sixth on the list, moving to fourth in 1998 and into a tie for second in 1999. *Fortune* did not compile a ranking in 2000, deciding "to wait for the results of the election and give the new President time to settle in before [testing] to see which . . . lobbying groups rose or fell in the new Washington."

Noticeably absent from the "Power 25" yet again are anti-gun organizations. *Fortune*'s Website (www.fortune.com) displays a list of 87 "Top Lobbying Groups" for 2001, but none of them are anti-gun groups. Neither the gun ban lobby—formerly known as Handgun Control, Inc., the self-proclaimed "largest citizens' gun control lobbying organization"—nor Americans for Gun Safety—the newest member of the

anti-gun community, founded on the checkbook of Internet billionaire and former HCI board member Andrew McKelvey—have found any perch on the list.

That solid victory for gun owners' rights crossed all political boundaries. It was best summed up by anti-gun Massachusetts [Representative Barney Frank who said, "The NRA does the best job of any group in lobbying members. They don't have marches, they don't have demonstrations, they don't shoot guns in the air. It's just good straight democracy."

Still, as Chuck Cunningham, director of ILA's Federal Affairs Division, noted, "We needed to get past the emotion of the tragedy and the ignorance surrounding gun laws. Once we dealt with just the facts, we won. If gun control worked, D.C.

would be a safe city, but the fact is, criminals don't obey laws, particularly gun control laws. Our task was to educate people on the abysmal record of the Clinton administration in enforcing the existing laws."

Defending Freedom Globally

Clinton's romance with global gun control fully blossomed when he gave his support to a new United Nations gun ban plan hatched by foreign governments. Behind the scenes and around the world, privately funded groups had been

During a U.N. firearms workshop in Sao Paulo, Brazil, local officials held an "unrelated" demonstration in which 1,700 firearms were destroyed. To counter international threats to the right to keep and bear arms, the NRA Institute worked hard to become an accredited U.N. "Non-Governmental Organization" in order to monitor gun control at the world body.

meeting under the auspices of the United Nations to devise a global summit on small arms, generally banning civilian ownership of arms.

NRA sought and won approval from the United Nations as an accredited "Non-Governmental Organization" (NGO) to gain the ability to observe the organization's activities firsthand and forewarn America's gun owners. As Wayne LaPierre put it, "The U.N. draws no distinction between legal guns and illegal guns, between a machine gun and your shotgun. To them, a bazooka and your Browning are both small arms. They want a

new global 'norm of non-possession.'" He vowed to fight any United Nations effort to redefine or diminish personal freedom, saying, "The global standard for personal freedom should be one standard—ours."

The global gun ban strategy of the Clinton administration would be swiftly rejected by the new Bush administration. At a U.N. conference on the Illicit Trade in Small Arms, John Bolton, Undersecretary of State for arms control and international security affairs, forcefully declared, "The United States will not join consensus on a final document that contains measures contrary to our right to keep and bear arms."

Seeing Results

Just as the 1994 congressional elections had witnessed strong voter reaction to the nation's failed criminal justice system, the same trend held in the 1996 campaigns in which nine of every 10 candidates backed by NRA won their races. As one syndicated columnist observed, "The NRA is like the Energizer Bunny. . . . They keep going and going and going and winning and winning."

A year later in Washington state, Initiative 676, which demanded that current and future handgun owners be licensed, tested, and approved by a government official, was defeated by a better than two-to-one margin. The lopsided victory was the political story of the year, with more than 80 percent of the state's police and sheriffs on NRA's side in opposing that bureaucratic invasion into gun owners' lives. Had the initiative passed, similar proposals would have spread like wildfire to other states.

With Jim Baker in command, the Institute for Legislative Action identified 2,576 candidates worthy of NRA's endorsement in the 1998 elections. An overwhelming 82 percent of these candidates were elected to office, along with 22 of 28 NRA-endorsed candidates for Governor. Pro–Second Amendment majorities in both the U.S. House and Senate were scored, once again keeping the gun ban forces in check.

To Wayne LaPierre, these victories were seen as manifestations of gun owners' united front in reaction to years of relentless attacks. While NRA's membership skyrocketed, national polling revealed that millions of citizens agreed with its mission. According to Mary Marcotte Corrigan, NRA Chief of Staff, "When asked, 14 million Americans claimed they were NRA members and 24 million said they were 'affiliated' with NRA, exposing a potent voting force well beyond our membership count. More telling, those surveys revealed that Americans had higher regard for NRA and a higher confidence in the organization than in the Republican party, the Democratic party, and the Congress as a whole."

From the mid-1990s, NRA's membership ranks had swelled to record levels—more than 3.5 million by the end of 1999 and soaring to an off-the-charts 4.3 million milestone in advance of the 2000 presidential elections.

Serving the Membership

Record numbers attended the 2000 Annual Meetings in Charlotte, North Carolina, in solidarity with NRA's leadership and clearly determined to make a difference in the upcoming elections.

"Our members knew those elections would be a watershed for our cause," said Jacqueline Mongold, NRA Assistant Secretary. She recalled the enthusi-

asm that well over 50,000 attendees brought to that meeting: "Members came from all over the country to be a part of that election rally. You could see great pride in their hearts for what the Association stands for, for what NRA accomplishes working with them, and for the tremendous role they play with their membership dues and donations. What you saw was total dedication and loyalty—a heartfelt sense of belonging and owning not just an Association but a movement that could make history."

"It's what I call the Washington phenomenon," said board member James W. Porter II of Birmingham, Alabama, who serves as a trustee for the NRA Foundation and chairs NRA's influential Legal Affairs Committee. "It's the membership that opens doors on Capitol Hill for our ILA representa-

When the media elite roundly predicted that Washington state voters would easily pass Initiative 676 and give their state the most restrictive handgun laws in the nation, they sorely underestimated the grassroots strength of determined gun owners. When the measure was crushed at the polls 71 percent to 29 percent, the media "spiked" the story.

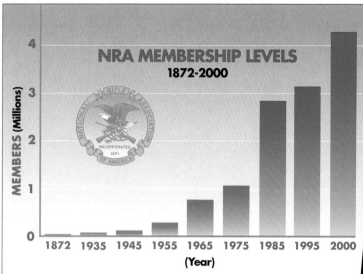

Above: NRA membership soared to the 4.3 million mark in advance of the 2000 presidential elections.

Right: NRA members who signed up a new member in a 1998 membership drive received an engraved silver .45 cartridge casting, signifying membership in the Charlton Heston Silver Bullet Brigade.

Below: G. David Tubb of Canadian, Texas, fired a 2380-112x and emerged as NRA National High Power Rifle Champion for an unprecedented ninth time at the 2001 National Matches at Camp Perry. He shot a rifle of his own design—the Tubb 2000, chambered for the 6mm X wildcat cartridge.

tives and gives them credibility when they're talking about political or legislative matters. Our members are the building blocks that translate into NRA success. They're good, solid, Americans—recognizable citizens in every community—people, who just believe in basic American values, what this country is all about." ILA's Jim Baker echoed that sentiment, saying, "Without our members, neither I—nor anybody else who represents this organization—could do what we do."

The broad cross section of America is wholly reflected on NRA's Board of Directors, noted David O. Boehm, a retired New York Appellate Division judge. He remarked on the depth of leadership he had seen during his many years of service: "Here were bank presidents. Here was someone who had formerly helped General Douglas MacArthur change the police force of Japan after the war. Here was an officer of the U.S. Border Patrol. Alice Bull was a woman from the state of Washington who was an outstanding rifle shot and made all kinds of records—all decent, good people, very principled people. They all had a quiet determination and strength and principle, working together to achieve a common goal."

"Fairfax to the Field"

Strength in numbers translated to dynamic and popular programs in the field. In its newly inaugurated "Fairfax To The Field" initiative, NRA General Operations accelerated its delivery of services in communities across the American landscape, using its volunteer networks in historic ways.

Under the stewardship of Craig D. Sandler, who was appointed by LaPierre in 1996 as Executive Director of General Operations, NRA expanded its

Above: The generosity of firearms genius and businessman William B. Ruger (right) helped make possible the creation and completion of the National Firearms Museum. "With Bill Ruger's commitment and generous support, our heritage of Second Amendment freedom will remain a living part of our proud history," said NRA President Marion P. Hammer at the check presentation.

Left: NRA's "I'm the NRA" advertisements continued to feature prominent Americans who support NRA and everything it stands for. "A constitutional freedom shouldn't be used as a political weapon to divide and label people," says U.S. Representative J. C. Watts Jr.

considerable reach with wide-ranging services offered through gun clubs, hunting clubs, and affiliated national, state, and local organizations.

Prior to his new assignment, Sandler had been Director of NRA's Law Enforcement Activities Division and was a distinguished 26-year law enforcement veteran who had served 12 years as Chief of Police in Nashua, New Hampshire. Among many achievements, he was responsible for implementing the new Law Enforcement Tactical Shooting Instructor Development Schools program

THE NATIONAL FIREARMS MUSEUM

O N A CRISP MAY EVENING IN 1998, CRAIG D. Sandler, NRA's Executive Director of General Operations, introduced NRA President Marion P. Hammer to a capacity crowd that had gathered at NRA's headquarters. The crowd was there to witness the ribbon cutting that would open the new National Firearms Museum to the public. It was a spectacular opening. The 15,000-square-foot National Firearms Museum showcased 2,400 firearms and related artifacts, all expertly displayed in 15 galleries and 85 exhibit cases.

The National Firearms Museum presents a historic chronology of Americans and their guns. Exhibits highlight the bravery of the early settlers to the New World, the fight for independence, the gold rush and westward expansion, the dawn of the industrial revolution, and the numerous wars and conflicts that Americans have fought to maintain their hard-won independence and freedom. Full-sized dioramas showcase the Jamestown Colony, Samuel Hawken's rifle shop,

NRA President Marion P. Hammer cut the ribbon that officially opened NRA's National Firearms Museum. She was joined by (from left) Executive Director of General Operations Craig D. Sandler, Executive Vice President Wayne R. LaPierre, Second Vice President Sandra S. Froman, and Dr. William L. Roberts, a major supporter of the museum.

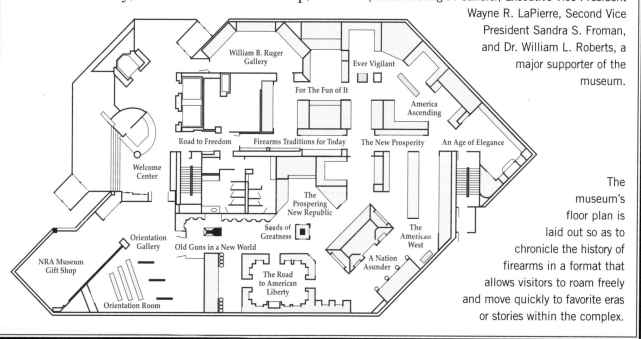

The museum's floor plan is laid out so as to chronicle the history of firearms in a format that allows visitors to roam freely and move quickly to favorite eras or stories within the complex.

the arms-making factories of the Civil War, a trench from World War I, and a heavily shelled Norman courtyard from World War II. A functioning Coney Island shooting gallery from 1903 and a full-scale replication of Theodore Roosevelt's library from Sagamore Hill let visitors step back in time and sense the importance of firearms to America's unique freedom.

The long journey that culminated on the museum's opening night began with one prize rifle in 1873, only two years after the Association's founding. This Remington Rolling Block rifle had been the award in the International Rifle Match of 1874, a competition that D. Barclay of the NRA's rifle team won handily. The rifle was donated to the Association and became the first firearm in what is now a collection of nearly 4,000 firearms and thousands more related artifacts and books.

From 1871 until NRA relocated from New York to Washington, D.C., in 1908, the museum grew slowly, just as the Association did. For a number of years the small collection of firearms, awards, and trophies was sporadically displayed

Right: In the National Firearms Museum, firearms are placed in historical context through a series of dioramas with life-sized figures. One depicts the men of the U.S. 29th Infantry Division at St. Lo, France, during World War II.

Below: America's role in keeping the world safe for democracy is chronicled at the National Firearms Museum, where visitors are able to view more American military arms on display than at the venerable Smithsonian Institution.

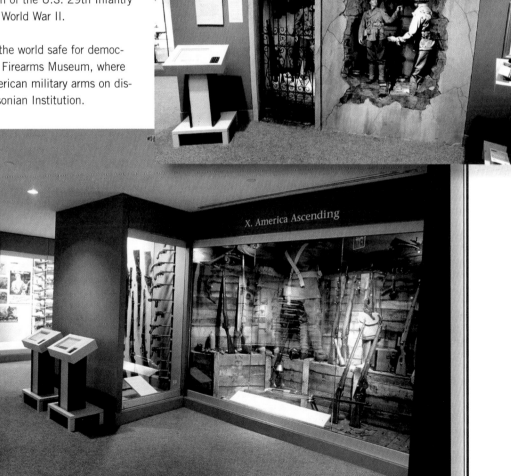

in the Association's headquarters in the Barr Building on Farragut Square.

NRA's flagship magazine, *American Rifleman*, began publication on a biweekly basis in 1923 and with each issue began a series of tests and evaluations of various products and firearms of interest to the shooting community. It wasn't long before the firearms industry began to send NRA publishers test guns to be used in the battery of rigorous trials. Those guns were maintained by the magazine for future use.

In 1937, NRA formally displayed the collection of test guns and those donated by both former officers and members of the Association in a museum. From 1937 until 1939, when NRA relocated to 1600 Rhode Island Avenue, N.W., in Washington, D.C., the collection was little more than window dressing in the offices of the Association's headquarters. There were no true curators—publishers, editors, and technical editors worked with the collection more as an assemblage of props than of artifacts. In the mid-1960s, a series of six-foot by eight-foot glass cases were designed and constructed by the

magazine staff to publicly display the burgeoning collection. From this design and display method, the museum served the NRA membership and public for some 30 years.

An effort to become a recognized museum in 1981 continued throughout the 1980s as NRA maintained a director and hired a professional curator and curator's assistant. A National Firearms Museum Fund was created, giving the museum a 501(c)(3) tax-exempt charitable organization status and thereby encouraging tax-deductible donations for construction of a new museum.

When NRA's headquarters moved from Washington, D.C., to the Virginia suburbs, new life was breathed into the concept of a world-class museum. The Leone Design Group of New York was hired in 1993 to design the proposed museum in the south tower of NRA's headquarters building. Within a year, design plans were completed, and fundraising efforts began in earnest to secure the $3.5 million required to complete the project. A white model of the museum prepared by the Leone Design Group was toured around the country in an effort to generate interest and contributions to the National Firearms Museum Fund.

By 1997, the museum's Director, Thomas "Whit" Fentem, had a complete set of plans and renderings provided by the design team, led by then-Curator of Exhibits Philip Schreier. Doug Wicklund, Curator of Collections during the design phase and later the museum's Senior Curator, had integrated the firearms collection and accouterments into the proposed 85 exhibits and 15 galleries.

In September 1997, the National Firearms Museum Fund was dissolved. The remaining assets and liabilities of the fund were assumed by the NRA Foundation, which had been estab-

One of the goals of the National Firearms Museum is to educate future generations on firearms, freedom, and the American experience. This youngster views a fine display of "Old West" Colts and Winchesters.

recently, a "Real Guns of Reel Heroes" collection of firearms used in well-known films and television shows opened, featuring the original *Dirty Harry* S&W .44 Magnum, John Wayne's Winchester 92 from *Stagecoach*, Mel Gibson's flintlock rifle from *The Patriot*, and Tom Selleck's rifle from *Quigley Down Under*.

The National Firearms Museum has grown from a small collection of test guns into a full-scale, world-class museum representing how the American history of firearms is so intimately intertwined with the freedom guaranteed by the Constitution in the United States.

Left: In the early 1800s, Jake and Sam Hawken formed a family partnership as gunmakers in St. Louis and began producing their soon to be famous "Hawken Rifle." A full-scale diorama of the circa 1830s rifle shop was recreated in the National Firearms Museum.

Below: This .38 caliber Colt official police revolver was used in NRA Life Member Robert Stack's *The Untouchables* television series and is on loan to the museum from Mike Papac.

lished in 1990 to provide a charitable umbrella for NRA program fundraising efforts. A National Firearms Museum Endowment was established, within the Foundation, and efforts to raise money for a construction fund began in earnest.

NRA President Marion P. Hammer assumed the leadership role in the museum's fundraising campaign, which successfully secured an initial personal donation of $1 million from legendary gunmaker William B. Ruger Sr. Other generous donations followed, and construction began over the Christmas holiday in 1997. Within five months, the first floor of the south tower of the NRA headquarters building had been transformed from a computer center into the National Firearms Museum. A project that normally would have taken nine to 12 months to complete was done in less than 150 days.

The William B. Ruger Gallery hosts exhibits that change every nine to 12 months. To date, the gallery has featured exclusive exhibitions of William B. Ruger and Dr. Ugo Gussalli Beretta's private and corporate arms collections. More

and revitalizing the National Police Shooting Championships. Sandler had joined NRA staff in 1992 at the urging of past President Richard D. Riley, who highly respected Sandler's no-nonsense style of management and business acumen.

"NRA's 178 educational programs are its secret weapon," Craig Sandler explained, "because every day we're in nearly every corner of the United States, teaching the safe and responsible use of firearms, teaching people how to become involved in outdoor activities, teaching law enforcement officers life-saving tactical techniques, and teaching citizens on how to defend themselves."

A staunch proponent of NRA's Project Exile initiative, Sandler contended that "a community sets its own norm for the amount of crime with

which it is willing to live. In Nashua and hundreds of places like it around the country, people have worked very hard for the American ideal, and they aren't willing to let gangs and other hoodlums take it away. When people have had enough of violent crime, they provide the resources to enforce existing laws. And when they do, they can cut crime in any city, of any size, any place in the nation."

With a renewed sense of partnership, NRA's positive influence among the law enforcement community continued to expand as officers from hundreds of agencies attended its Law Enforcement Firearms Instructor Schools in record numbers. Ron Kirkland, a 25-year veteran of the Federal Bureau of Investigation who served at its Training Academy in Quantico, Virginia, was named Director of the Law Enforcement Activities Division in 1998.

"We don't teach just one way of doing things," Kirkland said. "We teach many different approaches, and the firearms instructor makes the decision as to which technique suits the department's needs."

With its staff instructor and adjunct instructor programs—comprising former FBI agents, state troopers, and law enforcement officers—NRA liter-

The 1998 World Four Man Team Champions from the Los Angeles Police Department were congratulated by NRA Director John C. Sigler (center), a veteran law enforcement officer. The winning team members were (from left) Don Tsunawaki, Robert Barnes, Lou Salseda, and Richard Bennett.

Above: Myong-Sin Yi of MIT won the NRA Intercollegiate Women's Air Pistol Championship in 1996. NRA sponsors and/or supports the national collegiate rifle, pistol, and shotgun championships.

Left: Jacob Ryker (right), his brother Joshua, and three other boys subdued killer Kip Kinkel and ended his May 1998 rampage at Thurston High School in Springfield, Oregon. For his courage, Jacob, an NRA member, received the Honor Medal with Crossed Palms from the Boy Scouts of America. He was also honored with his family at the NRA Annual Meetings in Philadelphia.

ally "teaches the teachers" who work in police departments all across America. NRA-trained instructors are listed by the nation's major training entities, and each gives life-saving lessons to anywhere from 200 to 400 law enforcement officers each year.

Hunters continued to enjoy valuable NRA-sponsored programs. NRA's Hunter Clinic Instructor Program drew on the shared experience of hunters to not only improve hunting skills but also increase safety awareness and responsibility. In addition, the Association launched a Hunters for the Hungry Information Clearinghouse to assist hunters who wished to share game with needy families.

The organization was also on the forefront of hunting and shooting sports programs for disabled people through its Disabled Shooting Services. Spearheaded by Dave Baskin, the program has become a world leader in the research and development of shooting sports opportunities for people with disabilities. Baskin developed the

10-city NRA-Beeman Grand Prix Championship tour in 1997 as a way to improve public interest in the achievements of disabled Americans who participate in the shooting sports.

Presented with the Shooting Industry Academy of Excellence award in 2000, Baskin was credited with establishing rifle shooting as a tool for physical therapists in the rehabilitation of their post-injury inpatients. The first NRA Rehabilitative Shooting Unit was installed in 1994 at the Lakeshore Foundation in Birmingham, Alabama. Other public recognition of the Disabled Shooting Services program came in the form of a grant from the Eastern Paralyzed Veterans Association, the first grant ever from such a group for the shooting sports.

THE PRESIDENTS OF NRA

CAPABLE, COMMITTED LEADership has been a feature of NRA throughout its history. While some of the organization's early leaders, most notably military figures such as Ambrose E. Burnside, Winfield S. Hancock, and Ulysses S. Grant, were to an appreciable degree prominent individuals who brought to the office prestige rather than meaningful daily efforts, most of the 55 men and the lone woman (Marion P. Hammer) to serve as President have been anything but figureheads. That is especially true in the modern era, when presidents have consistently shown an incredible degree of dedication while working tirelessly as spokesmen and leaders. Most of these individuals have risen through the NRA ranks, "paying their dues" as committee and board members and in other ways. The list below covers the presidents from General Burnside down to NRA's 56th leader, Charlton Heston.

Name	Elected	Name	Elected	Name	Elected
Ambrose E. Burnside	1871	Benedict Crowell	1930	Bartlett Rummel	1963
William C. Church	1872	G. A. Fraser	1932	Harlon B. Carter	1965
Alexander Shaler	1875	Karl T. Frederick	1934	Harold W. Glassen	1967
N. P. Stanton	1877	Ammon B. Critchfield	1936	Woodson D. Scott	1969
Henry A. Gildersleeve	1880	Gustavus D. Pope	1937	Fred M. Hakenjos	1971
Winfield S. Hancock	1881	Littleton W. T. Waller Jr.	1939	C. R. Gutermuth	1973
E. L. Molineaux	1882	Nathaniel C. Nash	1941	Merrill W. Wright	1975
Ulysses S. Grant	1883	Hilliard Comstock	1942	Lloyd M. Mustin	1977
Philip S. Sheridan	1885	Thurman Randle	1944	John B. Layton	1979
George W. Wingate	1886	Francis W. Parker Jr.	1946	Keith M. Gaffaney	1981
Bird W. Spencer	1900	Emmet O. Swanson	1948	Howard W. Pollock	1983
James A. Drain	1907	Merritt A. Edson	1949	Alonzo H. Garcelon	1985
John C. Bates	1910	Harry D. Linn	1951	James E. Reinke	1986
Charles D. Gaither	1913	J. Alvin Badeaux	1953	Joe Foss	1988
William Libbey	1915	Morton C. Mumma	1955	Richard D. Riley	1990
Smith W. Brookhart	1921	George R. Whittington	1957	Robert K. Corbin	1992
Francis E. Warren	1925	Irvine C. Porter	1959	Thomas L. Washington	1994
Fred M. Waterbury	1927	John M. Schooley	1961	Marion P. Hammer	1995
Lewis M. Rumsey Jr.	1928			Charlton Heston	1998

"I'm really adamant about making sure we're the standard bearer in developing shooting programs for everyone," said James W. Porter II, a highly accomplished attorney and longtime board member from Birmingham, Alabama. "In Birmingham, we have a rehabilitation hospital called Lake Shore Hospital, where they are now building what's going to be one of the finest indoor shooting ranges in this country that will be available to disabled shooters. Shooting is a sport that anyone can participate in, regardless of gender or physical abilities. Shooting builds discipline, and it helps with self-esteem."

With urban sprawl threatening to close down shooting facilities, keeping ranges open became a high priority for the Institute for Legislative Action, according to Randy Kozuch, Director of State and Local Affairs. Since 1993, 37 states have passed range-protection legislation, for a total of 45 states that have enacted such laws.

"Young people and adult firearms owners need ranges to learn safety while recreational and competitive shooters need places to practice their sport," said Kozuch. "In an indirect but decisive way, our Second Amendment hinges on there being people who participate in the shooting sports, and places for them to do so." For ranges facing frivolous lawsuits, the NRA Civil Rights Defense Fund offers valuable legal advice, and NRA's Range Technical Team has assisted programs from the U.S. military and the Environmental Protection Agency on how to design, build, manage, and maintain safe, environmentally compliant shooting ranges.

On the Line: Youth Training

As testament to NRA's reputation and breadth of knowledge, in 1999 the Boy Scouts of America asked for NRA's expertise in preparing an outdoor skills book on the shooting sports. At the 2001 Boy Scout Jamboree, held at Fort A. P. Hill near Fredericksburg, Virginia, more than 50 staff members, certified instructors, and volunteers administered shotgun and rifle merit badge tests, handed out free gun safety materials, and managed the trap shooting venue. More than 1,110 Scouts a day lined up to shoot trap, making it the number one event in terms of participation at the entire Jamboree. Partnerships also grew with 4-H,

U.S. Jaycees, and FFA to promote youth shooting programs. NRA provides coach and instructor training, program design and materials, publicity, tournament sanctioning, and financial support, the latter through the NRA Foundation.

Giving youngsters a wholesome appreciation for firearms through its safety and education programs has been a hallmark of NRA's services. These services are organized and provided by an army of NRA's unsung heroes—its thousands upon thousands of knowledgeable adult volunteers. Where there was a need, a service was developed through programs such as the annual Youth Hunter Education Challenge; the Neighborhood Air Gun Program; the Marksman Qualification Program, which rewards shooters for reaching pre-established standards; NRA Shooting Sports Camps, which focus on specific curriculum such as safety and firearms education, hunting, competition, and other special interests; Junior Olympic Shooting Camps; Intermediate Junior Smallbore Camps for young participants of the Camp Perry National

NBA legend and NRA board member Karl Malone draws strongly on his experiences as a youngster hunting with his grandfather as he passes on his love of the sport to the youngsters of today through his namesake youth conservation program.

Matches; and the Summer Camp Shooting Program that can be set up in a typical commercial summer camp.

Providing training for adults who led youth shooting programs became more formal and more extensive in 2001 with a nationwide series of adult leadership workshops. "With these seminars," commented Matt Szyramoski, manager of Youth Programs Department, "when people go back to their clubs to start a junior program, they will have the tools and the resources to confidently get a

Right: Craig D. Sandler, NRA's Executive Director of General Operations (left) and Dr. Ugo Gussalli Beretta on the occasion of the opening reception for "The World of Beretta" exhibit at the National Firearms Museum on March 27, 2001. Also recognized on this occasion was the generous $1 million donation from Beretta U.S.A. and Benelli U.S.A. to the NRA Foundation to help endow the National Firearms Museum.

Below: Colonel Walter R. Walsh was named Outstanding American Handgunner in 1997. The former FBI agent and Marine Corps officer was a 1948 Olympian. Four years later, he won a silver medal at the World Shooting Championships and claimed the National High Power Rifle Championship at Camp Perry.

junior shooting program going, keep it going, and ensure that it continues for many years to come."

The National Outstanding Youth Achievement Award was inaugurated in 2001 to recognize NRA junior members who epitomized excellence. Robin Maly of Lodi, Wisconsin, received the first award. She was a champion high power shooter, had a 4.0 grade average, and had won several public speaking tournaments with a speech in defense of the Second Amendment. She was active in Friends of NRA and 4-H and was a student council officer and a member of the varsity math team. In his address to members at the 2001 Annual Meetings, Craig D. Sandler made Robin a key component of his speech, saying, "For all her wonderful work, for her spirit, for being a shining example of what is best about youngsters in America—now and throughout our history—we have honored Robin Maly with the NRA Outstanding Achievement Youth Award."

While designed to promote skill in the shooting sports, NRA youth programs provide sheer fun, an aspect all too often overlooked in the sharp-edged political climate involving Second

Amendment issues. As William F. Parkerson III, ILA Director of Research and Information noted, "One of the worst byproducts of gun control is that many kids, especially inner-city kids, grow up with no positive firearms experience."

"The urban centers with the heavy media concentrations, with the constant media propaganda against the Second Amendment, against guns, have developed a reflexive anti-gun culture," said board member Roy Innis, Chairman of NRA's Urban Affairs Committee and national Chairman of the Congress on Racial Equality. "Safety is so important, and adults need to give young people a consciousness about firearms so they can realize that."

Refuse To Be A Victim

With increased public concern over criminal violence, NRA had developed the Refuse To Be A Victim® program in 1993 in response to women who requested crime prevention and personal safety information. Refuse To Be A Victim® volunteers present a wide variety of strategies in three-hour seminars to community groups, educational institutions, associations, and corporations nationwide. These strategies cover security for automobile, home, personal Internet, fraud, and travel. As with every NRA General Operations program, Refuse To Be A Victim® experienced dramatic growth throughout the late 1990s.

"We developed that program to appeal specifically to women for whom firearms may not have been considered an option, but women who nevertheless wanted to learn how to protect themselves," said Sandra S. Froman, an experienced civil trial attorney from Tucson, Arizona, who was elected to the board in 1990 and elected NRA Second Vice President in 1998. "The program doesn't advocate that women protect themselves necessarily with a firearm, but teaches them to

create their own customized self-protection program that will work in their environment. The program does not advocate gun ownership, but it offers that as one option. And if women choose to own a firearm, the program leads them to NRA, where we'll provide the proper instruction."

A graduate of Stanford University and Harvard Law School, Froman came late to firearms ownership after a threat of violence touched her personally. As a litigator, Froman had seen close hand the consequences suffered by victims of armed criminals. "But as a near victim, I realized that I could not depend upon anyone else for personal protection," she said. As a direct result, Froman has become one of the most forceful and convincing advocates of firearms ownership in America.

NRA Director Susan Howard, known for her nine-year role on the television series *Dallas*, lent the visibility she earned through her acting career to being a spokesperson and activist for an issue near and dear to her heart: defense of the Second Amendment. She was featured in early Refuse To Be A Victim® promotional material and

In 1995, Marion P. Hammer, Executive Director of the Unified Sportsmen of Florida and a highly skilled lobbyist for gun owner rights, became NRA's first woman president. Hammer created the Eddie Eagle GunSafe® Program that has been taught to more than 15 million children.

helped the program gain national popularity among women from all walks of life.

NRA began offering women-only hunting and shooting events in 1997. Demand for these opportunities grew, spurring NRA to create Women On Target® in 1999. "Hunting and shooting are the perfect sports for women, yet many women don't have the opportunity or the mentors to make it easy to get started," said Stephanie Henson, Manager of NRA's Women's Programs Department. "So the women of the NRA created Women On Target®, inviting all women to participate in fabulous hunts and fun-filled shooting events."

Open to women of all skill levels, Women On Target® sponsors instructional shooting clinics at the range or on the sporting clays field, as well as charity shooting events across the country. Charity shoots benefiting organizations such as the Susan G. Komen Breast Cancer Foundation, Special Olympics, and Habitat for Humanity give women the opportunity to have fun while helping others.

With no comprehensive shooting and hunting video on the market designed for and by women, the NRA staff set out to create one in 2001, with funding provided by the NRA Foundation. Covering topics such as ammunition caliber, gauge selection, rifle sighting-in, shotgun patterning, and safety when afield, NRA's *Hunting with the Women of the NRA* video offered solid hunting information along with beautifully filmed, action-packed footage.

Sue King, a longtime NRA Director from Houston, Texas, lent her considerable expertise to the effort. "How I wish we could take every interested woman hunting with pleasant companions, good instruction, and share with them the pristine beauty of a sunrise and comfortably heavy game bag," she said. "But since we can't, this video allows us to show women not only the basics of safe gun handling when hunting, but the beauty and challenge of an adventure available to all women."

Eddie Eagle's Winning Ways

By the end of 2001, the Eddie Eagle GunSafe® Program had reached more than 15 million children. On local levels, the effectiveness of the program was recognized by many testimonial letters documenting cases in which children encountered guns without incident. In Bristol Borough, Pennsylvania, 11-year-old David Snyder and his

HUNTING
with the Women of the NRA

Learn what it takes to safely meet the challenges – and experience the profound joys – of hunting, the ultimate outdoor sport.

Texan Sue King (above), an NRA Director and expert hunter and firearms instructor, lent her skills to the creation of the *Hunting with the Women of the NRA* video. Designed for and produced by women, the informative film received funding from the NRA Foundation.

six-year-old sister were walking to school when they found a loaded revolver in a parking lot. The children then did exactly what they had been taught to do in the Eddie Eagle Program: "If you see a gun, **Stop! Don't Touch. Leave the Area. Tell an Adult."** They immediately notified a school crossing guard, who contacted local police. No harm came to either child.

In Euclid, Ohio, five youngsters were playing near their home when they spotted a gun in the bushes. Jarrell Minor, age seven, had been through the Eddie Eagle Program and remembered what he'd been taught, as reported in the *News Herald* on July 13, 1999. "I ran in the house and had someone call the police," he recalled. "The officers taught us that if we see a gun we are to stop, don't touch, leave the area and tell the cops."

In 2001, a nurse's study comparing several child gun accident prevention programs gave the highest marks to Eddie Eagle, according to the

October 2001 *Journal of Emergency Nursing Online.* And the National Center for Health Statistics reported that accidental gun deaths among children aged 14 and younger dropped more than 56 percent during Eddie Eagle's first decade of existence.

Yet another honor for the program came from the National Sheriffs' Association, which formally endorsed Eddie Eagle at its annual midwinter conference, held March 2, 2002, in Washington, D.C.

Sheriff John Cary Bittick, President of the National Sheriffs' Association said, "We are proud to partner with the National Rifle Association on this very important issue and we would like to express our full support for this program. The safety of our nation's children is of paramount concern and I can think of no better way to provide them with knowledge about firearm safety than through the Eddie Eagle GunSafe® Program. This program, which has proven to be most effective, simply teaches children not to touch firearms and to tell adults immediately if they should come into contact with a firearm of any kind."

The Eddie Eagle accident prevention message is taught each year by 20,000 elementary school teachers, law enforcement officers, and community activists, who use the program's colorful workbooks and video to get Eddie's message across to kids.

In 1996, NRA introduced the Eddie Eagle mascot costume to law enforcement agencies. While not necessary to teach the program, the costume provides law enforcement professionals a great opportunity to capture young children's attention while teaching them a valuable lesson. From 1996 through 2001, 104 costumes were sold to law enforcement agencies, and many costumes were purchased through grants from the NRA Foundation.

Pennsylvania Governor Tom Ridge attended the 1998 NRA Annual Meetings in Philadelphia and signed a commendation honoring the 10th anniversary of the Eddie Eagle GunSafe® Program. Attending the signing were (from left) NRA Director Susan Howard, Executive Vice President Wayne R. LaPierre, and Second Vice President Kayne B. Robinson.

Above: Nancy Johnson of Phenix City, Alabama, not only won a gold medal at the 2000 Olympic Games in Sydney, Australia, she was the first athlete at those Games to stand atop the award podium. To win the women's 10-meter air rifle, Johnson had to make up a two-point deficit in the finals.

Below: Kim Rhode, at age 17, became the youngest woman shooter ever to win an Olympic gold medal. She won her medal at the Atlanta Games in 1996, seven years after she first participated in an NRA marksmanship program.

Olympic Glory

For many years, NRA was the national governing body for international shooting sports in the United States. NRA conducted competitive events, selected national teams, and provided resources for medal-winning performances. In recent years, that role was transferred to USA Shooting at the U.S. Olympic Training Center in Colorado Springs, Colorado. NRA's Craig D. Sandler sits on its Board of Directors, and NRA still conducts numerous international-style competitions.

Shooting ranks as the third largest sport in the modern Olympic movement in number of athletes, events, and participating nations. Atlanta, Georgia, proved hospitable to American shooters in 1996, when Kim Rhode of El Monte, California, took the gold medal in women's double trap. At age 17, she was the youngest shooter ever on the U.S. Olympic Shooting Team and credited NRA with giving her a firm foundation in the fundamentals. Josh Lakatos of Pasadena, California, won a silver in men's trap, and Lance Blade of Vancouver, Washington, took the bronze in men's trap.

When the world's best shooters went head-to-head for Olympic glory in Sydney, Australia, at the 2000 Summer Games, four Americans came away with medals, including the first gold medal awarded during the games in women's 10-meter air rifle. That honor went to Nancy Johnson of Phenix City, Alabama, who credited an NRA-sponsored shooting program for helping her get started. Team USA brought home two other shooting medals. Three-time Olympian Todd Graves, a member of the U.S. Army Marksmanship Unit from Cusseta, Georgia, won a bronze medal in skeet. Three-time World Cup champion Kim Rhode won the bronze in women's double trap. And the U.S. team's Emily deRiel of Philadelphia, Pennsylvania, won a silver medal in modern pentathlon, which includes pistol shooting as one of its five disciplines.

Publications Take Center Stage

Serving up reliable technical information, useful tips, and robust entertainment remained staples of NRA's publications business. In 1997, *American Guardian* magazine made its debut, standing alongside *American Rifleman* and *American Hunter*.

Intended to appeal to legislative activists and address Second Amendment issues in considerable depth, the new magazine rapidly increased in circulation and was renamed *America's 1st Freedom* in 2000. NRA members could select the magazine of their choice as a membership benefit.

In January 2000, Joe H. Graham was named Executive Director of the NRA Publications Division and was charged with reinvigorating these official journals and expanding the reach of *InSights,* geared for junior members, and *Shooting Sports USA,* targeted for competitive shooters. Graham was uniquely qualified to meet the challenge set down by Wayne LaPierre. As Chief Operations Officer for Pentax Corporation, Graham had a proven track record in marketing and sales management, promotions, public relations, and strategic planning. He had also served as publisher for two outdoor magazines.

Straightaway Graham turned all the magazines into full four-color productions, increased their editorial length, gave staff writers and designers more creative freedom, recruited nationally acclaimed writers and photographers,

and attracted new advertisers while increasing the magazines' marketing strength with their traditional industry base.

"We asked some very well-known outdoor writers to craft features that attract a reading audience and lend veracity to what we're producing," said Graham. "But no matter who it is, we have everything checked out by technical editors because we have to be absolutely correct. Our readers are knowledgeable—they really know what's correct."

Within two years, the Publications Division had doubled its advertising revenue. In 2001, *Advertising Age* magazine ranked *American Rifleman* and *American Hunter* number two and number three, respectively, in the top 300 magazines by ad revenue growth. That year the division published the largest issue ever of *American Hunter* and the largest issue of *American Rifleman* since 1981. NRA also launched *Shooting Illustrated,* available on the newsstand and by subscription, to cover a variety of sport shooting interests.

Into the Arena

When Marion P. Hammer handed the gavel to Charlton Heston as NRA's 57th President in 1998, it was a solemn moment between two of the most important presidencies in NRA's long and proud history. Upon his election, Heston said, "I don't succeed Marion Hammer—I follow her," attesting to his respect for her accomplishments in office.

The membership overwhelmingly responded to Heston's and Hammer's joint call for unity and for an end to dissension. After two and a half years of strife in which Marion Hammer "called for, pleaded for, and at times begged for unity and an end to the malicious infighting," she finished her terms as President with the assurance that NRA officers and new representatives on the Board of Directors would stand united. Joining the leadership team was Sandra S. Froman of Tucson, Arizona, who was

Joe H. Graham took over the reins of NRA Publications in January 2000, bringing to that position years of experience in marketing and sales in the outdoor field. He had served as Chief Operating Officer for Pentax Corporation.

elected Second Vice President. Froman became the second woman to be elected to that office.

In his first message as NRA President, Charlton Heston unveiled his vision for the future and spoke of his immense pride in assuming the office. "I come here because I am proud," he said. "I believe the Second Amendment is America's first freedom. Among the entire Bill of Rights, it is first among equals. It is the one freedom that makes all freedoms possible, the one right that protects every other. I am proud of gun ownership, proud of how we use firearms and proud of what they stand for. No organization in the history of the world has done more to preserve individual freedom, to ensure personal security, to fight violent crime, or teach more youngsters and adults about firearms safety than your National Rifle Association."

Heston pledged to carry that message to every corner of America and called upon NRA members to "stand beside me, armed with pride in who we are and what we believe."

The Charlton Heston Endowment was announced during the opening of the "Real Guns of Real Heroes" exhibit in the National Firearms Museum, and Joel Morrow, President of Imperial Miniature Armory, presented President Heston with a miniature saddle commemorating his acting career and service to NRA.

Those words would remain at the heart of his historic presidency, as the Board of Directors twice voted to approve bylaw changes that kept Heston as President for an unprecedented four terms in office.

Heston proved almost immediately that he would be anything but a figurehead. He worked tirelessly and with great effectiveness as a spokesman for and a symbol of NRA and all it represented.

Heston's "tell it like it is" style came to the forefront in a speech delivered before the National Press Club, which the *New York Times* acknowledged as "a blistering defense for gun ownership" that "excoriated news organizations . . . for their gullibility in swallowing anti-gun arguments."

Though Heston was modest about the role he played, on the national political stage he commanded attention. With Wayne LaPierre, he set out to change the political equation, challenging without hesitation the Clinton administration's lax enforcement of tough gun law penalties against violent criminals even while it called for ever more restrictions on honest citizens.

Laying Down the Gauntlet

On ABC's nationally televised news program *This Week*, LaPierre laid down the gauntlet. He accused President Clinton of having "blood on his hands" for the murder of Northwestern basketball coach Ricky Birdsong in Illinois, a tragedy that could have been averted had the killer been prosecuted under existing federal gun laws.

"He's willing to accept a certain level of killing to further his political agenda, and his Vice President too," LaPierre said of Clinton. Raising the stakes, Heston lent his deep, sonorous voice in television commercials that echoed the theme, stating, "Mr. Clinton, when what you say is wrong, that's a mistake. When you know it's wrong, that's a lie."

Americans from coast to coast started asking why federal prosecutions of armed criminals had decreased so dramatically in the Clinton-Gore years.

Americans were also outraged to learn that two conservation trust funds—financed by an excise tax paid by anglers, archers, hunters, or sport shooters when they bought related equipment or supplies—were being abused and monies misap-

propriated by the Clinton-Gore administration. The problems surfaced during hearings by the House Resources Committee, chaired by Representative Donald E. Young of Alaska, an NRA Director. The General Accounting Office could not determine how much money was diverted or where it went. One of its investigators testified that the trust funds' administration was "one of the worst managed programs we have ever encountered."

NRA made sure the word got out, and, as always, NRA members responded. Members sent more than 200,000 postcards to the House Resources Committee. "It's the most correspondence we've ever had on any Fish and Wildlife Service issue," one staffer said. The individual effort of each NRA member made an enormous collective impression. On April 5, 2000, the U.S. House of Representatives voted 423–2 to pass the Wildlife and Sport Fish Restoration Improvement Act. It became law several months later.

Finally, when the administration went on record in federal court in the *U.S. v. Emerson* case

Alaska Congressman Donald E. Young, an NRA Director, with some of the more than 200,000 postcards his House Resources Committee received from NRA members protesting the outrageous abuses of the sportsmen's trust funds by the Clinton-Gore administration.

and asserted there was no individual right to own a firearm, Al Gore's fate was sealed in the presidential campaign against pro–Second Amendment candidate George W. Bush.

NRA members were so energized that they donated more than $12 million to NRA's Political Victory Fund for the 2000 elections. By contrast, MaryRose Adkins, ILA's Fiscal Officer, said that when the Political Victory Fund was created in 1976, it raised only about $1 million.

With the pivotal 2000 presidential elections in sight and the national media serving up a daily drumbeat against the Second Amendment, NRA launched an interactive, Webcasting news channel called *NRALIVE* to circumvent biased coverage. The news program was accessible around the clock and crystallized the debate by using high-tech tools to reach firearms owners in their homes. The *New York Times, Fortune, Time,* the *Cleveland Plain Dealer,* and other publications reported that the net newsroom was a trend-setter.

NRALIVE joined other innovative programming such as the syndicated *Wayne LaPierre Radio Show* and the *CrimeStrike* syndicated television series. Other public relations boosts came through the organization's Web sites—nralive.com, nrahq.org, and nraila.org—all of which proved highly popular, receiving tens of thousands of hits daily.

In the months, weeks, and even hours before the 2000 presidential election, NRA used every communications tool at its disposal to protect Second Amendment rights. Two weeks before the elections, ILA launched an NRAPVF.org Web site, which was visited by more than 200,000 viewers.

Though Gore tried to backpeddle his position in the campaign's waning days, he could not shake off history; he had spent eight years at Bill Clinton's side passing the most enormous set of new federal gun laws since 1968.

"At first, Al Gore thought the election might be decided in California, New York, and Massachusetts, but when he realized that it might be decided everywhere else, that's when he started peddling

his bicycle backwards from the likes of Bill Clinton and Handgun Control, Inc., as fast as he could, but it was too late," said ILA's Jim Baker.

NRA turned up the heat, exposing the Clinton-Gore legacy through hard-hitting infomercials aired in swing states and an advertising campaign that appeared in 13 million outdoor magazines in battleground states, with extra ad buys made in Florida. NRA's publications also provided state voter guides called Political Preference Charts.

Spearheaded by 375 Election Volunteer Coordinators nationwide, ILA's Grassroots Division mobilized volunteers to carry the message to the heartland, precinct-by-precinct. This voter education and registration effort primed new life into

Inset: NRALIVE.com, anchored by veteran newscaster Ginny Simone, bypasses the media elite's anti-gun bias with up-to-the-minute headlines and analysis of issues that affect gun owners.

Right: MyNRA.com is an Internet portal providing information and services important to NRA members. Other NRA sites are NRAHQ.org, providing information on NRA's 178 firearm safety, marksmanship, and hunting programs; NRAILA.org, an information clearinghouse for legislative, political and legal affairs, and grassroots activism; and NRALIVE.com, which provides up-to-the-minute news coverage, analysis, interviews, and commentary through streaming video and audio feeds.

Guess who's saving lives while you look the other way?
Richmond's murder rate was America's second worst. So the feds got fed up.

With a small army of federal prosecutors, the U.S. Attorney's Office in Richmond launched Project Exile. They used existing federal laws to impose an automatic five-year sentence on every felon caught carrying a gun. They took hundreds of names — but zero excuses.

They've cut Richmond's murders by 65%, and robberies by a third.

We're ready to work together. Where are you?
The National Rifle Association believes every American city deserves what's working in Richmond. We're not alone. Police groups, citizens, the Governor of Virginia, the leadership of both Houses of Congress — and even gun-ban groups — agree on this point.

So instead of giving us another press conference about more gun control laws, give us one city. Let us try crime-fighting our way — the Project Exile way.

How about Philadelphia? Mayor Ed Rendell is willing.

Are you?

Why support what doesn't work and refuse to do what works?
President Clinton supports gun bans and new restrictions on law-abiding gun owners. But not one has, can or will cut gun crime.

Meanwhile the White House has refused to do what NRA has claimed and Richmond now proves. Fierce enforcement of existing laws gets gun-toting criminals off the street. It may not make a great photo-op, but it truly saves lives.

Mr. President, why aren't you doing nationally what they're doing in Richmond? Why can you find resources to annoy honest gun owners but not to prosecute gun felons? In fact, why do we have to pay for this ad asking you to do your job?

CHARLTON HESTON
PRESIDENT
National Rifle Association of America

Mr. President, why have you turned your back on cutting gun crime?

NRA's grassroots power. "We educated our members, and we empowered them, and the enthusiasm was just incredible," said Glen Caroline, the division's Director.

NRA formally endorsed George W. Bush and, in high-profile editorials penned by the organization's leaders, made clear where he stood on Second Amendment issues. As Governor of Texas, Bush signed a law allowing law-abiding citizens to carry concealed firearms for protection. He secured legislation preventing frivolous lawsuits against lawful firearms commerce. He adopted the proven Project Exile model against armed violent criminals, among other criminal justice reforms. Richard B. Cheney, Bush's vice presidential running mate, was also a firm believer in the Second Amendment. When he was a U.S. Representative for Wyoming, the U.S. Congress

described his record on Second Amendment issues as "peerless."

With only a few days remaining before the November 7 elections, Charlton Heston, Wayne LaPierre, and Jim Baker left nothing to chance. They took to the election platform and led 16 "get-out-the-vote" rallies in key states. Massive crowds greeted them at "Vote Freedom First" rallies in the

Left: With Bill Clinton fixated on insisting that law-abiding gun owners pay the price for the acts of criminals, NRA produced ads asking why the President wasn't supporting proven crime-reducing measures such as Project Exile that threatened violent felons with expanded prison terms if they carried guns.

Below: Oscar-winning actor and tireless Second Amendment champion Charlton Heston—viewed by millions of Americans as the symbol of NRA—was elected President of the Association in 1998. Eight years earlier, he had been elected an NRA Honorary Life Member.

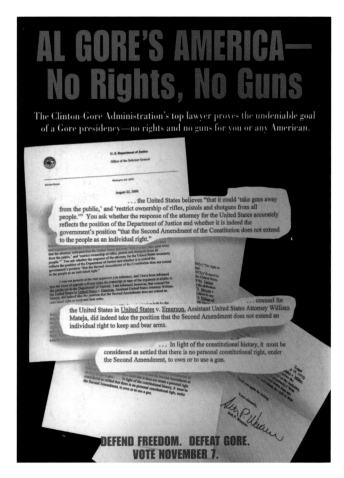

AL GORE'S AMERICA—
No Rights, No Guns

The Clinton-Gore Administration's top lawyer proves the undeniable goal
of a Gore presidency—no rights and no guns for you or any American.

DEFEND FREEDOM. DEFEAT GORE.
VOTE NOVEMBER 7.

When the Clinton-Gore administration, through Solicitor
General Seth P. Waxman, went on record claiming "there is no
personal constitutional right, under the Second Amendment, to
own or to use a gun," NRA made sure gun-owning voters knew
exactly what an Al Gore presidency would mean.

political reporter for the *Los Angeles Times* who was covering one of the "Vote Freedom First" rallies called his editors and issued a forewarning. "This is important," he said. "Something big is happening."

Indeed, something big was happening. A movement was reborn, and individual NRA members were its catalyst, helping to elect a pro–Second Amendment President in the nation's closest presidential election ever. More than 86 percent of the candidates who received NRA support took their places in the U.S. Congress, and 85 percent were victorious at state and local levels. State executive mansions also remained pro-gun by a better than two-to-one margin.

In its wake, Bill Clinton was uncharacteristically candid in assessing the result with CBS's Dan Rather: "I don't think there's any doubt that, in at least five states I can think of, the NRA had

pivotal states of Michigan, Pennsylvania, West Virginia, Tennessee, and Arkansas.

The rallies were an inspiration and a pleasure for Wayne LaPierre. "In all my years with NRA, I've never felt such overwhelming pride in our people, or our just cause—the preservation of freedom," he said. "Everywhere we went, the enthusiasm for NRA and our fight was remarkable." The whirlwind tour boldly swept the trio into Al Gore's Tennessee, Bill Clinton's Arkansas, and even West Virginia, where Democrats outnumbered Republicans two to one.

Even the national media woke up to the momentum of these events. A nationally known a decisive influence. . . . They've done a good job. They've probably had more to do than anyone else in the fact that we didn't win the House this time. And they hurt Al Gore."

Exit polls showed that a stunning 48 percent of those who voted had firearms in their homes—and they voted in force for George W. Bush, giving him the crucial edge in hotly contested states.

With the inauguration of George W. Bush as U.S. President, the fundamentals of the "gun control" fight waged from within the White House changed dramatically. But regulatory land mines were left behind by the Clinton-Gore administration and its entrenched operatives in the government bureaucracy. The closely divided U.S. Congress remained threatening, given its razor-thin margins in both the U.S. House and Senate.

Only a few weeks before Bush's inauguration, the Senate held confirmation hearings on

Above: An eight-year Clinton-Gore administration war on the Second Amendment was brought to an end with the election of George W. Bush and Richard B. Cheney. NRA's efforts to elect pro-gun candidates in the 2000 elections were unprecedented in their scope.

Left: Vice President Richard B. Cheney, a staunch supporter of the Second Amendment, meets with (from left) NRA Executive Vice President Wayne R. LaPierre, ILA Executive Director James Jay Baker, ILA Deputy Executive Director Patrick G. O'Malley, and ILA Federal Affairs Director Charles H. Cunningham.

former Missouri Senator John Ashcroft, whom Bush had nominated to the powerful post of U.S. Attorney General. Handgun Control, Inc., led a charge against Ashcroft's confirmation based on his staunch pro–Second Amendment record. In the end, Ashcroft prevailed.

True to his guiding principles and philosophy, Ashcroft later expressed his personal views on the Constitution in a letter to ILA's Jim Baker. In that letter, the Attorney General wrote, "Let me state unequivocally my view that the text and original intent of the Second Amendment clearly protects the right of individuals to keep and bear firearms."

Above: Senator Larry E. Craig (R-Idaho) spoke eloquently at the 126th Members Banquet: "With every Congress, it's NRA that separates the fact from the fiction. It's NRA that takes a stand against bad policy. It's NRA that does the heavy lifting. And it's NRA that most often wins."

Honoring a 35-year-old tradition, at the 2002 Annual Meetings and Exhibits in Reno, Nevada, Executive Vice President Wayne LaPierre hails six-year-old Raleigh Peterson (below), the youngest member in attendance at the Members Meeting, and Claude Willoughby (below right), the oldest.

That deeply held view would translate into policy at the U.S. Justice Department, marking a decidedly changed course in history for America's 70 million firearms owners.

Firearms owners welcomed another victory with the October 16 ruling in the *U.S. v. Emerson* case, which was central to the outcome of the 2000 elections. The Fifth Circuit Court of Appeals declared in clear and ringing terms that the U.S. Constitution's Second Amendment protects the individual's right to keep and bear arms "whether or not they are a member of a select militia or performing active military service or training." In its decision, the court forcefully rejected all interpretations of the "collective right" theory advanced by the anti-gun lobby.

The court exposed the real aims of those who advocate that the right to keep and bear arms applies to only government and not the people. Furthermore, it clearly recognized that the Clinton administration's position posed dangers to individual liberty when it said, "The Second Amendment poses no obstacle to the wholesale disarmament of the American people." In that one line, the court defined the end game of those who would deny Second Amendment rights to individual Americans.

NRA's General Counsel Office prepared and filed three separate *amicus curiae* briefs in the case, and the court twice cited a law review article authored by NRA's General Counsel Robert J. Dowlut. The NRA Civil Rights Defense Fund provided funding to this historic case.

Nelson Lund, a distinguished law professor at George Mason University, termed the decision, "the most important and favorable Second

Amendment judicial decision in American history. A federal court of appeals has . . . rejected the preposterous but judicially regnant theory that Second Amendment rights belong to government or can only be exercised in the service of government." It is a matter, Lund said, "of government officials catching up with what most of the nation already believed."

Defending Freedom

On the morning of September 11, 2001, as the world watched in horror, hate-filled suicidal terrorists launched simultaneous attacks on America that killed thousands of innocent victims in New York, Virginia, and Pennsylvania.

The National Rifle Association expressed its solidarity with President Bush and the men and women in uniform who would lead the nation against terrorist groups and nations bent on destroying America and its beliefs.

With equal solidarity, NRA vowed to battle those who would use the national emergency to demand the surrender of Second Amendment rights. LaPierre called for NRA members to "lead the nation in a fierce and fearless defense of personal freedoms." At the same time, gun prohibitionists were quick to twist all logic and all truth after the September 11 attack to justify renewed government infringement on Second Amendment rights.

Much to their chagrin, Americans chose freedom's road. All over the nation, rather than rolling over to terrorism, people signed up in droves for firearms safety courses, as handgun sales skyrocketed. Reportedly, instant background checks for firearms purchases increased 21 percent for the month following the attacks, compared to the same period the year before. As LaPierre observed, "On September 11, 2001, Americans awakened to the cruel truth that no government, no army, no police department, no technology, no security system can ultimately guarantee personal safety."

NRA vowed to expose the truth about those who claimed to "fight terror" as a cover for their real goal of destroying the Second Amendment in the name of national security. "We must always remem-

In the wake of the September 11 terrorist attacks, NRA's Law Enforcement Activities Division created two new trophies to be awarded at the National Police Shooting Championships. The Craig J. Miller Memorial Trophy is dedicated to the memory of federal law enforcement officers who died in the attack on the World Trade Center. The Walter Weaver Memorial Trophy honors the municipal law enforcement officers killed in the same tragedy. Miller served with the U.S. Secret Service, Weaver with the New York City Police Department.

ber that we cannot purchase a safe society paid for with the currency of America's Constitutional freedoms. We cannot make ourselves safer by making ourselves less free," LaPierre warned.

In the end, LaPierre reaffirmed Benjamin Franklin's admonition to a new nation that would be unlike any other in the world: "They that can give up essential liberty to obtain a little temporary safety deserve neither liberty nor safety."

With renewed determination, NRA stepped into the new century, more committed than ever to keep America safe and free.

Like America's founders, NRA members and its leaders were united in a singular cause—to pass the Bill of Rights intact to the generations that would follow.

INVESTING IN THE NRA FOUNDATION

TO RECOGNIZE SIGNIFICANT DONORS FOR their philanthropy, the NRA Foundation offers opportunities to donors to permanently name an endowment. Many significant names in NRA history, the firearms industry, and related manufacturing industries have named Foundation endowments, including the following:

Beretta Endowment
Established in 2001 by the Beretta USA and Benelli USA companies. This endowment sponsors the National Firearms Museum's "The Beretta Gallery: An Age of Elegance."

Blue Book Publications Acquisition Endowment
Established in 2001 by Blue Book Publications to fund the acquisition of items for the National Firearms Museum collection.

Board of Directors Endowment
Established and funded in 1998 by individual members of the NRA Board of Directors to support NRA's educational programs.

David P. Bookman Endowment
Established in 1998 by David P. Bookman to support the National Firearms Museum.

William S. Brophy Endowment
Established in 1991 by family and friends in memory of Colonel William S. Brophy to support the National Firearms Museum.

Brownell Family Endowment
Established in 1994 by the Brownell family and their company to support NRA's Youth Education programs.

Eldon L. & Hope T. Buckner
Established in 1999 by Mr. and Mrs. Buckner to support NRA's Youth Education programs.

Alice H. Bull Endowment
Established in 1999 by friends and family in memory of former NRA Director and Executive Council member, Mrs. Alice H. Bull. This endowment supports NRA's collegiate shooting programs.

Harlon B. & Maryann Carter Endowment
Established in 1997 by friends in memory of former NRA President Harlon B. Carter and his wife, Maryann, in recognition of their many years of service to NRA and to support NRA's educational programs.

Roosevelt, to support NRA's Hunting and Wildlife Conservation programs.

Robert F. & Ruth H. Rubendunst Endowment
Established in 1996 in honor of the Rubendunsts by friends to support the National Firearms Museum.

William B. Ruger Endowment
Established in 1996 by friends of William B. Ruger to support the National Firearms Museum.

Stehsel Family Endowment
Established in 1999 by Donald Stehsel to benefit NRA's junior firearms and marksmanship training programs.

St. Louis Big Game Hunters Endowment
Established in 1998 by the St. Louis Big Game Hunters Club to benefit NRA's Youth Hunter Education Challenge (YHEC) in Missouri.

Thomas L. Washington Endowment
Established in 1995 by friends in memory of past NRA President Thomas L. Washington. This endowment benefits NRA's Youth Hunter Education Challenge (YHEC) program.

R. L. Wilson Educational Endowment
Established in 1995 by Larry Wilson to support the National Firearms Museum.

James R. & Dorothy M. Wood Endowment
Established in 1996 by Mrs. Dorothy M. Wood in memory of her husband, James, to support NRA's Hunting and Wildlife Conservation programs.

John and Jeanne Wootters Endowment
Established in 1998 by friends of former NRA Director John Wootters and his wife, Jeanne, to support NRA's educational programs.

INDEX